# Magical Musical Tour

# Magical Musical Tour

## Rock and Pop in Film Soundtracks

**K.J. DONNELLY**

Bloomsbury Academic
An imprint of Bloomsbury Publishing Inc

# B L O O M S B U R Y

NEW YORK · LONDON · OXFORD · NEW DELHI · SYDNEY

**Bloomsbury Academic**

An imprint of Bloomsbury Publishing Inc

1385 Broadway
New York
NY 10018
USA

50 Bedford Square
London
WC1B 3DP
UK

**www.bloomsbury.com**

**BLOOMSBURY and the Diana logo are trademarks of Bloomsbury Publishing Plc**

First published 2015

**Library of Congress Cataloging-in-Publication Data**
Donnelly, K. J. (Kevin J.)
Magical musical tour : rock and pop in film soundtracks / K.J. Donnelly.
pages cm
Includes bibliographical references and index.
ISBN 978-1-62892-128-1 (hardback : alk. paper) – ISBN 978-1-62892-748-1
(pbk. : alk. paper) 1. Motion picture music–History and criticism. 2. Rock music–History
and criticism. 3. Popular music–History and criticism. I. Title.
ML2075.D663 2015
781.64'1542–dc23
2015014501

ISBN: HB: 978-1-6289-2128-1
PB: 978-1-6289-2748-1
ePub: 978-1-6289-2714-6
ePDF: 978-1-6289-2074-1

Typeset by Integra Software Services Pvt. Ltd.
Printed and bound in the United States of America

# Contents

# Acknowledgements

**M**uch of the material in this book has had a long gestation period, a large part of it going back to my teenage years and obsessive interest in rock and pop music and films. It is satisfying that this 'deep research' was ultimately useful.

Thanks to editor Katie Gallof for being consistently helpful and understanding. Many have helped over the years. Thanks to anyone who did who I fail to mention. Thanks to Wilfred Marlow, Beth Carroll, Daniel O'Brien, Ann-Kristin Wallengren, Neil Lerner, Claudia Gorbman, Jack Dubowsky, Glen Creeber, Jamie Sexton, Liz Weis, Peter Brygelsson, Bob Neaverson, Ron Sadoff, Gillian Anderson, Phil Tagg, Erik Hedling, Andrew Higson, Charles Barr, John Street, Christopher Natzen, Stefano Baschiera, Andy Curtis-Brignell, Liu Chu-Ying, Mike Allen, Steve Rawle, Mark Goodall, ex-colleagues at Staffordshire and Aberystwyth, ex-students who have had interesting discussions about music and film with me, and thanks to any musicians that I have ever played with. Special thanks go to Robert Donnelly, Joan Donnelly and Mandy Marler. Their encouragement and support was always beyond the call of duty.

This book includes material that I have sometimes been concerned with before, and a small amount of material has appeared in a different form in these publications:

*Pop Music in British Cinema: A Chronicle* (London: British Film Institute, 2001), *British Film Music and Film Musicals* (Basingstoke: Palgrave Macmillan, 2007), 'The Classical Film Score Forever?: Music in the *Batman* Films' in Steve Neale and Murray Smith, eds., *Contemporary Hollywood Cinema* (London and New York: Routledge, 1998), 'British Cinema and the Visualized Live Album' in Robert Edgar, Kirsty Fairclough-Isaacs and Benjamin Halligan, eds., *The Music Documentary: Acid Rock to Electropop* (London: Routledge, 2013). Other material has been presented at SCMS, Screen and MaMI conferences.

# 1

# Introduction

I am always surprised that there is not more writing about films and rock music, and in particular, the point where the two form a union.[1] To date, there have only been patchy attempts to deal with popular music's relationship with film, and perhaps this will patch up some holes or merely supply another patchy narrative. It is startling that there is so little written on subject that is so popular as a consumer item and thus has a significant cultural profile. This book attempts to engage the intersection of the two on both an aesthetic and industrial level, dealing with a wide range of material running from Elvis and the Beatles involvement with film to more esoteric intersections of popular music and film. While some chapters are historically inspired reviews, discussing many films and musicians, others are more concentrated and detailed case studies of single films. This book does not aim to be a systematic study of all areas of rock and pop music and film but aims to provide some analytical snapshots of notable instances and issues.

International popular music has been dominated by the United States and Britain since the turn of the twentieth century. The advent of rock'n'roll in the mid-1950s reinforced this dominance and was embraced by films that wished to add energy, show youthful credentials and make money. On one end of this spectrum, there have been forgettable exploitation films aimed at a quick buck, but on the other, there have been films that remain perennially popular and critically acclaimed, some of which even have credentials as 'serious' works of art. This book focuses on films using popular music since rock'n'roll in the mid-1950s, a relationship which grew from insalubrious exploitation origins to one of the dominant axes of contemporary culture. The categories of 'pop music' and 'popular music' have been challenged since the late 1960s, particularly by the development of more 'serious' (or rather more self-serious) rock music and some of its extreme forms of differentiation, such as progressive rock. The advent of 'concept albums', for example, tested the boundary of 'pop music'. Particularly though their pretensions and referencing of high art, concept albums manifest a rupture with 'pop music'.[2]

An important consideration is the relationship of the music and film as industries which have retained ties closer than most other industries and engaged in constant 'synergy' of cross-promotion. Indeed, the popular music industry has become completely interlinked with the film industry. The majority of mainstream films come with ready-attached songs that may or may not appear in the film but nevertheless will be used for publicity purposes and appear on a soundtrack album. Copyright has become one of the fundamental concerns of the modern music industry. While the merging of media companies has allowed some films to use a readymade roster of recordings that already belong to the company, in other cases, the rights for the use of particular songs have to be secured for a film, and in many cases, this does not extend as far as using the song on the film's soundtrack album. Indeed, there are some notable examples of the reuse of certain songs across a number of films. For instance, Cockney Rebel's *Make Me Smile (Come Up and See Me)* appeared in a series of different films and over a relatively short period of time (*The Full Monty* [1997], *Velvet Goldmine* [1998], *Best – The George Best Story* [2000], *Saving Grace* [2000] and *Blackball* [2003]).

Apart, but not totally disconnected from industrial aspects, is the relationship of aesthetics between the two media. Sensual and kinetic matters drive the commercial impetus. In many cases, popular music in films has made for some of the most striking moments in films and the most dramatic aesthetic action in cinema. Examples of some of the most memorable moments in cinema would include Mr. Blonde torturing a policeman to the strains of Stealer's Wheel's *Stuck in the Middle with You* in Quentin Tarantino's *Reservoir Dogs* (1991), the montage of Ben relaxing in the swimming pool and meeting Mrs. Robinson accompanied by Simon and Garfunkel's *The Sound of Silence* in *The Graduate* (1967) and the memorable potter's wheel sequence with the Righteous Brothers' *Unchained Melody* in *Ghost* (1990).[3]

These days, it is wholly unremarkable to hear rock or pop music in a film, just as it is not uncommon to hear musical underscore in a film that has incorporated elements from popular music. However, analysis can still often spend a great deal of time and effort pulling apart 'the music' and 'the images', but we should always remember that the two do not work as the sum of each added together. Instead, the fused elements redouble effects and create new configurations and significations. In actuality, music and images in film should never be considered 'two discourses' but a merged unity. This makes music an element of film and makes other film elements a part of music. In such as manner, an image can 'finish' a musical move, like a cadence, the same way that music can provide a comment or particular cast on an image.

# A long shot on developments

The history of pop-rock films to a large degree is defined by the history of pop-rock. This is hardly surprising, although there are certain points in the development of rock where films have had certain, crucial roles in the dissemination and development of the musical format.

Robust traditions have built and the relationship between the film and music industries remains as strong as it always has been. Indeed, even silent films sometimes included tied-in sheet music. The 'industrial' relationship has developed and surmounted the upheaval that rock'n'roll caused in the mid-1950s to create a strong and intimate bond. Apparently, DJ Alan Freed coined the term 'rock'n'roll' as a replacement for 'rhythm and blues' in his WWJ Cleveland radio show to avoid the racial denotation of the latter term. Nevertheless, it was a controversial form of music, and films had to work hard to 'defuse' any threat it was perceived to contain, while simultaneously exploiting its exciting possibilities. The tradition of film musicals, which arguably functioned primarily as vehicles to sell music, reshaped its traditional format to accommodate the new musical form. Examples of 'pop musicals' include Elvis's films in the United States and Cliff Richard's in the UK. In the early years after rock'n'roll, these would often employ 'realistic' stage performances (using the performance mode) rather than follow the 'MGM model' of bursting into song (the lip-synch mode).[4] Elvis's films such as *King Creole* (1958) exhibit both strategies for rendering songs. By the late 1960s, the selling of music through films increasingly had recourse to having tied-in songs appearing on the soundtrack as non-diegetic music, rather than as set-piece song sequences as were found in traditional musicals.

In the late 1950s, American films began to use rock'n'roll, either through featuring cameo appearances by groups in narrative films and backstage musicals or through building films around singing stars. According to Rick Altman, the number of musicals produced by Hollywood peaked in the late 1940s and early 1950s and peaked in terms of its creativity in the early and mid-1950s.[5] This was due to a number of determinants, and one of these clearly was the decline in sales of show songs in comparison to rock'n'roll songs. Barry Keith Grant points to the new popular music as an emergent form that hastened the destruction of the classical musical form and musicals as a viable genre:

> The rapid decline of musicals in the late 1950s seems to me more likely explained by the existence of an ever-widening gap between the music in the musicals the studios were making and the music an increasing percentage of the nation was actually listening to – rock'n'roll.[6]

The birth of rock'n'roll was closely tied to film. Bill Haley and The Comets's song Rock Around the Clock was used on the credits of delinquency film *The Blackboard Jungle* (1955) and came to some prominence. This led rapidly to a film built around the song: *Rock Around the Clock* (1955), while Elvis Presley's recording successes led to his immediate appearance in feature films, with *Love Me Tender* (1956) and *Loving You* (1957).

The British version of rock'n'roll had some slight differences. The culture centred on coffee bars, as evident in *The Tommy Steele Story* (1957), *The Golden Disc* (1958), *Serious Charge* (1958), *'Beat' Girl* (1959) and *Expresso Bongo* (1959). Britain's most successful singer in film musicals was Cliff Richard, although his film career declined after *The Young Ones* (1961) and *Summer Holiday* (1963), with *Wonderful Life* (1964) proving nothing like the success of its two predecessors.[7] As Cliff Richard's fifth film, it was released at the same time as the Beatles' debut film *A Hard Day's Night* (1964). The contrast between the two films could not be starker, with the Beatles espousing action, cinematic kinesis and a foregrounding of their songs, while Cliff Richard and his cohorts attempt to reconstruct a stage musical for the cameras in a similar manner to old-time Hollywood musicals. The Beatles' films, on the back on their music, changed the landscape of music's relationship with film. Concurrently in the United States, there was a spate of successful 'beach movies', such as *Beach Blanket Bingo* (1965) and *How to Stuff a Wild Bikini* (1965), which celebrated young people singing and dancing at the beach. In relation to the energetic Beatles' films, *A Hard Day's Night* and *Help!* (1965), these looked tame and juvenile. For pop music in the cinema, these films were highly significant, especially as films built around pop groups could be made relatively cheaply and were guaranteed a certain amount of success by the featured group's established history of record sales – they seemingly had a readymade audience.[8] The influx of American money and interest in Britain coincided with the Beat Boom, the Beatles spearheading the 'British Invasion' of the United States and Beatlemania signifying the power of the new pop music culture.[9]

If rock'n'roll in the mid-1950s firmly moved the most vibrant zone of popular music into a new demographic situation: a direct relationship with youth, the following decade further changed the notion of popular music as a vehicle for the tastes of all. Indeed, the whole of the popular music industry reconfigured in the following decade:

> In the mid-1960s the relationship between record companies and popular artists underwent a revolution. Rock musicians developed the capacity to act as self-contained production units. Many formed groups in order to write, arrange and perform their own music ... The revenues that rock

musicians generated from the sale of millions of albums, publishing rights, and large-scale concert tours provided them with their own economic base in the music industry. Many artists used the newly acquired power to build their own recording studios and to establish their own record labels.[10]

Edward R. Kealy characterizes this as an 'art mode of production', moving away from a craft industry and beginning a fragmentation of 'popular music'. In the 1960s, pop music went through significant shifts in the modes of production, with popular music increasingly becoming written, performed and recorded by the same individuals, rather than having specialist songwriters, session musicians and pop stars. Of course, this traditional division of labour never disappeared, but the production process of previous decades increasingly was replaced by alternative creative procedures. Ian Ingis notes that by the 1970s, 'rock' was considered something distinct from 'showbiz'.[11] The middle and late 1960s also saw a change in the way that popular music was conceptualized: it became increasingly the case that originality was lauded as a virtue in itself for recordings. Such a turn was concurrent with the increasing use of the term 'rock' to describe music that was not oriented towards immediate financial return in the singles chart. This privileging of the 'origin' was centred on the recording artist as an author and often (although by no means always) was dependent on their involvement with all stages of the aesthetic production process, specifically the writing and the performing.

The development of the Counterculture, from the middle of the 1960s onwards, heralded more radical developments in the use of pop and rock music in films. Large music festivals and extremely exciting performers led to rock documentaries such as *Monterey Pop* (1968), *Woodstock* (1970) and *Gimme Shelter* (1970). At this point, more experimental soundtracks with music by rock groups, such as *Wonderwall* (1968), *The Trip* (1967) and *Performance* (1970), heavily inspired by the culture of psychedelia. *Easy Rider* (1969) revolutionized the film soundtrack, by eschewing the use of especially written scored music for making dramatic and emotional effects. In its place, excerpts from existing song recordings were used across the whole film. This led to some highly memorable sequences, as well as some robust audiovisual models of accompanying certain kinetic images with certain forms of energetic rock music. This came in the wake of *The Graduate* (1967), where a few songs by Simon and Garfunkel had appeared effectively in extended montage sequences, perhaps the most notable being *The Sound of Silence* accompanying the protagonist's varied but relaxed leisure activities.

The following decade developed this process further, creating strong ties between film and popular music in both aesthetic and promotional terms. For instance, *American Graffiti* (1973) made a significant profit from having a soundtrack album of songs that had appeared in the film. This set a model that was to become highly influential. Rock musicals, including elaborate 'rock operas' developed, often from lavish stage show originals. Films like *Godspell* (1973), *Tommy* (1975), *The Rocky Horror Picture Show* (1975) and Brian DePalma's *Phantom of the Paradise* (1976) all took something from classical film musicals but infused a more modern sense, sometimes embracing the grotesque. In each case, the music was rock rather than show music.[12] These films tended to have a certain pretention towards artistic status, while simultaneously disco films merely exploited the current pop music trend for music for dance clubs. Films such as the highly successful *Saturday Night Fever* (1977), *Car Wash* (1976) and *Thank God It's Friday* (1978) set their narratives in clubs with plenty of dance sequences and distinctly resembled the traditional structural format of the backstage musical. An arguably less traditional approach was evident in the films that emanated from the outburst of punk rock with its intolerance towards convention. British films included *The Great Rock'n'Roll Swindle* (1980, the Sex Pistols), *Rude Boy* (1980, the Clash), while American ones included the documentary *The Decline of Western Civilization, Part One* (1981) and Susan Seidelman's drama *Smithereens* (1982).[13]

By the early 1980s, the pairing of pop songs with films was a strategy that dominated the marketing logic of the conglomerating film and music companies. Films like *Footloose* (1984) and *Flashdance* (1983) emblematized the strategy of 'synergy', which was also evident in the vigorous genre of 'high school movies', which included *Rock'n'Roll High School* (1979), *Footloose*, *The Breakfast Club* (1985), *Pretty in Pink* (1986), *Bill and Ted's Excellent Adventure* (1989) and *Pump Up the Volume* (1990), amongst others. MTV and other music television channels began in the 1980s and gave succour to films such as these that were exploiting popular songs for their publicity, as well as an important part of their attraction in the first place. The style of music video had an influence on film, with Jon Lewis noting that '*Purple Rain* [1984] is both a vanguard movie musical (the first to exploit so systematically the techniques and narrative structures of music video) ...'[14] Similarly, a review of *Highlander* (1986) noted that the director Russell Mulcahy '... has worked extensively in rock videos, which is evident enough in the way *Highlander* has been made as a succession of set-pieces'.[15] The film did not exploit musical song sequences, although its set pieces were often accompanied by loud, sometimes rock, music.

The 1990s began to see more films concerned with rock's past, such as *Back Beat* (1994), Oliver Stone's *The Doors* (1991), *What's Love Got to Do with It* (1993), Todd Haynes' *Velvet Goldmine* (1998) and Cameron Crowe's *Almost Famous* (2000), *Control* (2007) and *Nowhere Boy* (2009). Indeed, by the first decade of the twenty-first century, such rock nostalgia and musician biopic films had become common. Perhaps the most prominent other rock films were arguably traditional 'middle aged' rock films, such as Jack Black's films *School of Rock* (2003) and *Tenacious D: the Pick of Destiny* (2006), along with Disney musical *Camp Rock* (2008) and stage adaptation *Rock of Ages* (2012). Other traditional resurgences include the rediscovery of the dance film, with the highly successful *Step Up* films (*Step Up* [2008], *Step Up 2: The Streets* [2008], *Step Up 3D* [2010], *Step Up: Revolution* [2012] and *Step Up: All In* [2014]) and Disney's extremely popular television films *High School Musical* films (*High School Musical* [2006], *High School Musical 2* [2007], *High School Musical 3: Senior Year* [2008] and *Sharpay's Fabulous Adventure* [2011]).

Although this book concentrates on rock music, it is worth noting how far rap music has been influential in films. Some of these films focus on hip hop culture, such as *Breaking* (1984) about a female breakdancer and featuring rapper Ice T, and *Krush Groove* (1985) about founding a rap record label and featuring LL Cool J, Run DMC and the Fat Boys. Others, however, have used rap music as a sonic backdrop to urban violence and crime, such as John Singleton's *Boyz 'n the Hood* (1991), *New Jack City* (1991) and its battle against drug barons and *Juice* (1992) about a heist in Harlem and starring Tupac Shakur. Yet, there has been a significant interface between rock and rap, and both still can be used in films as a simplistic shorthand for social undercurrents outside of mainstream, respectable culture.

## Definitions, aesthetics and theoretical notions

There are a number of theoretical notions which are relevant for discussions about popular music (indeed, any music) and film. These include the basic division of diegetic and non-diegetic, whether the music appears to emanate from the world on screen or elsewhere as in the tradition of orchestral film scores which are not part of the represented illusory world in a film. In the film industry, these were traditionally termed 'source' and 'non-source' music and should not be confused with on- and off-screen sources for music. Despite the problematic nature of this distinction,[16] it is nevertheless still an important consideration, as conventionally the two modes have different assumptions and effects. Rick Altman wrote about the differences between diegetic and non-diegetic music: 'By convention, these two tracks have taken on a quite specific sense: the diegetic reflects reality (or at least supports cinema's referential nature), while the [non-diegetic] music track lifts the image into a romantic realm far above the world of flesh and blood.'[17] Although such functions are less well defined in recent cinema, the sense of more independence to non-diegetic music can allow it to comment on action or make stronger emotional effects.

While songs can appear as diegetic or non-diegetic music in a scene, what might be more pertinent is whether the music is 'scored' or 'tracked'. Production strategies involve either having a musician write new music for a particular sequence (scoring), or taking an existing piece of music and editing it to the images, or more commonly editing the images to fit the music (tracking). Examples that will be discussed in the book include William Friedkin's *To Live and Die in L.A.* (1985), which was scored by British group Wang Chung, and Dennis Hopper's *Easy Rider* (1969), which was tracked with existing rock songs. Tracking is often a simple option, while scoring a film using pop or rock music can be a difficult negotiation between two forms, even though there have been many crossovers and collaborations, and there is an assumption of equivalence at times between film and popular music. Prevalent musical structure in popular music is highly regulated and not particularly amenable to more fluid film structure, which is why written-to-picture orchestral scoring of precise dynamic developments in film remains prevalent. One notable product of this is that rock experimentation increasingly has found a place in cinema, with developing or maturing musicians aiming to stretch themselves and produce film music.

Arguably, there has been a convergence between incidental music in films (non-diegetic music) and the modes of the film musical. The musical may remain as a genre, but its impetus, aesthetics and attractions now also exist in many mainstream films. Indeed, one could argue that such characteristics have always been there, most clearly in mainstream films that included a featured song or two. With the recession of the musical as a perennial film genre, its role of selling music has migrated to mainstream films, taking with it something of the aesthetics that film musicals derived from their dominance by music dynamics and requirements.

## Rock and pop aesthetics

Film and rock music appear to go together remarkably well. While film has exploited music success and documented great rock performers, and music has exploited the charisma of actors singing songs and the success of films, there is also a sense where rock and film complement one another remarkably well on a material and aesthetic level.

It is tempting to imagine that the two were made for one another, but more convincing, that there has been some degree of aesthetic convergence which has been allowed by the virtues of each medium. In the opening chapter of their book on rock documentary films, Robert Edgar, Kirsty Fairclough-Isaacs and Benjamin Halligan include much discussion of music video, focusing heavily on the 1979–85 period, which is bookended by The Buggles' *Video Killed the Radio Star* record and video and the worldwide broadcast of the Live Aid charity concert. Their suggestion is that in the early 1980s,

> The visual would ultimately therefore demand the reinvention of the aural and what seemed to be a crude usurping of the priorities of form, in the domination of the visual over the aural, could be read as a survival mechanism or life-support system: only by completely transplanting popular music to the domains of the visual, no matter what damage would entail, would popular music continue to exist as an essential component of popular culture.[18]

They suggest that the advent of music video in the 1980s was an inescapable development which reinvigorated music. Yet, it also reinvigorated visual culture and was the embodiment of increasing close relationships between music and film as both aesthetic forms and industries. However, do not mistake this for teleology, a history written 'with hindsight', forcing events of the past ineluctably to lead to the present situation. Instead, this is noting that there was a certain inevitability which was in the heart not only of the technology that was developing over this period, but also certain desires and tendencies in the musical form itself. By this, I mean aspects to do with popular song structure and the culture of popular music increasingly incorporating visual aspects into the music. This is not to say that things might have taken a different form and developments could have led elsewhere, but broadly there has been an inexorable movement towards allying music and moving images. This less tangible aesthetic aspect may well have been as important as business decisions, changing technology and changing platforms of delivery.

Rock and pop are, more than much other culture, characterized by a distinct tension between creativity and commerce, one which at times can spur inventiveness but at other times dampen it. I remain convinced that the relationship between film and music is not simply one of financial exploitation. Film clearly was attracted to the energy of rock, and rock always had a notable visual component. The desire to make energetic film led to a unique relationship between rock and film.

A crucial aspect of popular music since rock'n'roll is a sense of dialectical relationship between beat and space. Beat provides a rhythmically compulsive element that divides and conquers time, while space in its various formats (in recording, live amplified sound and proximity to performers) articulates a spatial dimension. The relationship of the two delineates the time-space whole. This is given a stronger concretization when made into an audiovisual whole in film or music video. Heavily beat-based music privileges rhythm, 'groove', tempo and sense of movement in the music. This combines with and plays across rhythm of editing and movement of camera and objects on screen.

Newer forms of rock and pop in cinema have, at least partly, replaced some of the impetus that was there with film musicals. They exhibit aspects of traditional musicals increasingly being integrated with mainstream films (selling songs, foregrounded music, set-piece incidents and narrative). Classical musicals partly took the form they did due to the mode of production, where the Hollywood studio system's logistical basis dedicated regimented resources to making high-quality, standardized products based on distinct song sequences and the individuality of actors and actresses. Developments have taken place across rock's lifetime – becoming respectable, moving from being a downmarket contradictory mixture of a folk art and a crass exploitation industry to being an unproblematically dominant element of recent culture.

A development in the tradition, pop musicals used rock'n'roll songs yet followed the same means of rendering songs as traditional musicals. Rick Altman sees a continuity between the musicals of Hollywood's classical era and films that are based on pop music.[19] However, other commentators view pop music as providing a rupture with the traditional modes of musical film.[20] In an earlier discussion, I used two terms to differentiate between means of visual accompaniment to a song and/or dance sequence in musicals.[21] The term 'performance mode' designates an attempt to express an ineluctable connection between images seen and sounds heard, to indicate where images show the *production* of simultaneous sounds. Moving away from this, sometimes images show only some of the music's production. The clearest example of this would be the 'bursting into song' of the integrated film musical, which might be termed the 'lip synch mode', deriving from the industrial process of matching the lips to a pre-existing musical playback. Both the performance mode and the lip-synch mode offer a greater or lesser degree of the experience of the musicians performing the song or dance for the implied audience. The performance mode references a documenting of 'the real', while the lip-synch mode tends to signify a hyperbolic move to 'fantasy', the former being associated particularly with backstage musicals and the latter with integrated musicals such as *Seven Brides for Seven Brothers* (1954) or *South Pacific* (1958). The film of Andrew Lloyd Webber's *Phantom of the Opera* (2005) mixes the two, with operatic arias sung in public at the opera house using the performance mode and song sung intimately between characters using the lip-synch mode. As this description suggests, the two modes often work in different manners, with the former more amenable to use in mainstream dramatic films while the latter tends to indicate the traditional integrated film musical. Each approach tends to remain associated with different assumptions despite the breaking down of these as solid distinctions.

Rick Altman describes the process of 'audio dissolves' at the point where the song or dance starts in such integrated musicals. Here, the superimposition of the two distinct aural tracks signals a modulation of cinematic regimes, from that of the narrative to the song sequences, where from a conventional film style, the images actions reflect the music.[22] Altman's discussion of 'audio dissolves' in film musicals points to a profound shift in regimes (and concomitant emotional and mental states) at precise moments of entry to song sequences. However, something similar to this process has become evident in many films as a permanent state rather than a moment of transition. Altman describes the audio dissolve as a moment where the regime of mainstream film changes, with music moving into the foreground and diegetic sound and causality receding – a reversal of cinema's dominant regime:

> ... diegetic events, which seemed to be progressing according to an entirely causal scheme, slide imperceptibly, through an audio dissolve, toward the reduction of diegetic sound and the introduction of transcendent, supra-diegetic music. At this point, the events of the diegesis change motivation. Diegetic sound disappears; the only diegetic sounds which remain at normal volume are those which keep time to, i.e. are subordinated to the music .... The image now shows movements which depend more on the music than on one another.[23]

This equally can be applied to mainstream dramatic films,[24] bearing in mind Altman's description of the audio dissolve as a bridge from the prosaic everyday to the transcendent.[25] While it may not lead to full song sequences as in the film musical, such moments are marked by music's power, even if for a fraction of a second. The key is that loud music moves to the foreground to dominate the film's narration and aesthetics, even if only for a short time. The musical song sequence itself has a clear relation to the montage sequence, where constant visual action, collapsing many events into a short-time period, accompanies a distinct piece of music, which in much recent film is a rock or pop song.

'Audiovisual aesthetics' are something distinct from film aesthetics and from music aesthetics. They cannot be understood simply by looking at visual aspects and sonic process as separate entities. Indeed, particular rock and pop film aesthetics embrace a notion of isomorphism, embodied most clearly in the assumption that 'this goes with that', and that certain ideas or dynamics can be matched across image and sound. A strong tradition has built up, at least partly based on notions of 'congruence' between sound and image.[26] Dynamics and energy are regularly matched in both sound and image, with string contrasts proving rare. Sergei Eisenstein looked for a common denominator between music and image and alighted upon the idea of movement.[27] His sense of equivalence between film images and music was informed by a sense of structural resemblance at a profound level, allied to a sense of sound film's mixing of stimuli and sensation. Such combinations are apparent, but there are some distinctive aesthetics related to visualized musical performances. The 'on stage' rendering of rock or pop musicians has tended, for practical reasons, to follow the traditional 'tableau' that was used to 'record' performers from the early cinema, through to the classical musical and to television coverage of pop groups.[28] This format is a guarantee of the veracity of the performance context through the integrity of the shot as a discrete object in itself; film time corresponds to real time. This frontal stage-based shot often functions as a spatial anchor which is returned to intermittently as a grounding for the articulation of the other visual elements in comprehensible space. These other shots are primarily close-up shots of the musicians, particularly the singer, as well as often using interjected 'reverse shots' of audience. The on-screen audience's reaction can, in some ways, be seen as a model for the reaction of the film audience, as the on-screen audience can be seen as their replacement. This was a common device in the classical musical, as Jane Feuer notes: 'Long before television invented the studio audience and canned laughter, the Hollywood musical was putting audiences into the film for the purpose of shaping the responses of the movie audiences to the film.'[29]

The distinctive temporal schemes of rock and pop music are defining for their appearance in film, even if used in a fragmentary manner. Songs usually contain a continuous beat and tempo and conform to the loose pattern based around four-bar units that characterizes most Western popular music. The rhythmic continuity, cadences and changes in the song material are, to some extent, computed and anticipated by the audience. Recognition springs from the regularity of this temporal formation in popular songs and the logic that the music constructs for itself. The audience thus has a set of expectations which are, by and large, fulfilled by the music's relatively strict formalization into a set of presentations, repetitions and variations; this yielding a strict organization of time. As Adorno has noted in his negative appraisal of popular music, 'The whole structure of popular music is standardized .... The whole is pre-given and pre-accepted, even before the actual experience of the music starts .... The schematic build up dictates the way in which he [sic] must listen ....'[30] The traditionally established pattern for the presentation of songs and popular music, known as song form, is a format that encourages repetition as one of the prime means of comprehension.[31] This form allows the placement of material in specific relationships, governing a cyclical pattern of repetition of cells of music and a formula for the insertion of other material as a contrast to the principal material. Its succession of verses, choruses and variations are all sung, but traditionally almost all popular songs have a 'middle eight', a section of variation that commonly is occupied by an instrumental break and is so-called because of the convention that it was eight-bars long and in the middle of the piece as an aural contrast to its surrounding material (often an instrument solo, or a 'drop out' changing the instrumental texture of the music). The regimented repetition of material allows a maximized audience comprehension of form and recognition of the musical elements. These strong patterns are internalized by audiences and their appearance in film interacts with cinematic structures of time and senses of movement. In many cases, musical time substitutes for film time; particularly when music adopts the foreground. Musical time is profoundly different from the time schemes of cinema. It is continuous rather than flexible and gapped like time in films; time in pop music is for the song's duration a regime of the beat's rigorous reiteration. The continuity of the beat is the marker of time, held within song form's harnessing of the block repetitions of musical material that govern many forms of popular music.

Songs as a structure have an impact on film form. Song form is a relatively solid temporal format (often based on thirty-two bars and divided into alternating sections). Alan Williams notes that 'The popular song form ... [is] recognizable as a musical entity, since it is more structured both through tonality and repetition [than the motif used in classical film music].'[32] He goes on to note that '... the same procedures of music-diegesis interaction applied on the one hand to the short motifs typical of the symphonic score and on the other to the pop songs used in musical films will leave different effects and will be used to different ends'.[33] Associated aesthetics are good for certain techniques and less effective for others. The resulting aesthetics of the confluence of rock and pop with more traditional films scores include: often a lack of subtlety, a tendency towards drumbeats (often backbeats), a tendency for music (volume, beat and timbre) to dominate image and for sound to become autonomous. Songs are used regularly as underscore, along with pre-written mood pieces, in both cases mostly not conceived as 'accompaniment' in the traditional sense. Additionally, these pop musicians brought new timbres with them to films instead of writing music for the traditional orchestral ensemble, bringing the sounds of 1960s rock and pop music into the underscore as well as in the form of songs. The music for this series of films was trusted to musicians with no experience of creating film music in the traditional sense, and thus they produced music that bore more resemblance to the sort of music they had been producing already than it did to traditional film scores.

# Issues of commerce

Films have always had a musical dimension. Silent films were accompanied whenever possible and synchronized song films predated the coming of the 'talkies' by a couple of decades. The music industry had been involved intimately with films since the 1930s[34] but developed further with the selling of records superseding the selling of sheet music. The development of the LP record market in the late 1950s bolstered the situation and allowed non-diegetic scores to be released as a commodity together with the title song. Music appears perhaps to have been the most successful tied-in product in the cinema. Between the early 1950s and early 1960s, massive growth took place in the Disney merchandising division. *Kinematograph Weekly* pointed out that 'It was once estimated that a song from a Disney picture was played somewhere in the world every three minutes of the day ... [and now] top disc stars are being contracted to record the popular music, which has great hit potential.'[35]

Since synchronized sound films came into being, there has been a reciprocal relationship between music and films. Initially, this involved the mutual promotion of films and sheet music, and later cross-promotion between films and musical recordings. Indeed, Rick Altman notes that the film musical was inaugurated at height of piano sheet music sales.[36] Consequently, film musicals should perhaps be conceived less as musical accompaniment to images and narrative, but more image and narrative as emanations from or embellishments to the songs. The key might be to think of film musicals less in relation to general cinematic traditions than to see them in relation to the music industry and popular music traditions. Music defines the whole genre, and indeed, films were regularly built around pre-existing selections of songs.

How far are films simply a vehicle for selling music? Certain cases might beg this question more than others. In terms of synergy, the cross-selling of films and music makes good business sense, particularly in the light of conglomeration, where the two industries were in fact one company. Close relationships and buyouts between film companies and music companies run across the history of Hollywood, but this developed apace in the 1980s, which saw an acceleration in media company conglomeration. Tom Collins lists events:

> ... in 1988 the Sony Corporation purchased the CBS Record Group, which had recently acquired United Artists Music. The following year Warner Communications, which had already gobbled up influential independent music labels such as Atlantic Records and Elektra, was merged with the Time Inc. media empire. By 1991 six conglomerates were responsible for 91 percent on music sales in the United States. Music became one product alongside many others – cable television programs and movies, video games and magazines – in the conglomerate's entertainment stable: to create synergies, each was used to pitch the others.[37]

After a relaxation in the 1980s of the consent decrees that had dismantled the Hollywood studio system's control of production, distribution and exhibition (so-called 'vertical integration'), studios such as Paramount and Warner Brothers bought cinema chains. Universal's parent company MCA (Music Corporation of America) bought 50 per cent of Cineplex Odeon. Clearly, production of music and films was a crucial element of this maximization of control running through all levels of cultural consumption, even down to the magazine which review the films and music. In the UK, EMI, which had formed in 1931 as Electrical and Musical Industries Ltd., merged with Thorn Electrical Industries in 1979 (who made television sets and stereos), illustrating the desire to produce 'hardware' as well as cultural 'software', and owned the famous Abbey Road studios.

The soundtrack album industry has become one of the main ways to repackage existing music, and the expansion of the film soundtrack market has matched the contraction of the pop music market since the early 1970s. This has siphoned pop music back catalogues into the domain of 'film music' much like the way that silent film music cannibalized music from the classical concert hall. Cinema is now often a grab bag of effects, with music regularly being foregrounded and aspects such as pop music's regulated musical rhythm becoming critical in recent films. The surprising net effect of this has been to align increasingly autonomous forms of film music with the 'absolute' music championed by art music *aficionados*, moving it away from its perceived status as simply functional.

The development of MTV partnered the large-scale exploitation of record label back catalogues which was pursued aggressively in the late 1980s and

1990s. Cultural recycling was endemic in popular culture in the mid-1980s, and record companies were keen to exploit other markets.[38] Denisoff and Plasketes described the industrial strategy called synergy, involving the coordination of record releases from a film soundtrack as mutual publicity.[39]

# Book structure

This book's chapters are diverse, a selection of snapshots from a tout that testifies to the breadth and diversity of rock and pop's relationship with films. Some are clearly important musicians and films, near the 'centre', while some of those under scrutiny are less obvious, and perhaps more marginal. The chapter after this is 'Beat Boom Beatles: *A Hard Day's Night* and *Help!*' The Beatles were the catalyst not only for the explosion of new pop music inaugurated by the 'Beat Boom' but also for the impetus to put this new form of music into a new form of film rather than attempting to shoehorn it into existing film genres. Furthermore, the Beatles were important in that their first two (vehicle) films were conceived as a form of exploitation but (certainly their first film) increasingly is seen as 'art', cementing that the new youth-oriented popular culture of the 1960s instigated a new idea of art (as 'pop'). Later in the Beatles careers, they were involved in what is being discussed in the following chapter, 'The Psychedelic Screen.' In the late 1960s, bold steps were taken in both film and music, leading to some startling avant-garde-inspired experiments in the mainstream. Such a spirit of exploration was carried along by early Pink Floyd in to the next decade, as charted in the following chapter 'Obscured by Pink Floyd.' Their case illustrates how rock experimentation became tied to film from early on, while their sense of exploration in their first decade embodies a strong notion of rock's ambition as a medium. '"The Film Should be Played Loud": Rockumentary Films' looks into how rock and pop music developed its own particular form. Indeed, the rock documentary is often far removed from (non-musical) documentary tradition. Although rarely on cinema screens these days, it is one of the most vital areas of film-making – just that its films are released on DVD and more at home in record stores. The following chapter looks at a startling moment in film history, when films depicting urban African Americans had strident soundtracks by black artists to match the extremity and flamboyance of the images on screen. Indeed, the chapter 'Blaxploitation: Singing Across 110th Street' illustrates how these films demonstrate an unprecedented extremity and boldness of sound and vision. 'Falling to Earth: Bowie's Failed Film Soundtrack' looks into the audacious move where David Bowie was going to write the music for as well as star in *The Man Who Fell to Earth* (1975), although ultimately no music appeared, apart from a myth of the score. The next chapter, 'Cohabitation? The Resurgent Classical Film Score and Songs in the *Batman* Films,' looks into how many recent films (in this case the *Batman* series) are built around the use of pop songs and a specially written score, mixing tradition with commerce. After this, 'New Careers: Rock Musicians Become Film Composers' looks into how many ageing rock and pop musicians have opted for a career producing incidental music for films. This is a sign of rock getting old and also has instigated some changes in the modes and styles of film scoring, while 'Golden Years: 80s and 90s Hip Song Compilation Films' explores how some song usage in films are merely for commercial purposes, while others most definitely have a more imperative function. The final chapter, 'Copyright and Musical Censorship: Gangsta Rap and *Bad Lieutenant*' is about cultural ambiguity and how films might be 'misread', although it is also about how films can be amended later to uncertain effect.

# 2

# Beat Boom Beatles: *A Hard Day's Night* and *Help!*

The mid-1960s 'Beat Boom' saw an unprecedented amount of musical production and consumption, making the music industry the most lucrative culture industry against a background of the decline in fortunes in the film industry. This chapter will outline the clearest case of 'exploitation' of music by films during this period. The Beatles embody most of the processes across the period, from 'cash-in' films (*A Hard Day's Night* [1964]) to straight acting (*How I Won the War* [1968]), experimental film soundtracks (*Wonderwall* [1968]) and involvement in film production (*The Magic Christian* [1968]). The Beatles were aware of the possibility of using film to elevate their careers onto a different level. The band used cinema to differentiate themselves from other pop groups and pop music films of the time. Consequently, they espoused many cutting-edge techniques in their films, which also included *Help!* (1965), *Yellow Submarine* (1968), *Magical Mystery Tour* (made for television, 1968) and *Let It Be* (1970). Their success and innovation led to an explosion of films as a part of the beat boom and 'American Invasion' of the mid-1960s. This chapter will argue that during a short period the Beatles set the model and possibilities for later pop and rock musicians dealings with film.

Andrew Sarris famously called *A Hard Day's Night* (1964) 'the Citizen Kane of Jukebox movies', and it was unique in going into massive profit before its cinematic release through the presales of soundtrack LPs.[1] Two film vehicles, *A Hard Day's Night* and *Help!* (1965), for the Beatles are a significant point for the development of the relationship between music and film. The Beatles' films displaced the sturdy model of the classical film musical and offered an alternative: rough and ready action, fast-paced excitement and rapid change and fragmentation, all to the staunch beat of pop music rather than the smooth sophistication of show music.

Early examples of films that used rock'n'roll often set age-old narratives in a background of the youth or popular music world as in *King Creole* (1958) and *Expresso Bongo* (1959), or they were derivations of the Hollywood musical like *Rock Around the Clock* (1956), *The Girl Can't Help It* (1956) and *The Young Ones* (1961). These precursors to *A Hard Day's Night* and *Help!* were content at first to attempt to dilute pop music by mixing it into traditional forms of musical entertainment. Pop stars such as Elvis Presley and Cliff Richard made successful films that took the traditional musical film form and attempted to imbue it with a teenage orientation, often endeavouring to attenuate pop songs within a body of Tin Pan Alley songs in film musicals clearly deriving their impetus from the stage. *A Hard Day's Night* broke dramatically with the previous uses of pop music in cinema in a number of significant ways. It marked a point where pop music in films was not mixed with previously established musical forms, through the jettisoning of songs apart from those by the Beatles, while the film even ridiculed the traditional modes of 'family entertainment'. The film's significance can also be attributed to the template that it offered for pop music in films: the film style that paralleled pop music with dynamic visual activity and the articulation of songs as non-diegetic music. The success of the film put pop music firmly on the agenda of the cinema[2] or at least confirmed its importance for the cinema. This chapter will provide a detailed close analysis of sections of the film, looking to its use of music and accompanying articulation of the image.

## A Hard Day's Night

*A Hard Day's Night* is essentially a vehicle for the Beatles, its function being twofold. First, it shows the Beatles performing their songs in a form that is similar to the group's concerts, and second, it parades the Beatles as personalities, assuaging the thirst for intimate contact on behalf of their fans. The film's story concerns the Beatles travelling to London with Paul's grandfather in order to perform on television in front of a theatre audience. They have a number of incidental adventures: they are mobbed by adoring fans, have trouble with Paul's grandfather, are interviewed, lose Ringo and only just manage to be back at the theatre in time for their performance.

The Beatles' songs are foregrounded in the film in various ways. Four songs are performed in the concert sequence near the end of the film. Two songs are performed at the rehearsals at the theatre. There is another (impromptu) performance in the guard's van of the train which is motivated as a movement from the film's established reality into a fantasy moment, while at a club, the group dance to their own hit records. Beatles' songs are also utilized four times as non-diegetic music: in the opening/title sequence, in the sequence where the Beatles have 'escaped' their professional confines and gambol on a field, in the 'chase' sequence where they go between the theatre and the police station to retrieve Ringo in time for their concert appearance and lastly during the end titles. Apart from these four occasions, songs appear diegetically, most using the performance mode and making a point of reproducing the group performing live, an example of which is *I Should Have Known Better* being played in the guard's van of the train on the way to London. Nine different songs appear in the film (some are repeated), and each is suitably foregrounded as a distinct object in itself married to the spectacle of performance or action, as a discrete entity or micro-narrative within the body of the film. Micro-narratives (songs, in this case) may be defined as relatively autonomous narratives within films, distinct episodes within a film that make sense without specific reference to the framing (overall) narrative.

In terms of the second primary function of the film, the Beatles are represented as distinct and individual personalities with an emphasis on their bonding together as a group. Their collective identity is channelled through their hair and dress and through the projection of a strong provincial image (Liverpudlian/northern English), bolstered by their youth, humour and their constant verbal repartee. The film provides a further dimension to the Beatles as individuals, which develops the star image circulated by magazine profiles and television interviews. What the film offers to fans is a virtual contact with the Beatles.[3] The ambiguity between the group acting and as non-actors 'being themselves' allows *A Hard Day's Night* to function both as a dramatic film and as a succession of spectacles of the group.

This dual function of the film, showcasing the songs and displaying the Beatles, is paramount and as a consequence *A Hard Day's Night* is not geared to a complex developmental narrative but utilizes a loose narrative that meanders through a number of incidents rather than progresses in any purposeful manner. This means that the music and the spectacle of the Beatles articulate much if not all of the film, relegating narrative development to a function of simply unifying disparate songs and incidents.

The film has a strikingly visual impetus to complement the musical drive, having a consistently fast pace and using a number of self-conscious techniques.[4] An example of this is the press conference, where the moving image of photographs being taken is converted into a series of still images representing those photographs. Handheld camera is utilized constantly, and there is a simultaneity of action within the frame that gives the film an improvisational quality, suggesting a 'capturing' of actual events. The film was shot very quickly, fitted into a break in the Beatles' schedule and consequently uses predominantly first (and only) takes.[5] The film's director, Richard Lester, had been successful in television and advertisement production,[6] and it is probable that his experience of the latter in particular added to the sense of visual excitement in the film, achieved chiefly through its fragmenting of the classical spatial and temporal systems. Lester, although American, had already made two films in the UK, *The Running, Jumping, Standing Still Film* (1959), an eleven-minute surrealistic and Oscar-nominated short starring Peter Sellers and Spike Milligan, and *It's Trad, Dad!* (1962), a narratively framed feature length showcase for 'trad' jazz and pop songs.

*A Hard Day's Night* established a model and standard for pop music in film, not only setting standards of quality but the means by which pop music and groups could be represented in the cinema. This is achieved chiefly through generic hybridization, blending documentary-derived techniques with the form of the dramatic fiction film, the former elements guaranteeing the pop group and their performances while the latter functions as a frame containing these elements. The visual style that *A Hard Day's Night* establishes for itself is a hybrid of the documentary conception of 'recording reality' and the dramatic film form of mainstream cinema. This was a pragmatic move as it attained the principal aim of portraying the Beatles as themselves for an audience that desired a relationship of proximity to them, and it managed to sustain a feature film by taking the Beatles' repartees, activities and performances and framing them with a narrative derived from dramatic cinema. *A Hard Day's Night* created a substantial legacy: film style paralleling pop music with speed and kinesis, and a specific procedure for the articulation of pop songs in films. As John Hill has noted, '... the film successfully challenged many of the old conventions of the pop film by introducing a new approach to both plot and visual presentation .... For possibly the first time, the pop film demonstrated that it was possible to present a musical number without the illusion of actual performance'.[7] *A Hard Day's Night*'s film style certainly established it as a foundation of sorts for pop music in visual culture that followed, and its influence can be detected as early as *Catch Us If You Can* (1965) and American television's later virtual facsimile of the Beatles and the film style of their first two films for the Monkees.

Music appears within the film as autonomous performances, set pieces which either halt the progression of, or at least do nothing to further, the narrative, much as is the case with song and dance sequences in the backstage musical.[8] Yet, at certain points, songs are utilized as a replacement for the traditional cinematic non-diegetic music; that is to say they replace cinema's traditional 'background music'. This is of prime significance as the use of pop songs as non-diegetic music, which had become widespread by next decade, had not previously been used as a coherent strategy in feature films. Apart from the film's beginning and ending, Beatles' songs are utilized twice as non-diegetic music in the body of the film: first, in the playing field sequence and second, for the 'chase' sequence. On all of these occasions, the songs supplant diegetic sound almost totally and parallel the kinesis of the images and cutting. The images were cut to the music's demand (to the music's duration rather than rhythm[9]).

Most songs in *A Hard Day's Night* are presented as group performances, using the performance mode, rather than using the lip-synch mode.[10] The contemporaneous Cliff Richard and Elvis Presley films tend to adapt the classical musical form, utilizing the lip-synch mode, sometimes semi-diegetic, supported by minimal diegetic sources (like a guitar) but using substantial non-diegetic music as the principal form of song backing. On a practical level, this solved the problem posed by the stardom of the Beatles as a group of recognizable individuals, rather than a single foregrounded individual. The lip-synch mode could have marginalized the group members who were not singing at a given moment, the tendency of this strategy being to focus on one person as the vocal and visual centre – and yet, that option was taken up for a song in *Help!* in the following year.[11]

The song *A Hard Day's Night* opens the film, as the title song, articulated non-diegetically and being accompanied by footage of the Beatles running away from a mob of their fans. As a statement of intent, visual style here signifies what will follow in the rest of the film: speed and kinesis, fragmentation and an exciting array of action and songs. Screen space is made chaotic through disparate shots and confused screen direction as well as by the use of fast panning shots of moving bodies and body parts that are often indistinct images and spatially ambiguous. Continuity is not provided by space or editing but by the song which is the main device for continuity and unity in the sequence. Space is thus articulated in terms of the visual objects (the Beatles and their fans); rather than establishing a space for action, it is the action that provides the spatial system of the sequence.

This highly active title sequence establishes speed as a central strategy and narrative theme of the film, with a large amount of kinetic activity and virtually no static images. After the three of the Beatles have run into the railway station (a low-angle long shot) followed by their fans, there are shots that appear to be close-ups of disembodied legs in fast motion. These shots are indistinct, blurred by the speed of activity and the large size of the image in the frame, and create a non-representational image of the speed and kinesis that is established in the title sequence and is a significant feature of the film in general. This particular process works intermittently throughout the sequence; when George Harrison, John Lennon and Ringo Starr hide from their pursuers in telephone kiosks, there is a slow pan across the three adjacent booths but with the shot or image constructed as a double plane of image and action: the booths in the background are in focus, while the fans rushing past in the foreground are out of focus and cannot be distinguished. This is a repeat of the kinetic processes already in circulation in the film, but rather than being constructed as an interjected shot, the image, of movement rather than of a specific object, is incorporated into the shot of the Beatles, as a visual equivalent of noise or distortion.

In a *Sight and Sound* review at the time of release, Geoffrey Nowell-Smith's verdict on *A Hard Day's Night* was: 'It can hardly be called well directed, unless you believe that the rapid gyrations of a hand-held camera are intrinsically more cinematic than the usual methods, which is patently not true.'[12] His concern with 'the cinematic' was symptomatic of film culture at the time, which was less than impressed with a film that attempted to reorient its whole film style around music. Indeed, here very clearly the visual track has become partially abstract in order to better accompany the song. This approach announces a new form of cinema to match the very novelty of the Beatles.

At *A Hard Day's Night*'s conclusion, there is a climax towards which the narrative inexorably has been moving: the television broadcast, a performance in front of a theatre audience. This is a straightforward reward for Beatles' fans in that it simulates the concert situation that the audience might have expected from the film.[13] Overall, this is perhaps more conventional than the rendering of songs in the rest of the film. It is substantial, involving the performance of four songs (*Tell Me Why, If I Fell, I Should Have Known Better* and *She Loves You*). The visual strategy for showing the group is 'classical' in that space is articulated around an establishing shot showing the Beatles on stage and varied close-up shots of the different group members. Allied to this, it is crucial to show the 'reverse shot' documenting the audience's reaction to the performance. This offers a screen surrogate for the cinema audience and facilitates a direct simulation of the concert experience.

The concluding song of the concert sequence is *She Loves You*, which had been a massive hit for the Beatles in the year before *A Hard Day's Night* was released.[14] The visuals are simultaneously a representation of and a confirmation of the phenomenon of Beatlemania, showing an extreme reaction. The emphasis on the Beatles performing the songs is lessened in favour of a heightened representation of the relationship between the group and their fans. The most remarkable aspect of the image track in the *She Loves You* section of the concert is the amount of audience shots when compared to the number of shots that constitute the group's performance. After the inaugurating shots that establish a situation of mass audience hysteria, the film seems intent on reinforcing this.[15] In stark contrast with the chasing fans at the start of the film, members of the audience are portrayed as individuals rather than being represented as an undifferentiated mass of an audience. Concentration on the audience serves, first, to manifest Beatlemania in the film as a reality and, second, guarantees the veracity of the performance (and the whole film itself) through the utilization of quasi-documentary techniques, which are at the heart of the film's strategies.

While *A Hard Day's Night* included some songs that were not on the soundtrack LP (previous Beatles' hits), the album itself contained a whole side of songs that did not appear in the film, so in reality it was only a semi-soundtrack. The record was highly successful and remained at the Number One position in the charts for over nine months, spawning two Number One singles that were both featured in the film.[16] The film too was also an unqualified success. *Kinematograph Weekly* announced shortly after the film's release: 'The Beatles picture ... is overtaking the outstandingly successful *Tom Jones* and is hard on the heels of the record-breaking *From Russia with Love*.'[17] Two weeks earlier, the same organ announced that at the London Pavilion, *A Hard Day's Night* had 'exploded into the big money ... On Saturday and Sunday house records were broken ...'[18] In addition to its massive financial success, *A Hard Day's Night* was nominated for Academy Awards for Alun Owen's screenplay and George Martin's musical direction. The popularity of *A Hard Day's Night* was largely due to the Beatles' cultural status at the time, the film's release being at the height of 'Beatlemania', which is figured within the body of the film itself, while in fact 'Beatlemania' had also been the film's working title.[19]

## *Help!*

The success of *A Hard Day's Night* was such that another Beatles' film followed within a year with a larger budget and consequently superior production values.[20] This manifested itself principally in the use of colour film stock and exotic locations for the shooting of the film, while the ten-week duration of *Help!*'s shoot was significantly greater than its predecessor. However, the sequel broadly follows the initial film's blueprint which became standard for pop group vehicles. This includes being constructed around an existing pop group using the individuals as characters that are nominally themselves; having a narrative that does little more than frame the songs and the representation of the group; and the group's songs appear as a central pillar of the film, being constructed as performances that reproduce their concert performances and, on occasions, the group's music becomes a non-diegetic accompaniment to visual action sequences.

Since *A Hard Day's Night*, the Beatles' career had gone from strength to strength with two more massive hit singles between the material from their two films (the double A side *I Feel Fine/She's A Woman* and *Ticket to Ride*). They had produced a string of hit records and had toured the United States, and the world had caught up with Britain and America's 'Beatlemania' hysteria. *Help!* takes the possibilities of pop songs use in films a step further than *A Hard Day's Night* while developing the film featuring pop stars a step away from where musicians simply play musicians. It was produced by the same people as the group's first film venture, specifically producer Walter Shenson and director Richard Lester.[21] There is a progression of sorts between the vocabularies of the two films; increased production values and the success of *A Hard Day's Night* ensuring that *Help!* would need to be an aesthetic 'progression' commensurate with the Beatles' increased success. One of the key differences is that the film has a far more developed narrative, and although the Beatles play themselves, they act within a general comedy framework. The film's story concerns the religious followers of 'Kaili' trying to get a sacrificial ring from Ringo's finger. This group of people is represented as what at the time was considered comic versions of south Asians and are white actors with dark facepaint. This aspect of the film severely limits its current popularity, fixing the film as an enduring index of attitudes at the time.

The film's soundtrack album was also the official Beatles' album, as had been the case with *A Hard Day's Night*, and similarly contained seven songs out of fourteen that are not featured in the film. Both the film and the album included the hit before the film, *Ticket to Ride*, yet the album failed to include their other inter-film hit *She's A Woman*, which appears in the film. The film uses only half of the group's songs that appear on the album, and it clearly was considered that George Martin's orchestral music, which is predominantly based on Beatles' melodies, could not have been combined with the film's songs into a successful commodity outside of the film. This underlines the relationship of the film and the music, the situation being that the film is sold on the back of the Beatles' songs, accessed as almost a secondary product to the music. The album was thus able to benefit from film publicity (and, of course, vice versa), while being essentially the successor to the *Beatles for Sale* album rather than an accurate document of the music that appears in the film.[22]

*Help!* includes the display of exotic elements that were lacking in the fairly dour *mise-en-scene* of the first film, specifically the locations, the colour photography and a variety of costumes. However, the narrative is much more traditional and the first film's pseudo-documentary style is jettisoned while the construction of the musical performance sequences is more extravagant. *Help!* includes title cards and words appearing on the screen, what are often seen as 'alienation effects' like the short 'interlude' sequence. This starts with a title card reading 'Interlude,' has no diegetic sound but overtly overdubbed birdsong, while the Beatles play around for a matter of seconds before another title card appears, reading 'Part 2' and the film's development is reengaged after the narrative-destroying insert. The film is more fragmented than most musicals but crucially is built around a series of song sequences. The Beatles perform *Help!* at the start, *You're Gonna Lose That Girl* (in a recording studio), *You've Got to Hide Your Love Away* (in their house), *I Need You* and *The Night Before* (in succession on Salisbury Plain) and *Another Girl* on the beach in the Bahamas. Two songs appear as a non-diegetic accompaniment to the action: *Ticket to Ride* and *Help!* at the film's conclusion.

The *Ticket to Ride* sequence in *Help!* is pioneering in its use of a pop song as non-diegetic music tethered to a distinct sequence of visual spectacle with no real narrative impetus. Indeed, this sequence is eminently removable from the film and resembles later pop promos.[23] The sequence is inaugurated by the song's appearance on the soundtrack, which cues a succession of shots of the Beatles doing a variety of things in the snow. The four group members play about around a piano on snow-covered mountainous terrain, fall over in the snow, ski, do the body semaphore signals that appear on the album cover and in film publicity, ride in a horse-drawn cart, have a picnic and run around a train. The sequence is described with no little difficulty, because of the lack of any unifying logic in the visual track. This is not an inconsequential 'episode' where the narrative drifts from a progressive development but a fully blown spectacle that denies the power of narrative in the film.

All the action appears to take place in a similar space (a ski resort) and has no diegetic sound, its continuity and cohesion being provided solely by the foregrounded non-diegetic music on the sound track. This sequence is similar to the song and/or dance sequences of the film musical, in terms of a set-piece spectacle replacing the film's narrative impetus. However, instead of the song being sung and danced, the group cavorts entertainingly. In this sequence, the soundtrack and image track have become uncoupled, with the image track becoming subordinate to the demands of the song and evacuating narrative development and coherence in favour of merely offering the audience a selection of images as accompaniment to the song. Reviewing *Help!* in *Sight and Sound* in 1965, Peter Harcourt noted: 'What is the effect of all this endless running and jumping, this refusal to stand still? Up to a point, it seems an attempt to render in visual terms some of the energy of the Beatles' music . . .'[24]

The most temporally sustained section of music in *Help!* is a recording session held in the open air on Salisbury Plain with the Beatles surrounded by the army. Two songs (*I Need You* and *The Night Before*) are performed in succession, and there is an interpolated appearance of portions of another of their songs (*She's A Woman*) played on a tape recorder. This sequence demonstrates vividly the conflict in the film between performance (showing the group performing music) and narrative (film as logical progression), as the space of the autonomous spectacle is intruded upon by the drive to retain narrative progression. The Beatles are being protected by the army, an oblique development for the narrative but an opportunity for the film to display them in an unfamiliar environment and add the military firepower to the spectacle of the group. Whereas *A Hard Day's Night* had a substantial section representing a concert performance, *Help!* went beyond the quasi-documentary style of its predecessor and was able to have narrative take the wildest of turns purely for the sake of variation in the parade of spectacles on display for comedic purposes.

As the Beatles perform the songs, the followers of Kaili have dug a tunnel for a bomb with which they hope to kill Ringo. A cultist sympathetic to the musicians convinces their leader that the tunnel is already beneath the Beatles by playing a tape recording of their record *She's A Woman*. This is intercut with the Beatles' song performance and breaking the homogeneity of the song sequence. Each song contains a continuous beat and tempo and conforms to the loose song form pattern based around four-bar units that characterize most pop music. The rhythmic continuity, cadences and changes in the song material are, to some extent, cognized and anticipated by the audience.[25] However, the interlocution of one song into the aural continuity of the other two destroys an overall coherence that the music tends to provide in song sequences. Such a strategy in a song sequence is rare indeed, and perhaps the conflict between the film's narrative and its presentation of the Beatles' music is apparent at this point, and indeed precisely this conflict was perceived as one of the problems of *Help!* with John Lennon later remarking that the Beatles felt like extras in their own film.[26] Indeed, Neil Sinyard points to the exotic locations and unbelievable house interior as potentially alienating locations for four normal working-class young men.[27]

# Conclusion

*Help!* must essentially be seen as a sequel to *A Hard Day's Night*. While it develops various elements from the previous film, it retains the same characters (the Beatles playing themselves), the foregrounded song format and much of the film style and comedic routines from its predecessor. *Help!* betrays a conflict between the demands of its narrative, which is more developmental and conventional than that of *A Hard Day's Night*, and the demands of the film functioning essentially to provide spectacles of the Beatles and their music. To parallel the narrative's increased demands, as part of the process, the song sequences are more elaborate and fantastic.

Together these two films can be seen as setting a model for the pop group vehicle, one where the group members form a character unit (often playing a pop group) and the film narrative runs in parallel to (or in conflict with) the film's principal aim of showcasing a succession of songs. In addition to this, these two Beatles films set a standard through their cultural prominence and financial success that other films using pop music had to be aware of and in some ways follow. The first two Beatles' films have to be seen as a foundation upon which pop music in cinema and specifically pop group vehicles was built, testified to by the later neglect of the more traditional forms and strategies used by Elvis Presley and Cliff Richard in favour of the foregrounding of visual and musical materiality used in the Beatles' films. Other pop group vehicles that have followed this format include *Ferry Cross the Mersey* (1964) for Gerry and the Pacemakers, *Catch Us If You Can* (1965) for The Dave Clark Five, the Monkees TV series and their film *Head* (1968) and more recently the Spice Girls' vehicle *Spice World* (1997). In this process, *A Hard Day's Night* and *Help!* utilize the principal means of representing pop songs in films that has perpetuated up to the present day. In the case of using pop songs as non-diegetic music, these were the first films to establish this as a strategy for the cinema; and in the case of the *Ticket to Ride* sequence and the hybrid form used in the *Another Girl* sequence, *Help!* demonstrates the principal visual language that has been used by pop promotional films from the late 1960s to music videos of today.

*A Hard Day's Night* and its sequel *Help!* broke significantly with many of the established modes for presenting songs in the traditional film musical. Both films utilize a minimal amount of orchestral non-diegetic music, but notably, at certain points, the Beatles' songs are utilized as a replacement for it. When the Beatles' songs appear as non-diegetic music, a reversal in the relationship of the film's elements takes place: the songs marginalize and destroy diegetic sound and dominate the image track, whose function it now is to 'double' the musical energy with kinetic images and decoupage. The beat of the music becomes the principal articulator of time for the sequences and the songs mark off the sequences as discrete objects. The images are subordinated, cut to the music's requirements, which means that the music has become the central agent of filmic action. Not only does it articulate the image track, but it mediates between the audience and what bear more than a passing resemblance to silent cinema sequences through their lack of diegetic sound, namely the spatially chaotic succession of shots that comprises the title sequence and the procession of incoherent images in the later playing field sequence. Although the rhythm of the editing does not double the song rhythms and structures, the endings of the songs cue the return to narrative-based cinema; the songs refuse to fade out and be subordinated to narrative development.

In the mid-1960s, popular music increasingly became written, performed and recorded by the same individuals, rather than professional ranks of songwriters and session musicians in addition to the pop star 'faces'. This was part of a process of gradually seeing pop, and its more 'serious' sibling rock, as having artistic status. Consequently, authenticity and originality became valued. This privileging of the 'origin' was centred on the recording artist as an author and often (although by no means always) was dependent on their involvement with all stages of the aesthetic production process, but specifically the writing, recording and performing. The Beatles were certainly one of the vanguard in this shift in production and cultural perception, having initially fought against producer George Martin to replace the established songs that they were contracted to cover with their own songs and then going on to experimentation in the studio later in the decade.

*A Hard Day's Night* and *Help!* can be seen as a part of this cultural elevation process, with film bringing a certain amount of prestige as well as further dissemination to a group who were a household name but were initially lacking in being accorded any artistic merit. Testament to the increasingly legitimate status of the Beatles was the awarding to each group member of an M.B.E., while the start of the next decade saw a Cambridge University professor of music, Wilfrid Mellers, write a book that analysed the group's music in a way that had previously been reserved for classical composers.[28] As the 1960s progressed, it is impossible to deny that the Beatles' music progressed too, a trajectory of gradually increasing complexity. By 1966, the Beatles had already announced the abandonment of live concerts as their records were so complex they were no longer reproducible in a performance context.[29] By the time of *Help!*, the group had already begun this process, although the songs in the film bear little resemblance to their later more self-consciously 'original' product. The films perhaps helped move pop music some way towards being taken seriously, as the medium of film was somehow considered more respectable than popular music. After all, it is hardly an uncommon situation for a cultural form to gain legitimacy through the annexing of a more legitimate form. Films have regularly attempted to attain a legitimate status, to be deemed 'art', through the high-profile adaptation of literature, and it is possible that the Beatles' films worked in a similar way.

# 3

# The Psychedelic Screen

'Psychedelia' is not an easy thing to define, and indeed, there appear to be different definitions for a vague object. Michael Hicks notes that by the late 1960s, 'it was a household term that people used to describe almost anything, from neo-expressionist paintings to strip shows'.[1] It was commonly imagined to mean 'drug-inspired' (particularly hallucinogen LSD) or 'multi-coloured' and has implications of using a certain type of collaged visual design and espousing a sense of being 'revolutionary' and breaking with tradition. In 1967, The Beatles had produced *Sergeant Pepper's Lonely Hearts Club Band*, arguably the ultimate psychedelic LP and widely regarded as a musical landmark. This was a key part of the cultural explosion associated with psychedelia, a predominantly visual culture inspired by hallucinogenic drugs that became prominent during the 'Summer of Love' in 1967.[2] As a cultural trend, psychedelia was a massively influential idea for a few years in the wake of the 'Summer of Love', which sometimes was also known as the 'Flower-Power summer' and was a watershed for the cultural underground.[3] The most concise definition of psychedelia available is 'the musical response to LSD'.[4] In film, this manifested itself often as hallucinogenic interludes that resemble surrealist cinema in their stylization and grotesquerie. However, it also involved a very direct use of music associated with psychedelia and the counterculture.

Although 1967's 'Summer of Love' is considered the birth of psychedelia and the counterculture, according to Mark Kurlansky, 1968 is a watershed year that defines much of what happened in ensuing years.[5] In terms of events, during 1968, there was the Prague Spring and subsequent Warsaw Pact invasion, the Paris student rebellion that nearly was a revolution, Martin Luther King and Bobby Kennedy were shot, the Yippies attacked the Chicago Democratic Party convention, there was the My Lai incident (massacre) in Vietnam, Nixon was elected president, the Vietcong began the successful Tet Offensive and there was a high-profile feminist attack on the Miss America pageant. 1968 was also an interesting year for popular music, particularly in Britain. There was a mad rush of counterculture and psychedelia. It was in the middle of an outstanding period of creativity and aesthetic bravura. The Beatles made their own film, *Magical Mystery Tour*, which depicted the effect of drugs in close-up for bemused audiences across Britain when it was broadcast on BBC2 on Boxing Day 1967. The protean energy of pop music and 'Swinging London' films came into intimate contact with a trio of films that boldly decided that their musical scores should be constructed and performed completely by popular musicians with a total lack of experience in making film music, and thus following radically different procedures from the dominant film music patterns evident in mainstream Hollywood films.

Some musical recordings associated with psychedelia were characterized by certain distinctive sound effects, including phasing and the use of magnetic tape recordings run backwards. Phasing effects were evident in The Small Faces' *Itchycoo Park* or Status Quo's *Pictures of Matchstick Men*, while backward tapes were evident in Jimi Hendrix's *If 6 was 9* and the Beatles' *Tomorrow Never Knows*. Pink Floyd's debut album *The Piper at the Gates of Dawn* (1967) embraced child-like naiveté and an interest in space as well as diversity in music as well as lyrics. Their second album *A Saucerful of Secrets* (1968) had a more psychedelic cover of distorted colour imagery. Similarly, a visually distorted 'psychedelic' cover adorned Spirit's *The Twelve Dreams of Doctor Sardonicus* (1970), which also contained highly varied musical material, although American bands tended to rely less of studio possibilities as the counterculture often involved more straightforward rock.

Michael Hicks notes: 'By late 1967 the word "psychedelic" already suffered from overuse. Virtually every rock band was calling itself – or allowing itself to be called – "psychedelic", no matter what the band's actual style or whether its members used drugs.'[6] Roky Erickson's band's debut album was self-consciously titled *The Psychedelic Sounds of the 13th Floor Elevators* (1966). Arguably, the dominant groupings of this music were American 'Acid Rock', such as the Grateful Dead and psychedelic pop/rock, such as the Strawberry Alarm Clock. Acid rock exerted a massive influence on British 'underground' music, particularly in fostering a sense of working outside of normal channels of culture and publicity.[7] If musical sounds of psychedelia were not so easily summarized, then the design art of concert posters would more easily be seen as a coherent visual approach, with this form of culture being easily differentiated by its use of bold and often abstract graphics with strident use of (sometimes clashing) colours.

The twin developments of increased importance of popular music (with its expanded market) and the burgeoning counterculture meant that psychedelia entered film as an object regularly tied to music. During the 1960s, there was pressure for 'up-to-date' soundtracks. Probably, the most famous instance of this was Hitchcock's *Torn Curtain* (1966), where he fell out with his musical collaborator Bernard Herrmann over the desire for an 'up-to-date' score or the film. While such pressures and aspirations may have had a negative effect, they also led to a degree of experimentation. This involved the introduction of some pop musicians to the medium of film. Indeed, this was enabled by the protean character of rock and the counterculture from the middle of the decade. The advent of the more serious 'rock', allied with counterculture sensibilities and drug use for 'mind expansion', led to different assumptions about how popular music should and could relate to film. Some film-makers decided boldly that their musical scores should be constructed and performed completely by popular musicians, marking radical experiments within mainstream cinema and following radically different procedures from the dominant film music patterns evident in mainstream Hollywood films. For some films, this meant a score and for others a series of songs that provide character and can often adopt the foreground of the film. For a relatively short period, this coalesced into a distinctive sensorium of sound and vision. Psychedelia on film often embraced short hallucinogenic interludes that resemble surrealist cinema in their stylization and grotesquery, and music could often play a part in the out-of-the-ordinary status of such sequences. The visual repertoire of psychedelia included mixtures of different colours, fragmented and obscured vision, and juxtapositions of objects from different contexts, often mixing the very new with antiquated objects, as part of a distinctive design ethic. While this was evident in set design,[8] particular film style also included the use of disorientating camera movement, use of particular lenses that distort images, self-conscious sunbursting from shooting into the sun and fast and discontinuous editing.

The late 1960s marks a moment of experiment in the use of pop songs in films that were not musicals in the traditional sense of the term but in most cases mainstream narrative films. In the United States, *The Graduate* (1967) had songs by Simon and Garfunkel used as non-diegetic music, along with a small amount of score by Dave Grusin, while *Easy Rider* (1969) was fitted up with a succession of pop and rock songs. This is not to say that these were the first to use such techniques, as Kenneth Anger had 'fitted' pop songs to film a few years earlier.[9] Similarly, Woody Allen's film *What's Up, Tiger Lily* (1967) had taken the image track from a Japanese film and added comic dubbed dialogue and music by The Lovin' Spoonful. This was a period, though, of aesthetic experiment, when more in the way of 'avant-garde' techniques found their way into mainstream films or films at the margin of the mainstream.

# American psychedelia

Roger Corman's *The Trip* (1967) was made by AIP (American International Pictures) as an exploitation film. It begins with a spoken and written warning about LSD; the film was controversial at the time of release but made money.[10] The film's screenplay was written by Jack Nicholson and concerns Paul (Peter Fonda) taking LSD at his friend John's (Bruce Dern) house after meeting Max (Dennis Hopper). The acid trip sequences afford the film many opportunities for visual flourishes, including regular use of kaleidoscopic lenses, fast cutting and juxtaposition of divergent images. *The Trip* also required significant support form music in depicting the alteration of perception engendered by LSD. The film's music was by Electric Flag – billed as 'Mike Bloomfield and the Electric Flag (An American Music Band)'. Having recently been formed, the soundtrack was the ensemble's first studio recording. Led by guitar player Bloomfield, they were a blues rock group that had been inspired by black artists such as Booker T and the MGs and Otis Redding and were a rarity in including horns with the blue rock band format prevalent in the late 1960s. Oddly, the band appearing at the start of the film is the International Submarine Band (with Gram Parsons as singer) rather than Electric Flag, although it is the sounds of the latter. Electric Flag provide an effective score, adopting many different musical styles, not only blues but also jazz, experimental music, electronic music and rock. *The Trip* starts with music that alternates dreamy keyboards and more assertive sections of brass. It is initially uncertain as to whether this is music from the advertisement appearing on screen but it then persists, with its volume being moved crudely up and down to allow for dialogue's audibility. The onset of the LSD trip involves a distinct visual strategy of communicating things being beyond normality. These involve primarily coloured light effects including flickering strobing, kaleidoscopic lenses and rapid and discontinuous editing providing a strong sense of fragmentation. For example, at one point, an extremely short shot (virtually a flash frame) appears of a lizard shooting its extended tongue at an insect. This is unrelated to shots surrounding it, although near the end, there are a couple more isolated shots of this lizard, which appears not to share the same diegetic space as the characters. While these aspects add up to a psychedelic dreamworld, *The Trip* has some clear psychedelic décor on the walls of the clubs and Max's apartment, involving murals and multicoloured designs and swirls of colour, as well as hanging beads and diverse objects. The dreamlike images are accompanied by some atmospheric music which initially involves violin and guitar arpeggios, and for the beach sequences organ and electric guitar and bass. These appear to be distinct pieces which are edited to fit the action rather than music scored to fit the images precisely. During the sequence of the couple on the bed, the music involves scraping sounds with electronic echo, as well as a dull hammering drum beat and electric guitar sounds. The images are enhanced and obscured through having images and patterns projected onto them. The extraordinary images are accompanied by some unusual music, including prototype Moog synthesizer played by pioneer Paul Beaver, as well as electric violin. The score's eclecticism is striking, though, with the tour-de-force of extremely rapidly edited montage at the film's conclusion when Paul comes down from his trip involving first a piece of Dixieland jazz and then a Chicago blues-style instrumental.

Another AIP production, *Psych Out* (1968) showcased American west-coast psychedelic culture and included some of those involved in *The Trip* (Jack Nicholson, Susan Strasberg and Bruce Dern).[11] The film follows Jennie (Strasberg) who is looking for her brother in the Haight-Ashbury district of San Francisco. She is helped by Stoney (Nicholson) who plays guitar with a band called 'Mumblin' Jim'. *Psych Out* showcases the psychedelic culture of the time, in many cases using locations, such as the street and park scenes which open the film. In the café and Stoney's house, chaotic collaged psychedelic décor is highly evident with painted walls with hanging objects like carpets, hanging beads and at the café a fast cutting sequence showing many posters (saying things like 'Flower Power'). Ronald Stein's incidental music is rock-based, and includes guitar, organ and sitar. This includes some ethereal music by Stein featuring The Storybook when some women decorate the house with strings of beads. The house décor is characteristically fragmented and juxtaposes diverse objects, while in the sex sequence between Stoney and Jennie (which features the film's opening song again) obscures visuals through superimposed images, blurred images, light effects and even the use of non-diegetic inserts, of a corn field and sunset.

The Seeds appear and perform *Two Fingers Pointing at You* at the 'funeral', while the Strawberry Alarm Clock perform *Rainy Day Mushroom Pillow* on stage in a club with psychedelic 'op art' lights on their backdrop. There are a large number of shots of the dancing audience, illustrating the attraction of seeing people dressed in 'hippie' garb as much as seeing the band. The Strawberry Alarm Clock provided four songs for the film, including their hit record *Incense and Peppermints*, which appears non-diegetically for a montage of fly-posting. One, *The Pretty Song from Psych-Out*, opens the film with the titles and Jennie's view of the street activity of Haight-Ashbury, while another *The World's on Fire* appears to be played by Mumblin' Jim. There is a remarkable sequence in a club where Mumblin' Jim perform illuminated by some strobing oil lighting. The music is a remarkably close instrumental pastiche of Jimi Hendrix's *Purple Haze*, an iconic piece from the period that had been released in early 1967.

One piece of music by the Electric Flag that had appeared in *The Trip* (called *Flash, Bang, Pow*) was reused in *Easy Rider* (1969), a film which strikingly was made by three of the people involved in *The Trip* (Fonda, Hopper and Nicholson). Indeed, a small cohort of people occupying Hollywood's margin were evident in these late 1960s 'counterculture' films. *Easy Rider* was extremely successful and made on a small budget. A large amount of footage was shot, rendering the post-production process crucial in organizing material. Here, the film's musical strategy was also significant in that pre-existing recordings were edited to fit the film and sections of the film were edited to fit the sound recordings. The film concerns two men on motorcycles (Fonda as Wyatt and Hopper as Billy) crossing America. Crucially, the film used a compilation of contemporary or fairly recent songs as accompaniment, adding an extra dimension to the film. Songs included Steppenwolf's *The Pusher* and *Born to Be Wild*, Jimi Hendrix's *If 6 Was 9*, Roger McGuinn's *Ballad of Easy Rider* and cover of Bob Dylan's *It's Alright, Ma (I'm Only Bleeding)* and his band The Byrds' *Wasn't Born to Follow*, The Electric Prunes' *Mass in F Minor* and Smith's cover of The Band's *The Weight*, amongst others.

Songs appear in a sustained manner for the sequences of motorcycles driving across the country. These are in effect montage sequences, with a concentration on landscapes and the interplay of the bikers. For instance, The Byrds' *Wasn't Born to Follow* accompanied the two bikers driving through mountain scenery, picking up and taking a hitchhiker credited as 'stranger on the highway' to a commune where he lives. Later, when Billy and Wyatt take George Hanson (Jack Nicholson) with them on the road, the song *If You Want to Be a Bird (Bird Song)* by the Holy Modal Rounders (1969) appears, marking the moment when George, wearing a gold football helmet, flaps his arms on the motorcycle pillion seat. In both cases, diegetic sound is marginalized, allowing for the foregrounding of the music as loud accompaniment to spectacular sequences of landscape and travel.

*Easy Rider* was not produced along the lines of conventional films. Much of it was improvised using the script merely as a guideline. Some of the cast are non-actors, and a massive amount of footage was shot, leaving the construction process to post-production where editing became an extremely protracted process. The film style adopted by Easy Rider is one of constant fragmentation, which can be seen as a direct psychedelic characteristic. Indeed, possibly even an analogue for drug experience. Camerawork is usually handheld and often unstable, there are regular jump cuts, elliptical editing with flashback and even a flash forward (where in the New Orleans brothel Wyatt experiences a premonition of the film's conclusion). This approach is most pronounced when dealing with a drug effect. The memorable sequence where the protagonists take LSD in a graveyard illustrates that it is not a happy trip through fragmented and rapidly edited images, sometimes with tone effects, and through the use of bizarre sound effects. Peter Biskind notes that 'LSD did create a frame of mind that fractured experience and that LSD experience had an effect on films like *Easy Rider*.'[12]

Painted as sometimes competitor with the Beatles, the Monkees also became involved in psychedelia. Formed in 1966, as a manufactured band for the eponymous television show, after initial great success the series was cancelled in February 1968. As an appendix to the series, the band made the uncharacteristic *Head*, which debuted in November of 1968. The film makes something of a continuity with their self-consciously 'zany' TV show through being a succession of fragmented incidents and routines. However, *Head* is far more confounding and tessellated, with the general narrative constantly breaking down or being partly interrupted by a succession of cameos from people like boxer Sonny Liston, beach movie actress Annette Funicello, muscly actor Victor Mature, musician Frank Zappa (as a 'critic') and footballer Ray Nitschke. Directed by creator Bob Rafelson,[13] one evident aim was to give the Monkees some credibility with the counterculture at the expense of alienating their existing child and young teen audience.

*Head* opens and closes with *The Porpoise Song*, which was also released as a single before the film's release. This was written by experienced professional songwriters Gerry Goffin and Carole King, who had written *Will You Still Love Me Tomorrow* (the Shirelles, 1961), *Halfway to Paradise* (Tony Orlando, 1961), *The Locomotion* (Little Eva, 1962), and *Pleasant Valley Sunday* for the Monkees in 1967. The song has a psychedelic quality with lead vocals from Monkees drummer Micky Dolenz. The song has a whiny droney quality and appears to suggest the group's demise with its chorus of 'Goodbye, goodbye, goodbye!' The accompanying imagery of Dolenz jumping off a bridge and slowly drowning is poetic and ethereal but hardly a positive image of the sort that had characterized the Monkees previously. Indeed, this song and accompanying images appear at the end of the film, too, giving a cyclic narrative structure. The first appearance of *The Porpoise Song* is followed by a rapid montage sequence dominated by still images and split screens, alongside the recited *Ditty Diego – War Chant*, which revels in ironic celebration of the group as 'manufactured'. This immediately runs into a live performance of *Circle Sky*, including striking intercut images from the Vietnam War amongst other things. Fleetingly, Dennis Hopper appears, walking in front of the camera while the film was co-written by Jack Nicholson, who also had an important role in compiling the soundtrack album. The ironic chant the Monkees make near the start was based on their self-description in the theme song that opened their TV shows: 'Hey, hey, we're the Monkees. You know we love to please. A manufactured image with no philosophies.' The band made a TV special in the wake of *Head*, called *33 1/3 Revolutions per Monkee*, which repeated some of the film's ideas but perhaps for a different audience, and then also appeared in a TV commercial alongside Bugs Bunny. Although they wrote and played their songs more than they had at the start of their career, and despite Head's ironies, the Monkees remained still very much part of the commercial machine.

# British psychedelia

*Yellow Submarine* (1968) still looks a startling film, using bold and innovative animation. The involvement of one of the Beatles in such innovation was no surprise, since, a year earlier in 1967, the Beatles had produced *Sergeant Pepper's Lonely Hearts Club Band*, arguably the ultimate psychedelic LP and widely regarded as a musical landmark. British psychedelia was in some ways qualitatively different from its American counterpart. It was perhaps less overtly drug-inspired and less 'multi-coloured', and more multimedia, more of an arts collaboration. The emblematic *Sergeant Pepper's Lonely Hearts Club Band* album cover designed by pop artist Peter Blake suggested that British psychedelia was perhaps more design oriented and interested in stylistic juxtaposition more than its American counterpart and had a less overt political agenda.[14] The Beatles' next film prescribed a revolution of the mind that had little to do with the dramatic events of civil unrest in both Europe and America during 1968.[15] *Yellow Submarine* was the Beatles' third film, although it was animated and its production concerned the group minimally. The voices of the animated Beatles' characters are even spoken by doubles, and the group was unhappy about their contractual stipulation to supply new songs. This led to the group contributing some of their substandard material, like an out-take from *Sergeant Pepper*,[16] which then nestled among the film's roll call of the group's hits and famous songs. The essence of the film comes directly out of the *Sergeant Pepper* LP, using almost all the songs and cobbling together a story from the nonsense-words of the song *Yellow Submarine*, which had appeared on *Revolver* in 1965. Psychedelic imagery forms the basis for the film's visual style, as it consistently uses bright, garish primary multi-colours as well as baroque fashions and designs. The irony of this was that the British film that most fully develops a sense of indigenous psychedelic culture was made virtually without the Beatles, one of the prime movers in British cultural activity throughout the decade. It was produced by a team of animators under the control of Canadian George Dunning, who apparently had little interest in the Beatles or contemporary youth culture.

The film was built around a compilation of songs by the Beatles, many of which were well-known. This accounts for the rather contrived narrative which often moves quite crudely between songs. However, there are some extremely striking animated sequences for songs such as the haunting one for *Eleanor Rigby*. The film's highly colourful and imaginative imagery became accepted as textbook psychedelia, with the band having to travel to Pepperland to battle the evil 'Blue Meanies'. The film's ultimate battle concludes with a song, the whole film climaxing with *It's All Too Much*, one of the handful of out-takes from *Sgt Pepper* that the Beatles gave to the film. According to Ian Macdonald,

> *It's All Too Much* is the *locus classicus* of English psychedelia: a cozy nursery rhyme in which the world is a birthday cake and the limits on personal transformation are settled in the line 'Show me that I'm everywhere and get me home for tea'. The revolutionary spirit then abroad in America and Europe was never reciprocated in comfortable (and sceptical) Albion [England], where tradition, nature and the child's-eye-view were the things which sprang most readily to the LSD-heightened Anglo-Saxon mind.[17]

*Yellow Submarine* certainly appears to encourage something less than political revolution and suggests a solution with the song *All You Need is Love*. Despite the showcasing of a large number of the Beatles' best-known songs and some imaginative visuals, *Yellow Submarine* was something of a failure, although it quickly became a perennial children's film. Perhaps it betrays something of the film-makers approach to the Beatles' 'revolution in the head' that *Yellow Submarine* is cast as a children's fantasy more than a statement of novel culture and the cutting edge of the counterculture.

The Beatles' project that followed was the television film *Magical Mystery Tour* (first broadcast on Boxing Day 1967). In sharp contrast to *Yellow Submarine*, the group puts its full energies into the project. While the result was less than the absolute success that was expected, the television film treats the new psychedelic culture seriously.[18]

In *Wonderwall* (1968), the protagonist says, 'Music is just organised noise and noise is poison to the mind.' The film included visually strident and hallucinogenic sequences which foregrounded incidental music. *Wonderwall* has a singular and striking soundtrack, a full score by George Harrison, the Beatles' guitarist, with the opening titles announcing it is by 'George Harrison MBE'. Rather than the simple provision of songs for a film, Harrison provided very distinctive music as a self-conscious contemporary soundtrack to the film. He used popular music techniques and collage to build a musical fabric for the film using Indian sitar music, experimental music resembling *musique concrete* and parodies of generic music. The story concerns a scientist who has psychedelic fantasies about his young woman neighbour and watches her voyeuristically through a hole in his apartment wall. These fantasy sections of the film allow for musical and visual spectacle, Harrison's music being predominantly non-diegetic in a filmic scheme that *Kinematograph Weekly* pointedly described as 'Designed for with-it tastes ...'[19]

George Harrison remembered Massot saying 'Anything you do, I will have in the film'. Harrison agreed despite worry about not knowing 'how to do music for films'.[20] He saw a rough cut and then composed music – clearly not to precise timings as it was 'uncut' – yet George Harrison claimed that he used a stopwatch to spot-in music and then composed and recorded it. Some of the music was recorded in London, some in Mumbai (then known as Bombay).[21] In London, Harrison used musicians including the Remo Four (including pianist Tony Ashton), Tommy Reilly on harmonica, Eric Clapton and Ringo Starr. So, this marks a project where Harrison oversaw a number of musicians and produced the recordings on both continents. The music mixes and alternates metal string drones of Indian music mixed with Western-styles,[22] recorded partly in London and partly in Mumbai (then known as Bombay). The score includes many distinctly Indian pieces as well as country-inspired music and some strident honky-tonk piano. Harrison's music was released as an album, the first on the Beatles' Apple record label, and included some stereo effects that exploited studio capabilities as much as the possibilities being offered by stereo sound in the cinema and increasing availability of high-quality stereo equipment for home consumption. He followed this up with another experimental solo album, *Electronic Sounds* (1969), which is based around the use of a prototype Moog synthesizer. George Harrison had often had his songs marginalized in the Beatles by Lennon and McCartney. However, this music was the first Beatles' solo recording, as well as being the first album on their Apple record label, the Beatles' own record label.[23]

*Wonderwall* is a paramount example of psychedelia on film. Its astonishing art direction was by Dutch art collective 'The Fool', who had also painted the mural on the Beatles' Apple building and provided defining psychedelic design for the scientist's neighbouring flat.[24] This is doubled by film techniques which include a few sequences of speeded-up action and little in the way of dialogue scenes, which allows for sustained and often unsynchronized music. This uncoupling of sound and image track leads to an experience of aesthetic and sensory counterpoint. Thus, the music becomes a notably powerful element in the film, empowered well beyond its traditionally assigned role as a support to the image in the cinema. The assumption in mainstream films is that sound and music are synched. Eisenstein discusses the notion of parallel and counterpoint in film music.[25] The latter is where music can work irrespective of on-screen dynamics and action, thus creating something of a dialectical relationship – a counterpoint – between image and music. In *Wonderwall*, the degree of separation between image and music is at times quite strident. The fact that Harrison's album contains a number of stereo experiments which would not have been apparent for almost all British cinemas, where monophonic sound overwhelmingly dominated, merely underlines that this was not simply 'accompanying' music, and that the experience of it in tandem with the film was perhaps only a secondary experience.

*Performance*, released in 1970 but shot two years earlier, made explicit the destructive and self-destructive aspects of the late 1960s culture.[26] It mapped the confluence of the decadent, drug-inspired rock psychedelia and that of the glamorous British gangster as made famous by photographer David Bailey. In the same year as the film began production, one of the film's stars, Mick Jagger, with his group the Rolling Stones, had released an LP called *At Their Satanic Majesties' Request*. This was the band's only self-consciously psychedelic album and, irony aside, appeared to suggest a sinister direction for the Rolling Stones.

In the run-up to the shooting of *Performance*, there were reports that the film's star Mick Jagger was writing the score for the film.[27] While this finally was not the case, the Rolling Stones studio arranger Jack Nitzsche provided the music and was on the project fairly early.[28] Nitzsche was known primarily as an arranger, most notably for producer Phil Spector, rather than a film composer. After *Performance*, he went on to score films including *The Exorcist* (1973), *An Officer and a Gentleman* (1982) and *Star Man* (1984). So, the choice for scoring was a figure peripheral to the pop music scene rather than a skilled musician with experience of writing music for films. Nitzsche produced a singular and highly eclectic score for the film, which I have elsewhere termed a vaguely coherent 'composite' of diverse bits and pieces,[29] including rock, early rap, electronic, rhythm and blues, Delta blues, Indian sitar, middle-eastern Santur, echoed discordant piano, 'improvised' music (guitar, jaw harp and wailing) and 'Muzak'. Nitzsche assembled an impressive cast of musicians, most of whom were Los Angeles-based session musicians and friends. They included singer Buffy Saint Marie, who was Nitzsche's wife, guitarist Ry Cooder who had played with Captain Beefheart. Indeed, one piece from the film is a bottleneck solo by Ry Cooder accompanied by Indian tablas, and the second is a more rhythmic blues rock piece. Exactly the same slide guitar line is used again by Cooder at the beginning of *Sho' Nuff 'n' Yes I Do*, which opens Captain Beefheart's *Safe as Milk* album from 1969. Cooder later claimed that Nitzsche did not write a score for much of the film but asked musicians to improvise and develop their own material.[30] This underlines that Nitzsche's music for *Performance* is a diverse assemblage, not constructed in any way that resembles the through-composed especially written scores traditional to dramatic films. By its mere eclectic and fragmented character, the film's music embodies something of the psychedelic spirit, paralleling the diverse array of object compiled together as the décor to Turner's house. The musical juxtapositions include the sort of ethnic music that was becoming fashionable in counterculture circles in the late 1960s while the sense of constant musical change was like the montage procedure which was evident in experimental culture but increasingly has become dominant in the mainstream since that time. *Performance* is surely one of the ur-films of psychedelia. Its breaking of conventional narrational style to include irrational and more subjective elements, and its constant tendency towards fragmentation and pulling away from unified, stable points of view mark it out as a film that appears to embody this remarkable period in culture.

## Conclusion

Some films from this period appear radical. If the politics is not radical, then the aesthetics most certainly are. This impetus was primarily centred on US and British films, but also illustrates some profound differences of the two, reinforcing traditions of both. While the American appeared to suggest the possibility of radical change, in some ways the British seemed to deny or discount that possibility. Perhaps the archetypal psychedelic film was Roger Corman's drug exploitation film *The Trip*, which not only used film techniques to simulate hallucinogenic drug experience but also included contemporary rock music as an essential part of the experience. On the other hand, if a film summed up British psychedelia, it would be *Wonderwall*, with its multicoloured set design, voyeuristic nudity, pop surrealism and eastern-inflected music by a member of the pop music aristocracy (Beatle George Harrison). Here, the film is less clearly about drugs, although arguably adopts its whole diegetic and narrative style from drug experiences. In addition to this, Harrison's music is less 'rock' and more an experimental mixture and juxtaposition. The situation for Harrison's score for *Wonderwall* ('do anything you want') was clearly unique. There were almost no films that followed suit. The aftermath of this short but creative period saw pop musicians occasionally score films, although more often they would simply provide songs for a film. It was extremely difficult to adapt the techniques of pop music to fit in with the exigencies of film scoring. The pop musicians involved in the films under scrutiny were not film scorers: they had no experience of the craft of writing music to accompany film.

Consequently, they used different techniques, and the music in these films is not really conceived and constructed as an accompaniment to the image but is conceived as having a more loose relationship than most film scores. If these are not 'ruptures' in convention, they certainly involve marginal practices in film scoring at the time.

The embracing of psychedelia by certain film-makers during the late 1960s produced some startling films. These marked an isolated moment of experiment, although nominally these remained mainstream films. Such activity took place against a backdrop of the solidification of industrial and aesthetic relationship between popular music (and especially record sales) and film. While exploiting the counter culture and psychedelia, cinema catalysed the process of recuperating the counterculture. For example, American films which dealt quite positively with the novel culture and psychedelic drugs, such as *The Trip* and *Psych-Out*, were matched by more successful films that had exploited this culture as a negative and indeed criminal object. A fine example is *Coogan's Bluff* (1968), directed by Don Siegel and starring Clint Eastwood as a cowboy policeman searching for a miscreant in New York's countercultural underworld. The 'flower children' are portrayed as freaks, psychologically disturbed and violent, while the counterculture is reduced to a number of stereotypical signifiers, summed up by the club called 'The Pigeon-Toed Orange Peel', which strangely appears to make people dance to a song about itself. In addition to such incorporating recuperation, as Brian Hogg points out: 'As the sixties drew to a close, what had once been the counter-culture gradually became the dominant artform, and groups and filmmakers once on the fringes were now considered commercially viable.'[31] Indeed, some of the techniques and concerns of psychedelic films moved across into the mainstream as did some of the film-makers and musicians. It is interesting to note that the visual and sonic bravura of this period showcased a number of film techniques that over a decade later became associated with music television, and indeed became decried by some as 'MTV aesthetics' when they began to creep back into the arsenal of film techniques in the 1980s and 1990s.

# 4

# Obscured by Pink Floyd

**A**s one of the most successful and ambitious rock groups, Pink Floyd have had an interesting relationship with film throughout their career. They were one of the first rock groups to provide incidental music for films (including *The Committee* [1968], *More* [1969], *Zabriskie Point* [1970] and *The Valley* [1973]). Pink Floyd were making film soundtracks during their early years, although many of these remain obscure. Some films, like *More*, are now known for their Pink Floyd music rather than the film itself. This chapter will chart how far Pink Floyd's music was inspired by film soundtracks, and how far their music has had an impact on film soundtracks. It will conclude with a discussion of their bestselling landmark album *Dark Side of the Moon* (1973), which not only had something of the character of a film soundtrack but actually included music they had written for a film. A successful concept album from the end of that decade was made into a film musical, *Pink Floyd: The Wall* (1982), which was a bold and late entrance in the rock opera cycle of films. This chapter will review Pink Floyd's use of film and its influence upon their musical style and ambitions. Indeed, I argue that making music for films (in Britain, Europe and America) was crucial in changing Pink Floyd from drug-inspired psychedelic acid rock to 'serious' coffee table superstars.

Progressive rock blossomed during the late 1960s and early 1970s, with groups accelerating to excess, particularly in terms of length of songs, instrumental complexity and references to high art. Concept albums were loftily conceived narrative song cycles, sometimes consciously similar to art music, and their production values became conspicuously high. The emblematic album for this form of pop music production is probably Pink Floyd's *Dark Side of the Moon* (released 1973), which included both songs and instrumental pieces, special sound effects, brand new synthesizer technology, snatches of film-like dialogue, a gatefold sleeve with lyrics and posters and a vague overall unifying concept. *Dark Side of the Moon* sold by the million, breaking the record for time spent in the LP charts.[1] It was a pioneering aural cultural item, something like a sound sculpture for a stereo set, exploiting new 'hi-fi' systems and standards. It was also a soundtrack LP without a film, constructing something that approximates a cinematic experience within domestic space.

The late 1960s was a period of exceptional experimentation for both pop/rock music and cinema. Between 1967 and 1972, Pink Floyd provided music for nine films and television programmes. While the group attempted to reformulate the musical soundtrack as an aesthetic object, ultimately they ended up carrying the film soundtrack's influence over into their tremendously successful albums of the 1970s. Yet, Pink Floyd were a significant agency in the reinvention of the film soundtrack at this time, through their concern with sound quality and 'high fidelity', a characteristic that partially inspired the momentous developments in film sound in the late 1970s.

From the late 1960s onwards, large numbers of pop and rock musicians began writing music for films. Pink Floyd were a pioneer of groups creating film music, after which they went on to be one of the definitive rock groups, achieving the rarity of both critical acclaim and massive record sales. They ended up carrying some of the film soundtrack's influence over into their albums of the 1970s, most notably *Dark Side of the Moon*, one of the bestselling albums of all time.

Instrumental excesses and the desire to transcend the thirty-two bar, three-minute pop song meant that progressive rock was open to a fruitful two-way interaction with films. The primary concern of this musical substratum was to differentiate itself from mainstream pop music, which was achieved largely through playing extended songs rather than following the three-minute format that characterized the pop chart and, indeed, popular music more generally. They consequently became patronized through album sales, the format allowing for long and unfolding musical pieces, along the way attracting more mature audiences.[2] In the 1970s, LPs rather than singles became the principal means of pop and rock song dissemination. The growth of LP sales in the late 1960s consolidated through the expansion of the market in terms of age range, crystallized by the 1970s development of AOR ('adult oriented radio') in the United States, aimed almost entirely at the demographic bulge of the Baby Boom generation.

The concluding section of Pink Floyd's piece *Saucerful of Secrets* is called 'Celestial Voices' and finishes a noisy instrumental with a repeated series of chords with wordless choir-like vocals. Non-diegetic music manifests 'voices from heaven', and indeed, this piece sounds something like film music. It certainly has clear potential as 'accompanying music' or 'complementary' music. It is music that does not overwhelm images and carries ambiguous meaning, making it more of a blank slate than a clear communication of particular ideas. Such music is capable of forging a symbiotic relationship with other media, particularly moving images. Pink Floyd's albums often cohered into a conceptual unity, even if the unifying principle was obscure. This, along with the group's experimental edge, led them quickly to work with film. Indeed, it seemed the fate of much rock experimentation from the late 1960s onwards was to end up in film.[3]

Pink Floyd's career in films at this time elicits little more than a footnote in the band's history and has barely registered in histories and studies of film. This paper will attend the aesthetic and historical trajectory into screen music taken by Pink Floyd during this period and the developments in the interzone between pop/rock and film music which arguably led to music that was more visual and films that were more musical. It is my contention that involvement with film soundtracks inculcated a visual, conceptual and narrative sense in the group that was essential to the development of rock music during the 1970s and beyond. In turn, Pink Floyd were not an obviously influential agent in some of the subsequent developments in film soundtracks. These developments in the sector between pop/rock and film music arguably led to music that was more visual and films that were more musical.

## Form conducive to film

The dominant history of the group's early development concerns their negotiation of the departure of singer Syd Barrett and their manoeuvring into the forefront of progressive rock. In fact, Pink Floyd had a seemingly unique trajectory for a group of the time, first developing from being a traditional rhythm and blues group into a challenging avant-garde improvising group to being a psychedelic pop group with some big hit singles. Subsequently, they developed into an 'albums band', producing extended instrumental pieces as well as songs, often creating a conceptual unity to their output.

In 1967, The Pink Floyd – as they were then known – broke through with two major hit singles, *Arnold Layne* and *See Emily Play*, both written by and sung by Syd Barrett. This commercial success inculcated a schizoid character in the group, whose live performances were dominated by extended improvisations wholly lacking the pop accessibility of their singles. Pink Floyd's interest in avant-garde and improvised music manifested itself in their repertoire's mixture of large-scale pieces and shorter, more conventional pop songs. One influence derived from British improvising group AMM, whose guitarist Keith Rowe played the instrument horizontally and highly unconventionally. There was a direct connection in that the Pink Floyd's management was connected with AMM. On a more pragmatic level, improvisation allowed Pink Floyd to build a longer set from limited material.[4] However, their improvisation bore little resemblance to the modes of jazz improvisation, as it was not based on instrumental virtuosity but instead was based on instrumental density, rhythmic impetus, dynamics and individual sound qualities. Very quickly, the group exploited musical technology, with the use of Binson 'Echorec' echo units, very expensive devices based on multiple magnetic tape heads providing intense echo for instruments. This was a feature on both Barrett's Fender Telecaster guitar and Rick Wright's Farfisa Compact Duo organ.

The turn of 1968 saw the momentous change in the group, when they parted company with their increasingly erratic singer Syd Barrett. This left them without a clear front person and without a successful songwriter. This development set the group on a path towards more in the way of extended instrumental pieces rather than discrete pop songs that could be made into hit singles. After the failure of the single *Point Me at the Sky* at the end of 1968, 'The Pink Floyd' (as they were known) became a dedicated 'albums band' and gradually dispensed with the definite article in front of their name. While Barrett's exit cannot be overestimated in its importance in Pink Floyd's maturation, their later development followed logically from elements present before Barrett's replacement by the more traditionally styled guitar playing and singing of Dave Gilmour.

According to commentators, The Pink Floyd's stage shows in the late 1960s were notable for their fusing of music and lights, yet they also included film projections as an integral part of the multimedia sensorium. Peter Wynne-Willson pioneered projections for the group at London's UFO ('Underground Freak Out') Club[5] and appeared with the group to showcase some of these on *Tomorrow's World*.[6] Liquid lights were characteristic of the psychedelic culture of the time, of which Pink Floyd were an avatar. Such lights commonly used oil on slides, but experiments also used latex, paint and mirrors. Wynne-Willson, Mark Boyle and Russell Page lit the UFO club, and the house lighter Boyle also worked with Jim Haynes in avant-garde theatre.[7] Wynne-Wilson's innovations included individual lights for each group member, projecting coloured shadows of the group on a backdrop as well as using polaroid effects. However, this light and film show tended to obscure the individuals in the group and became an important catalyst in the group's personal anonymity in the wake of Barrett's exit. Lacking the ubiquitous personality cult of rock and pop groups, Pink Floyd instead exploited their anonymity to produce fairly abstract 'progressive' music and film music, neither of which required the personal identification of audience with individual performer. Significantly, this freed the music to be accompanied by something other than merely its instrumental production, leading to dramatic on-stage visuals, striking album covers and accompanying visuals, not to mention films. Their highly distinctive LP cover designs from *Saucerful of Secrets* (1968) onwards were made by 'Hipgnosis' (founded by the group's friends Storm Thorgerson and Aubrey 'Po' Powell). These covers showed how important visual facets were for the group, as well as demonstrating their determination that albums should be fully integrated objects. The group's live activities not only included lights but also projected films, making the show into a multimedia 'happening' or singular event rather than a more traditional concert.[8]

In 1969, Pink Floyd began to create extended musical pieces, often filling a whole concert themselves, which necessitated extending their set. This required a sense of overall cohesion and unity that was allowed by the 'song cycle' form and its recorded counterpart, the concept album. At this time, Pink Floyd's set was a single bipartite piece called *The Man and the Journey* (also known occasionally as *The Massed Gadgets of Auximenes*). This was in fact a number of songs and pieces strung together into a compound piece comprising the group's full set, the first section being *The Man* and the second *The Journey*. It was unified by a loose narrative concept and never received an official recording or commercial release. There is an illicit recording of *The Man and the Journey* that can be found through peer-to-peer file sharing on the internet. Upon discovering this bootleg recording, I felt that I was beholding something of a Rosetta Stone that translated Pink Floyd's early career into the terms of their later career. One can hear the process taking shape where large-scale formal pieces are unified through loose concepts, songs are tacked together with long instrumental sections and atmospheres. This extended piece not only brought together their songs and mood pieces, but also unified their more traditional popular music aspects and their multimedia ability to join with other products or activities. It included adaptations of pieces that appeared on the *Saucerful of Secrets*, *More* (1969) and *Ummagumma* (1969) albums, some already recorded and some not. These songs had their contexts modified, titles altered, and were reset among atmospheric fragments of sound effects, making the set a sonic continuity rather than the traditional set of a succession of songs. The music is integrated with speaking voices and sound effects and, indeed, at times sounds more like a film soundtrack than a rock album. It resembles the 1960s and 1970s phenomenon of soundtracks recorded from the television set, a common practice that thrived before the widespread availability of video, as a means for home consumers to relive the experience of films or television shows. This practice of enthusiasts is responsible for the BBC's ability to release soundtrack recordings of programmes that have lost their visual track, most notably episodes of *Doctor Who* (1963–89), where the BBC destroyed their copies of the programmes.

# Musical recordings

We can build a historical matrix based on most prominent historical artefacts associated with Pink Floyd: their recordings made commercially available on disc. This creates something of an 'Official History', one that would be recognized by the group's fans.

### Pink Floyd's Album Releases 1967–73

1967 – *The Piper at the Gates of Dawn*

1968 – *Saucerful of Secrets*

1969 – *More*

      *Ummagumma*

1970 – *Atom Heart Mother*

1971 – *Meddle*

1972 – *Obscured by Clouds*

1973 – *Dark Side of the Moon*

Taking its name from Kenneth Grahame's *The Wind in the Willows*, Pink Floyd's debut album *The Piper at the Gates of Dawn* was released on 4 August 1967 and reached number 6 in the UK charts. The album's working title was 'Projection',[9] which suggests something of a film inspiration, or at the very least a visual, multimedia influence. The group's second album, *Saucerful of Secrets*, was released in June of 1968 and reached number 9 in the UK charts. Although Barrett had left, it included some material recorded before his exit. According to Nicholas Schaffner, 'The one inescapable conclusion to be drawn from the album as a whole (and its successors through at least to *Dark Side of the Moon*) is that the melody and the poetry in the Floyd went out with Syd Barrett, a deficiency for which the band, to its credit, found compensations.'[10] These 'compensations' were what set the group on a path to international success and included an increased reliance upon instrumental and conceptual pieces of large scale. This allowed for the sort of music that easily could be used as accompaniment to other activities. Their next album was a film soundtrack.

*More*, the group's first soundtrack, was released on 13 June 1969 and peaked at 9 in the British charts. This album included many quiet acoustic songs and certainly sounds nothing like a traditional film score. The film itself as a concept provided a unity to the album, although it remained a recognizable and marketable rock album comprising a succession of songs. It was quickly superseded by double album *Ummagumma*, which reached number five in the British charts, having been released on 1 November 1969. It was an unusual mixture of self-indulgent solo material by each group member and live recordings of older songs. The album includes some very long instrumental pieces, extravagant solo spots and atmospheric texture-based pieces. The extended studio pieces are programmatic, most notably Nick Mason's multi-tracked percussion solo *The Grand Vizier's Garden Party* and Roger Waters' soundscape called *Several Species of Small Furry Animals Gathered Together in a Cave and Grooving with a Pict*, neither of which have much to do with contemporaneous pop or rock music.

Pink Floyd's first number one album was *Atom Heart Mother*, which was released on 10 October 1970 to publicity that included a herd of cows being moved along Pall Mall in central London. The cover marked an aesthetic move towards a certain oblique strain in modern advertising, as it featured a photograph of a cow with no writing to denote the artist or the album title. Seemingly a fully blown concept album, it used an orchestra and brass band and was a collaboration with Scottish experimentalist Ron Geesin. It was a success and a notable incidence of 'symphonic rock', following Deep Purple's *Concerto for Group and Orchestra* (1969). The opening of the lengthy title track was based on a chord sequence that the group's guitarist Dave Gilmour referred to as 'Theme from an Imaginary Western',[11] suggesting an awareness of film scoring and the possibility of their music being an accompaniment for images as well as standing alone. Furthermore, it suggests the influence upon their music that film was having at the time.

The next album was *Meddle*, released over a year later, on 13 November 1971 in Britain (earlier in the United States), where it peaked at number three in the charts. It took advantage of developments in multitrack recording technology, being the group's first album to use a sixteen track recorder rather than eight track.[12] This facilitated more complexity in sound and an increasing move away from the limits of their guitar, bass guitar, organ and drums concert instrumentation. Michael Watts's review in *Melody Maker* called it 'a soundtrack to a non-existent movie'.[13] Indeed, the mostly instrumental track *Echoes*, which took up a whole side of the LP, not only sounded like the sort of atmospheric music that could enhance films, but parts of it were also used as incidental music in films and television, even in recent years. *Meddle* opens with *One of these Days*, which is inaugurated by a fabric of wind sound interrupted by a highly individual repeating pattern on echoed bass guitar. The piece finishes by retreating the way it started and demonstrates a sharp dramatic sense rather than a proclivity towards the attractive 'hook' of popular music.

*Obscured by Clouds*, the group's second film soundtrack album, was released in June 1972, and reached number six in the UK charts, but, significantly, was the first Pink Floyd album to make an incursion into the American album charts, reaching 46. This was and is, of course, the real road to financial success. Like *More*, despite being a soundtrack album, it sounds more like a traditional album of songs. This was followed by *Dark Side of the Moon*, which was released in 1973 and reached number one in Britain and the United States, remaining on the former chart for a record-breaking 700 weeks. It is a highly distinctive recording, mixing fairly conventional songs with experimental pieces and field recordings. As an aesthetic and financial success, *Dark Side of the Moon* was not an inevitable culmination of Pink Floyd's activities. However, guitarist Dave Gilmour declared, 'If you take [the track] *Saucerful of Secrets*, the track *Atom Heart Mother*, then the track *Echoes* [from *Meddle*] – all lead quite logically towards *Dark Side of the Moon* and what came after it.'[14] Bass guitarist Roger Waters also suggested that each album was a successive step towards *Dark Side of the Moon*.[15] It is perhaps also too easy to draw a trajectory straight from Pink Floyd's music for films to *Dark Side of the Moon*. Pink Floyd's development towards *Dark Side of the Moon* was not a clean and straightforward trajectory but was uneven. Ironically, the film influence on the extraordinary sounds of that album manifested itself most obviously in the use of speaking voices, tape sound effects and overall (LP-wide) extra-musical logic. While film might be seen as a staging post in the development of progressive rock, it is worth noting that some of Pink Floyd's rejected film music ended up on *Dark Side of the Moon*. Michelangelo Antonioni rejected a Richard Wright piano piece, called *The Violent Sequence* on bootleg recordings, written for his film *Zabriskie Point* (1970) that became used as *Us and Them*, while *The Body* (1970) included some of what later became the track *Breathe*, both of which later appeared on *Dark Side of the Moon*.

# The films

The collapse of the Hollywood studio system with its standardized blueprint for music in films encouraged the gradual appearance of different styles of film music and roles for music in films. The context for Pink Floyd's involvement with films was one of cultural experimentation. In Britain in the late 1960s, a number of films made bold explorations in terms of their music, embracing popular music and empowering pop groups to produce their music. In 1966, Paul McCartney (with help from George Martin) produced some fairly traditional incidental music for *The Family Way*, while *Here We Go Round the*

*Mulberry Bush* (1967) had music by the Spencer David Group and Traffic, and George Harrison produced a quite experimental score dominated by sitars and synthesizer for *Wonderwall* (1968). Even *Performance* (shot in 1968 but released in 1970) was originally to have a score by Mick Jagger.[16] Ultimately, it did not, but he produced an austere synthesizer score for Kenneth Anger's *Invocation of my Demon Brother* in 1969. These were substantial developments beyond films simply featuring pop groups in films and matched similar events in the United States at the time, such as *The Graduate* (1967) and *Easy Rider* (1969). In almost all cases, pop/rock group involvement was isolated and rarely added up to systematic or sustained collaboration with film.

In contrast, Pink Floyd's work for film (and television) over the five-year period under scrutiny was extensive and extraordinary, yet has never received much in the way of comment.

### Pink Floyd's Film Work 1967–72

*Tonite Let's All Make Love in London* (1967, Peter Whitehead)

*San Francisco* (1968, Anthony Stern)

*The Committee* (1968, Peter Sykes)

*More* (1969, Barbet Schroeder)

*Omnibus*: 'So What If It's Just Green Cheese?' (BBC1, Tx. 20 July 1969)

*Zabriskie Point* (1970, Michelangelo Antonioni)

*The Body* (1970, Roy Battersby)

*Pink Floyd: Live at Pompeii* (1971, Adrian Maben)

*Crystal Voyager* (1971, David Elfick)

*The Valley* (1972, Barbet Schroeder)

*Tonite Let's All Make Love in London* (1967) was directed by Peter Whitehead as an impressionistic documentary about 'Swinging London' and in particular a 'happening' at Alexandra Palace. (This was the famous '14-Hour Technicolor Dream' on 29 April 1967.) The film was released in February of 1968 and included two excerpts from Pink Floyd's evocative extended instrumental piece *Interstellar Overdrive*, one appearing as backing for Allen Ginsberg's narration of his poem that supplied the film's title. The next film to use Pink Floyd's music used the same piece. It was directed by Anthony Stern, who had been the assistant director on *Tonite Let's All Make Love in London*. It was a short film called *San Francisco*, which was made and registered in 1968 but did not receive a release as such until May 1971.[17] The film concerns a day in the life of the city in the film's title, using copious amount of montage and freeze frame. For the length of its fifteen minutes, it used the musical accompaniment of a recording of *Interstellar Overdrive* from late 1966.[18] This instrumental piece lent itself to being used as accompaniment, with a wide range of dynamics and impressionistic use of instruments, while its space/ astronomy title lent it a cinematic edge.

In 1968, Pink Floyd were assigned to write and record the whole score for a dramatic film. *The Committee* was an hour long and based on illustrating abstract and philosophical ideas. It starred Paul Jones, who had been singer in Manfred Mann and had starred in Peter Watkins's *Privilege* (1967). It was directed by the young Australian Peter Sykes, who went on later to direct the Hammer horror film *To the Devil ... a Daughter* (1976). The music for the film was mostly either variations on the Pink Floyd song *Careful with That Axe, Eugene*, or sparse instrumental textures for momentary atmosphere. It was recorded quickly during May of 1968, and they supplied just over seventeen minutes for the film.[19] Owing to the brevity of material and its uncommercial character, the group elected not to release on disc the music they had provided for the film.[20] *The Committee* had its premiere at the Cameo Poly, Oxford Circus, London, on the 26 September 1968, although it never received a proper distribution.

Next, Pink Floyd were asked to provide all the music for the debut feature by the Swiss-born Barbet Schroeder, who previously had worked with Jean-Luc Godard. *More* (1969) was an art film concerned with hippies and hard drugs in Ibiza. While Pink Floyd supplied a considerable amount of music, as the release of a soundtrack album attested, Schroeder chose not to use their music to great advantage in the film. Indeed, *More* includes some different versions of the songs on the album (and one song that did not make it onto the album), but what is notable is Schroeder's desire to use the music predominantly as diegetic music to give some authentic sense of youth culture and the hippie *milieu*, with it appearing recurrently at parties on record players. There is a clear discrepancy between what the group conceived as the album *More* and what Schroeder wanted from them for the film. Indeed, the desire for some independence from the requirements of the film allowed for the production of an album that stood up well on its own, rather than merely having the character of an appendage to the film. The album's pieces have their own integrity; they do not need the film. Consequently, songs dominate rather than instrumental atmospheres. *More*'s low-key drama does not really require dramatic or atmospheric music and thus eschews utilizing Pink Floyd's music as underscore, apart from in one or two places.

*More* made its debut at the Cannes Festival on 13 May 1969 and shortly afterwards Pink Floyd were creating music for television. The BBC asked the group to provide a piece for an episode of the documentary series *Omnibus*, called 'So What If It's Just Green Cheese'. This was a special episode celebrating the Apollo 11 moon landing, and linking up German and Dutch television with some satirical endeavours from the BBC.[21] The Pink Floyd piece (often called *Moonhead* by fans) was recorded in a day, probably partly improvised and never officially released. The BBC1 broadcast took place on 20 July 1969, between 10 and 11 PM. Actually, by this point, Pink Floyd's music had appeared as incidental music in many television programmes, including *The Gamblers* (ATV, 1968), *Horrorscope* (Granada, 1968), children's drama *The Tyrant King* (ITV, 1968), Tony Palmer's doc for *Omnibus: All My Loving* (BBC1, November 1968). The sheer volume of screen activity for Pink Floyd's music suggests that there was something in its character that was most conducive to its appearance in films and on television.

Next, Pink Floyd were engaged to provide the music for Michelangelo Antonioni's *Zabriskie Point* (1970), a film about the Californian counterculture and something of a sequel to his portrayal of 'Swinging London' in *Blow Up* (1966). Antonioni was certainly interested in the distinctive flavour of the time, furnished by its radical cultural and social developments. It was perhaps surprising that initially he chose a British group to provide the music for the film. In Rome, during post-production, Antonioni constantly rejected the work Pink Floyd showed him, and ultimately, he used little of it in the film's final version,[22] instead getting the indigenous Grateful Dead to provide some music, along with some contemporary pop songs and other pieces. However, Pink Floyd's music provided a suitable, prominent and memorable accompaniment to the film's startling climax of slow motion explosions.

Immediately before this, Pink Floyd's bass guitarist and sometime singer, Roger Waters, collaborated with Ron Geesin on the soundtrack to *The Body* (1970). This is an experimental recording for a most singular biology documentary about the functioning of the human body that ran for 112 minutes. Geesin, who subsequently worked with Pink Floyd on *Atom Heart Mother*, had a reputation for experimental music, using electronics as well as unconventional and innovative practices. Although there are some characteristic acoustic guitar and vocal songs from Waters, the soundtrack appears to be a collaboration in the true sense of the word. The recording that was released as an album was in fact a re-recording of the music that appeared in the film, being recorded nearly a year after the music for the film's soundtrack. *The Body* was scripted by Tony Garnett and directed by Roy Battersby, having its premiere on 29 November 1970 at Piccadilly. The music appears prominently in the film, although much of it has more of the character of sound effects rather than music in the traditional sense. While the music is not by Pink Floyd in the strictest sense, it was made by one of their most prominent members and marked the group's third soundtrack album released within a year.

At the start of 1970, Pink Floyd were committed to scoring cartoon series *Rollo* (by Alan Aldridge) but ultimately were not involved, and in 1971, there was a rumour that Pink Floyd were going to score a film of Frank Herbert's *Dune*.[23] At the time was a project going to be directed by Alexandro Jodorowsky but over a decade later finally was realized under the direction of David Lynch, and without Pink Floyd. Clearly, their film work constituted a success seeing as these film music projects were mooted, even if they failed to mature.

The vast majority of successful progressive rock groups made live albums, often double live albums, showcasing their instrumental proficiency. As an innovator, Pink Floyd instead made a live film, *Pink Floyd: Live at Pompeii* (1971). This was recut a number of times and, surprisingly, was not matched by a release of the music on disc. It was originally made for European television, directed by Adrian Maben and made its premiere at the Edinburgh film festival in September of 1972, but its widespread release was then held up for another two years. As live concert films go, *Live at Pompeii* was extraordinary. Instead of presenting a live 'on stage' situation of the group on tour, Pink Floyd were removed to the emptiness of the deserted amphitheatre of Pompeii's ruins. Many of the songs include insert shots of the town and surrounding landscape that converted the live soundtrack into a non-diegetic accompaniment.[24] This is a rarely noted phenomenon that can be found in some musical films and rockumentaries and involves the inversion of the conventional conception of sound and music in cinema, as an accompaniment to the primacy of the images. In the case of films like *Pink Floyd: Live at Pompeii*, the images are without doubt secondary to the music. Yet, their music has a notable 'accompanying' quality that is able to make for a constant dialogue between music and images.

After their live film vehicle, Pink Floyd had some of their music used as the spine of David Elfick's film *Crystal Voyager* (1971), a twenty-one-minute-long Australian short documentary about surfing. This consisted of a succession of impressive visuals, some achieved through mounting a camera on an active surf board. The film used one piece of music, *Echoes*, taken from the album *Meddle*, exploiting the music's highly evocative quality. The group then went on to score Barbet Schroeder's next film, *La Vallée* (*The Valley*, also known as *The Valley Obscured by Clouds*) (1972). The film concerned a company of hippies questing for an inaccessible valley paradise in New Guinea and included some remarkable anthropological documentary footage of indigenous tribes. Pink Floyd's music is hardly more prominent than it had been in *More*. Again, their music appears almost wholly as diegetic music, on radios and at parties – materializing precisely as recorded music. The music was recorded, and most of it was written in less than a week in Paris.[25] Although the music on the soundtrack album *Obscured by Clouds* seems to follow the film's narrative development, this is obscured in the film itself. In fact, only four tracks from the LP are employed in the film and another piece that is not on the LP makes a brief appearance.[26] The music works well as a disc uncoupled from the film, and clearly the group was unwilling to provide more traditional incidental music that would follow and emphasize on-screen action and emotion when they could produce 'film music' that to all intents and purposes was no different from an album of songs unrelated to a film, and thus not a commercial risk. This dual-purpose soundtrack album was a hybrid product, as film music and as a rock record, although any connection to this film is not strictly necessary. Indeed, whole generations of Pink Floyd fans since have bought this album while the film has been little seen and drifted into obscurity.

Since the early 1970s, Pink Floyd have been involved in films, ballet, plays and opera. Their rock opera *The Wall* (1979) was made into a film in 1984, and Waters did incidental music for *When the Wind Blows* (1987) and more recently wrote an opera, *Ca Ira*. Between 1967 and 1972, Pink Floyd did not try to create traditional film music. They worked on their own terms and were unwilling to change musical style the way that many other pop musicians have done since (see a detailed discussion in Chapter 9). Their film music was produced quickly and had something of a rough and ready quality to it. Significantly, film work was good money. Keyboard player Rick Wright pointed out that film soundtracks were more lucrative than concert tours, while Dave Gilmour noted that Pink Floyd wanted to break into 'big time movie scores'.[27] They never would. While their music for films was never really matched to film dynamics and conventions for musical accompaniment in the cinema, it nevertheless still had a certain quality that allowed it to accompany images.

Bass player Roger Waters regretted that Pink Floyd did not supply the music for *2001: A Space Odyssey*.[28] Later, however, their music was fitted to the film by anonymous enthusiasts on the internet. The phenomenon of what might be called 'slash soundtracks' or 'slash MPegs' is recent. These involve individuals adding a piece of music as soundtrack to existing images and then make them freely available across the internet. This can provide a vivid illustration of the 'accompanying quality' of a piece of music well. On the internet, I have found Mpeg files which weld together Pink Floyd's *Meddle* with *2001: A Space Odyssey*, *Dark Side of the Moon* with *The Wizard of Oz*, *Dark Side of the Moon* with *Doctor Who: The Web Planet* (from 1965), and *Goodbye Blue Sky* with footage of the 9/11 attack on the World Trade Center in New York in 2001. This procedure of adding soundtracks to emotive images can be traced back to the wide availability of video recorders in the 1980s and was most evident in The Cars' *Drive* being used as accompaniment to starving Ethiopians at Live Aid in 1985. The process became easier with the proliferation of the internet through the World Wide Web as well as basic audiovisual computer software in the mid and late 1990s. This twilight world of slash soundtracks on the internet also includes the footage of the beheading of American journalist Nick Berg in 2004. While there are many different combinations of sound and images, Pink Floyd seem to be more prominent than others in supplying the music.

# Accompanying music: *Careful with That Axe, Eugene*

Pink Floyd's early music was particularly suited to accompany images.[29] Often characterized by little in the way of consistent dramatic musical development and often avoiding the clear four-bar and alternating structures that usually define popular music, their music was conducive to being layed into a film's soundtrack. Indeed, Pink Floyd's instrumental music tended to lack changes in dynamic emphasis that might cause a negative relationship with a piece of film footage, as illustrated by the history of a single piece of the group's music.

Pink Floyd's song called *Careful with That Axe, Eugene* was in its early incarnations also known as *Murderistic Women*, *The Murderotic Woman*, *Beset by Creatures of the Deep*, *One Chord Wonder* and *Keep Smiling People*. In November of 1967, Pink Floyd toured with a package including Jimi Hendrix and The Nice. It is likely that *Careful with That Axe, Eugene* originated as a reply of sorts to The Nice's song *The Cry of Eugene*.

This piece was used as the basis of Pink Floyd's music for *The Committee* (1968), recorded in May 1968 and called *Keep Smiling People* (and significantly lacked the final recording's screaming).[30] The group opened a live appearance on Radio 1's *Top Gear* programme with the piece on 11 August 1968. It appeared as a recording on the B-side of *Point Me at the Sky*,[31] released on 17 December 1968 (having been recorded over a month earlier). A live version of the song appeared on *Ummagumma* in late 1969, and then the same piece was used in *Zabriskie Point* (1970), called *Come in Number 51, Your Time is Up*, where, as already mentioned, it appeared as accompaniment for the film's startling conclusion, where a succession of objects is blown up in extreme slow motion. Another live version of *Careful with That Axe, Eugene* appeared in the film *Pink Floyd: Live at Pompeii* (1971).

It is a remarkable piece of music in many ways. John S. Cotner wrote a chapter about *Careful with That Axe, Eugene* in Kevin Holm-Hudson's book *Progressive Rock Revisited*. He noted that '... the beauty of the piece is that it allows for multiple readings'.[32] It certainly has a general ambiguity, bringing together Pink Floyd's tradition of improvisation with the more conceptual character their music would take in the future. Most versions contain the same core musical elements, including a single chord harmony, a continuous beat and bass line, an improvisatory organ melody, a build-up in dynamics and back down again, and after quiet vocals early on which consist of the whispered title, a section of climactic vocal screaming.[33] The musical aspects of *Careful with That Axe, Eugene* encapsulate Pink Floyd's evolution in that there is no real 'musical development' in the traditional sense. Instead, the piece is based on atmosphere, dynamics and, most notably, concept. This loose musical format lent itself to a fair degree of improvisation, and the piece's lack of traditional song focus certainly makes it more conducive to being used as accompaniment to images. While it may not necessarily be 'filmic', it certainly has a representational dimension. The screams suggest that the care urged in the title was not taken, while the live version of the song on *Ummagumma* has the snare drum produce a 'chopping axe' rimshot sound. As Edward Macan noted in *Rocking the Classics*, programmatic music, which had extra-musical inspiration, entered popular music from art music.[34] Yet, one could also argue that the 'programme', the music's representational aspects, could have been inspired at least as much if not more by film.

Although it is not based on song form alternation of material, the song retains 4-bar structures and is dominated by 4/4 time. It never has the flexibility of a traditional film score, yet *Careful with That Axe, Eugene* has proved itself a notable piece of music for accompanying moving images. As the above list of its appearances suggests, the piece is adept at being both 'accompanying' (fitting with images) and 'foregrounded' (standing on its own, like absolute music). Their live film *Live at Pompeii* is where these two strands come together with some pieces being foregrounded and others including film as an accompaniment, and it is no surprise that *Careful with That Axe, Eugene* appears. However, the song made an isolated appearance in an episode of British period television cop show *Heartbeat*,[35] where it accompanied a violent robbery, with the explosive breaking into screams being synched dramatically with a person being hit on the head on screen.

## Conclusion

Pink Floyd were tied to films immediately, and not just providing music for them. In 1967, a Melody Maker report noted that they were to start shooting their first feature film, the thirty-minute long *The Life Story of Percy the Ratcatcher*.[36] This project came to nothing or may have been an idle boast to the press. A couple of years later, keyboard player Richard Wright stated, 'We also want to make our own film ... there was some definite talk about us doing a film and then writing the music around it.'[37] This also failed to materialize but their 'cinematic' interests persisted. Indeed, their interest in sound quality and spatialized sound predates later film notions of 'sound design'.

Quadraphonic sound (known as 'quad' for short) was the heir apparent to stereo in the early 1970s, and Pink Floyd were one of its spearheads, both in concert and on recordings. The group had always been interested in spatialized sound. At the 'Games for May' event on 12 May 1967 at the Queen Elizabeth Hall, London, they used a 'Periphonic surround sound system' of four channels with multiple speakers which allowed for peripheral sound. The speakers at the back of the theatre produced mostly pre-recorded sound effects compiled by Waters, including birdsong, wind, waves and footsteps. Later, Pink Floyd used the 'Azimuth co-ordinator',[38] which was a massive innovation in popular music, as it spatialized the group's performance and projected elements of it behind the audience.[39] This was an absolute rarity in rock music, where spatialized concert sound was far less of a concern than aiming for clarity at high volume. Indeed, spatialization had been more of a concern for art music, with Vaughan Williams's separated orchestras on *Fantasia on a Theme by Thomas Tallis* (1910) and Stockhausen's musical forces surrounding the audience in *Gruppen* (1957).

From *Atom Heart Mother* in 1970 onwards, Pink Floyd released quad versions of their albums. On 17 October 1971, a press presentation of *Meddle* was staged in quad at the Roundhouse, Chalk Farm, London, while Pink Floyd were on tour in the United States.[40] Indeed, Pink Floyd always betrayed an intense interest in sound itself, later embracing Dolby technology and even the more esoteric Zuccarelli 'Holophonic' recording in the 1980s (a form of binaural recording using microphones in a dummy head).[41] Indeed, *Dark Side of the Moon*'s mixture of songs and sound effects might be approached merely as software to show off the hardware of a hi-fi system. The interest in high-quality and spatialized sound evident in this record, like the barrage of effects on hi-fi demonstration discs of the time, doubtless fed into expectations regarding film sound at around this time. It would not be too fanciful to suggest that *Dark Side of the Moon*, which appears like a soundtrack to a non-existent film anyway, might have provided some of the inspiration for the developments in hi-fi film sound.[42] Gianluca Sergi suggests that the impetus for technical progressions in film sound in the 1970s, such as Dolby stereo, came from the fact that: 'Consumers, spectators and participants could now [in the 1970s] enjoy better quality sound at concerts and in their homes than in the vast majority of cinemas.'[43] With rock concerts and the overwhelming majority of recordings, the interest would have been more in volume and quality than in spatialization. Questions of sound quality had been of paramount importance in popular music's technical circles since the widespread availability of multitrack sound recorders since the mid-1960s. Alan Parsons, engineer on *Dark Side of the Moon* noted in 1975:

> Pink Floyd have recently used back projected film behind the stage with a 35mm four channel sound track. This has proved very successful but problems do arise with run-up times of up to ten seconds when attempting to bring in a sound on a musical cue. Film and multichannel sound are now commonplace of course, as in the new Ken Russell picture of *Tommy* and its use of a 'quintophonic' system – doubtless an indication of things to come.[44]

Pink Floyd were almost unique in using spatialized sound effects on disc and in concert, with *Dark Side of the Moon* marking the domestication of that part of their live experience. It is worth noting that Pink Floyd's film work was of lower sound quality than their 'pure' recordings. Ultimately, Pink Floyd's involvement with films had more of a concrete effect on popular music than it had on film more generally. It rightly should be seen as part of the long-term historical development in rock and pop music towards visualization on screen and ultimately away from live concert performances. Pink Floyd were an important part of the cultural developments that enabled and inspired the reinvention of the film soundtrack at this time. Their foray into film music did not change the way film scores were produced. Instead, their influence materialized in the form of their pursuit of high quality 'hi-fi' sound (that on disc culminated in *Dark Side of the Moon*), and most notably in spatialized sound, where they had used a form of surround sound live for a number of years.

# 5

# 'The Film Should Be Played Loud': Rockumentary Films

The opening screencard for *The Last Waltz* (1977) reads: 'The Film Should Be Played Loud'. The development of the rock documentary was where rock music, and to a lesser degree perhaps pop music, found its own specific film form, derived from the music itself. The form is highly specific and not merely a derivative of the documentary tradition or the film musical genre, although it is most definitely related to both.

The rock documentary became a notable genre of film in the late 1960s and 1970s. In more recent years, it remains vibrant and successful but almost wholly on DVD rather than in cinemas. Sometimes made by acclaimed film directors, films such as the Maysles brothers' *Gimme Shelter* (1970) and Martin Scorsese's *The Last Waltz* (1978) and *Shine a Light* (2008), these 'rockumentaries' included festival and live concert documents, as well as the spoof *This is Spinal Tap* (1984) and its sequel. Film historians have shown little interest in the genre and popular writing has more often than not been negative.[1] One reason for such a dismissal is that they mis-recognize these films through an assumed comparison with mainstream narrative cinema whereas they are more of an emanation of the music industry. Although rarely registered, other film formats derive directly from music apart from only the film musical. A whole zone of cinema makes more sense when approached from the perspective of the music industry rather than the film industry. Indeed, one might interpret some existing music formats as simply being translated into celluloid form: concept albums led to rock operas and live albums became filmed live concert-based rock documentaries.

Prominent in the 1970s, rock documentaries or 'rockumentaries' had emerged in the previous decade. It seems that in its first years, the rock documentary was essentially North American, with such notable films as D. A. Pennebaker's British-shot but American-registered *Don't Look Back* (1967, about Bob Dylan), *Woodstock* (1970) and the Maysles' brothers' *Gimme Shelter* (1970). These were event-based films and included much besides the on-stage performance.

# Distinctive form

A crucial issue when considering rock documentaries is the relationship these films have to the music industry. A significant proportion of these films were funded and produced by record companies rather than film companies, suggesting that they should be approached and understood in the context of the music industry rather than seen as purely another 'film'. Furthermore, there is a clear and close relationship between rockumentary films and live albums. Indeed, it makes sense to see some of these films as direct counterparts to live albums.[2] In aesthetic terms, there are clear similarities, while some live albums are in effect the soundtrack of the film made available in a commercial form. In the 1960s and 1970s, the format of vinyl discs set a limitation on the form, with albums being of roughly 30–50 minutes' duration. This often meant that a band's live set, as well as a concert film, would often be translated into a double album release. The set-length for a live concert varied but was more easily encapsulated by a film, most of which ran from just under an hour to nearly two hours. A common strategy to bolster the duration of a film was to supplement the live concert footage with additional material such as interviews or footage from backstage. In the case of some rock documentaries, these aspects can dominate and displace the recording of musical performance, which nevertheless remains the defining characteristic of the film genre. The showing of musicians performing has been the most defining aspect of rock documentaries, although there are exceptions which fail to show any performances. The rock documentary has been built around a dual approach: on the one hand, showing the musicians performing live on stage as a transmission of the original concert, while on the other showing them in a 'backstage' close-up that goes beyond the concert experience (for instance, in interviews, caught in unsuspecting moments outside the performance situation) and which are not accessible to people attending a concert. Such a format illustrates a clear resemblance to the traditional classical backstage musical film, which leavened the 'on stage' musical set-piece performances with complementary 'backstage' events and insight behind the show and the performers.[3] Indeed, there is an unacknowledged antecedence for the rock documentary in the film musical, another example of which is the similarity to the 'revue' film, which merely showed a succession of acts on stage. This was quite prominent in the 1930s and had something of a revival in the mid-1960s but then was replaced by rock documentaries of events which showcased a song or two from a succession of acts.

The more often cited antecedent is the tradition of documentary films. As a film form, the documentary has its origins in the earliest 'actuality' films such as the Lumiere brothers' films, which recorded actual events as they took place. As a specific form, it was solidified by directors such as Robert Flaherty's *Nanook of the North* (1922) and *Man of Aran* (1934) and Dziga Vertov's *Man with Movie Camera* (1929) and *Three Songs about Lenin* (1934). The British documentary film movement of the 1930s and 1940s developed the format further, with films such as *Song of Ceylon* (1934) and *Fires Were Started* (1943), while Leni Riefenstahl's Nazi films *Olympia* (1938) and *Triumph of the Will* (1935) illustrated how far actual events could be choreographed for the camera in service of political propaganda. More recent proponents such as Jean Rouch, Michael Moore and Werner Herzog have defined the form, while television has come to dominate documentaries with amongst the most successful programmes internationally being produced by the BBC Natural History Unit.

Documentary films carry a distinctive repertoire of assumptions and issues. There is a supposition that on some level the film will transmit 'the real' and provide a window on reality. This often involves a sense of dispassionate, critical distance, meaning that documentary films should involve a minimal amount of fabrication. Of course, while for some documentary film-makers these have been solid principles, for others, they have been 'rules' to be broken. However, the sense of transmitting 'the real' is at the heart of the power of the film form itself. This has led to certain stylistic aspects in terms of both sound and vision. A particular audiovisual style has dominated, based on the notion of 'caught action' in opposition to the system prevailing in mainstream narrative films, that of variations upon 'classical continuity' and 'classical narration'. This approach often encompasses the use of mobile, often handheld camera, shooting at specific locations with natural lighting and using location sound. In terms of post-production traditionally, there was little non-diegetic music supplementing footage as this would make it seem more like film 'fantasy' than a recording of reality. The editing together of diverse and 'captured' footage often meant that documentaries would seem more fragmented than mainstream cinema, and indeed, in some cases, the very chaotic character of the footage and sound and image aspects became a defining attribute.

The rock documentary in the 1960s involved some respected documentary film-makers, such as D. A. Pennebaker, who made a foundational film for the genre: *Don't Look Back* (1967), which recorded aspects of Bob Dylan's UK tour of 1965, where he had controversially begun to use electric instruments and incorporate aspects of rock music into his folk *oeuvre*. Similarly, direct cinema film-makers Albert and David Maysles made *Gimme Shelter* (1970), a document of the Altamont festival in 1969, which collapsed into violence. The film's direction is also credited to Charlotte Zwerin, who edited together a massive amount of footage recorded by a number of cameras as the event was taking place. Indeed, the proliferation of large-scale special musical events in the late 1960s was a fillip for documentary film-makers. Not only were these events interesting in themselves, both in musical and anthropological terms, but they could also be documented for posterity in that they seemed like they were 'making history' at the time.

Other films included Pennebaker's *Monterey Pop* (1968), *Woodstock* (1970) and *Concert for Bangladesh* (1972). The late 1960s big festivals in the United States embodied the optimism of the generation and the counterculture. While the Woodstock free festival had been 'three days of peace and music' in early 1969, the west-coast counterpart at Altamont had proved a disaster.[4] After the early 1970s, large-scale festival events became less prominent and increasingly moved onto television.[5]

While these films are documentaries, many rock documentaries are highly distinctive in being music-centred. This defines the film form. The music track dominates, and indeed the image track is in the vast majority of cases cut to it. Rockumentary films also require guarantees of the reality of the 'live' performance situation. This usually involves not just convincing onstage sequences but also behind scenes sections to further 'flesh-out' the concert as an actual event. These backstage aspects can include interviews, concert preparation (such as travelling and building stage sets), and musicians dealing with problems or writing songs. Some of the most memorable sequences in rockumentaries can be backstage sequences, such as those in *Don't Look Back* where Bob Dylan argues with a fan backstage or in *Gimme Shelter* where Rolling Stones drummer Charlie Watts listens to and comments on a radio interview with the leader of the Hells Angels who had seemingly stoked tension and violence at the Altamont festival. Adrian Wootton noted that in rock documentaries '... most attention was given to the paraphernalia surrounding the concerts. Thus, the logistics of constructing a stage set, people arriving at the event, interviews with fans, promoters and occasionally musicians were all interspliced with the music itself'.[6] While this bipartite form may not always be evident in rock documentaries, it is certainly common. Indeed, rockumentaries often appear like DVDs of concerts but with optional DVD extras cut intermittently into the film. An interesting example of this is Marc Bolan and T. Rex's *Born to Boogie* (1972), which includes a selection of out-takes integrated in the film. However, the film is essentially a live concert recorded for posterity despite its inserts and bizarre paddings.

The tension between transmission of 'reality' and fabrication, which is evident in most documentaries, is also important for rock documentaries, if not for the film itself for attempts to understand these films on a more profound level. The sense of fabrication is compounded particularly by rock documentaries that feel they need a 'supplement' to add to the actuality footage. These can include fantasy sequences or special visual effects. A good example of this is *Genesis: On Stage* (1976), which includes some old silent film footage cut in quite crudely during the extended instrumental section of The Cinema Show. Although on one level it might be inspired by the song itself, its relation to previous events is at best tenuous.

The use of handheld camera in rock documentaries to 'catch the action' transmits some of the excitement of the live concert situation, as well as taking inspiration from *cinema verité* and direct cinema approaches to making film a direct window on reality. In contrast with this, the more formal set-up static camera can sometimes mark out interviews or 'official' footage. The technological development of 16 mm cameras in the early-to-mid-1960s was crucial in their ability to be mobile and handheld. This was allied with the development of portable magnetic tape recorders, and the increasingly technological character of rock concerts, using light shows and sound channelled through a multi-speaker set-up from a single mixing desk. An event could use multiple camera visual recording and also record high-quality sound, mixing 'live' microphones among the audience with high fidelity mixing desk recordings of the musicians. Bearing some resemblance to current recording of sport events, cameras would shoot during the event and the editing stage would mix footage from different vantage positions, blending it into a seamless continuity built around the soundtrack. Sometimes the camera activity is very clear, for example in *Gimme Shelter* once the event becomes more violent and congested in front of the stage, the cameras increasingly shoot from behind the musicians (a safer position), while in *The Great Rock'n'Roll Swindle* (1980), the short piece of 'professionally-filmed' footage of the Sex Pistols live in the United States looks distinctive in its use of crane shots and slow crossfades. Warner Brothers had clearly invested money in this footage and it contrasts notably with the more mundane style of other live footage in the film.

In many cases, the stereotypical film style does not matter as the footage is about the contents of the shot rather than its style. There is, in effect, a form of onstage filming which makes for what might be called a theatrical 'classical space'. This is a strong and very practical tradition for the visual recording of music ensembles and is based on the principal of the establishing shot and the closer cut-in shot. The establishing long shot is similar to the tableau shot of early cinema and defines the overall stage space, while the closer shots showcase individual activity by musicians.

Some films can be highly regimented in the way they do this, while others can be less strict. In most cases, it will depend on what footage has been secured by the camera operators. The establishing shot is an 'audience' point of view of the whole stage, while the close-ups are better than an audience point of view and usually involve mobile cameras on the stage and among the musicians. There is, of course, one more vantage point: that potentially of the musicians, looking back at the audience. Shots of the audience can become dominant in some rock documentaries, often depending on how interesting the film-maker assume the audience to be and how far they are considered to be a crucial and active part of the event. This interplay of these three shots makes up the onstage sections of rock documentaries and allows for a sense of dynamic development. John Caughie has described the interaction of the documentary and the dramatic narrative in the television documentary drama form:

> Within the conventions of documentary, the objectifying look is part of the support of truth and neutrality. For documentary drama, however, two looks are in play, and they come to constitute a hierarchy: the rhetoric of the drama operates an exchange of looks between the characters ... [while the] rhetoric of documentary, the fixed and fixing look, constitutes its object ....[7]

There is a similar but not quite the same situation for rockumentaries. Concert sequences involve two looks: one towards the performers on the stage, which is enhanced to allow an enquiring view backstage, but also, significantly, a reverse shot looking backwards at the audience of the concert. However, this is not a point-of-view from the band so much as it is a guarantee of the veracity of the concert event. Not only does this show an (often excited) audience for the music, but it also fleshes out a culture surrounding the music. Also, as in the film musical, the figuration of the audience in musical sequences provides an analogue for the film spectator watching, cementing them into the event, but also making the event appear more like a real live event and less its recording on film.

## Two films

Emerson, Lake and Palmer were a 'supergroup' formed by members of The Nice, King Crimson and Atomic Rooster. They released *Emerson, Lake and Palmer* (December 1970), *Tarkus* (June 1971), and then *Pictures at an Exhibition* (November 1971). The last had been recorded live in March of

1971 and was a dramatic rearrangement of Mussorgsky's *Pictures at An Exhibition*, a late nineteenth-century concert hall piece originally for solo piano, but better known in its orchestral arrangement by Maurice Ravel. This was a loose 'concept album' rather than a collection of unrelated songs. Mussorgsky's piece had been used in rehearsals at the time of their debut LP's release and was recorded live at Newcastle City Hall. Distinct from the album, the corresponding film had been released in February of 1971, before the recording of the LP. It had been shot in December of 1970 at the Lyceum Theatre in London, at the time when their debut LP was on release. It was ninety-five minutes long, although some versions in existence are as short as forty minutes (the VHS video is short, and the Japanese Laserdisc is long).

*Pictures at an Exhibition* contains some startling visual effects, which are reminiscent of psychedelic light shows. These swirling patterns which on occasions overlay the images of the group on stage were based on the post-production creation of feedback patterns using a television camera. Indeed, the film was shot wholly on video, and two cumbersome television cameras on dollies are fitfully visible in shot to 'catch the action' of the live event, much like in televised sport. According to a *Melody Maker* article, their use of video was due to the future arrival of video as a medium as well as its technological possibilities.[8] This is a production that has little to do with film-making in Britain and more connections to the television industry. It was filmed by band's friend producer Lindsey Clennell, for 'Visual and Musical Entertainments'. The visual recording equipment was television standard, and it was directed by television director Nicholas Ferguson. Drummer Carl Palmer commented on the film:

> There are lots of basic shots of the band ... we had a lot of ideas about modern filming techniques which we wanted to see done, but instead ... it was done as a straight film, like the early Beatles films ... Because a friend of ours is doing it is the only reason we let him release it.[9]

So, it seems that 'progressive' music embraced a 'regressive' film style. There was an air of uncertainty about the whole endeavour. According to Palmer, the group did not intend to release the live LP, as it was not their original material. More significantly, perhaps, their normal engineer Eddie Offord was absent and the sound recording quality of the film was poor and hardly acceptable to the increasingly 'hi fi' demands of progressive rock audiences. The demand for a soundtrack album stimulated by the film led to a plan to record a coming live show, with the aim of achieving excellent sound, and indeed the LP apparently was used as a demonstration disc in some hi-fi shops.[10] *Pictures at an Exhibition*'s corresponding soundtrack LP, rather than existing as a supplement and advertisement for the film, was in fact the principal commodity itself.

For British progressive rock groups, *Pictures at an Exhibition* set something of a precedent. Musicians wanted films to showcase their abilities and imaginations, but also there appears to have been an extra tier added to rock's product chain: the repeated normality of album and associated tour could include a feature-length film as part of rock groups' intermittent bursts of product.

Led Zeppelin's *The Song Remains the Same* (1976) had a release in 4-track stereo, in this case with the music on the magnetic strip of the film print rather than synching up a magnetic tape recording to a silent print. The album was billed as the 'original soundtrack', and the record and film are closely related, although some parts of the double-LP are different from the film. Footage was taken from a few nights at Madison Square Garden, New York, at the conclusion of Led Zeppelin's 1973 tour.[11] *The Song Remains the Same* is first and foremost a recording of a live concert, although, significantly, it contains fantasy sections which embellish the primacy of the performed music. These are bold and remove the focus from the productive origins of the music. For instance, Jimmy Page's sequence in *Dazed and Confused*, during an extended solo where he plays the guitar with a violin bow, has images of the group on stage replaced by a short film depicting a shrouded figure climbing to the top of a mountain and swinging a sword that looks remarkably like the light sabres that appeared in *Star Wars* the following year. For just over four minutes, the music has remained constant while the images have become in effect non-diegetic, like an accompaniment to the soundtrack emanating from an elsewhere.

Despite rock music's appeal to authenticity and the self-proclaimed 'honesty' of many bands during this period, *The Song Remains the Same* was dramatically 'sweetened'. The album is a composite of not only songs from different days mixed together with audience noises to sound like a continuous event, but individual tracks are comprised of edited together sections of different performances.[12] Similarly, the images are an amalgam of shots from different performances. Furthermore, some shots are from a re-staging of Led Zeppelin's show at Shepperton Studios in London, where a facsimile of the Madison Square Garden stage was recreated to allow for more in the way of close-up shots. Bass and keyboard player John Paul Jones had cut his hair short after the original concerts and was forced to wear a wig at Shepperton to aid the illusion of continuity. While we may imagine we are watching a straightforward document of a concert that happened in front of the camera as a real pro-filmic event, we should be aware of how far illusion might be taken, although it is doubtful that many rock documentaries went to these lengths.

An isolated article by Adrian Wootton discusses key aspects of rock documentary (such as backstage and 'setting up' components) and cites *The Song Remains the Same* as a 'classic example' of films '... being produced by the so-called dinosaur groups [which] were often pretentious, uninteresting and uncinematic'.[13] Yet, these films were for fans rather than general film audiences (or indeed film critics) and directly reflected their interests in the music involved. *The Song Remains the Same* is first and foremost a recording of a live concert, although it also includes fantasy sections which function as inserts while retaining the continuity of the live soundtrack recording. Wootton's comment confirms that these films fail to 'make sense' as 'cinema'. Some of these films make more sense as live albums with added images. Indeed, many of them were compounded by the simultaneous release of the soundtrack album, which arguably is the primary product. In terms of distribution, the discs far outweigh the films: that is where most of the profit is being made. Consequently, it is no surprise that the overwhelming majority of these films were produced by record labels rather than film companies. In fact, live concert-based films could be characterized simply as counterparts to live albums. Furthermore, most of these films could also be characterized as glorified fan films, aiming not to please a wider audience so much as supply a very specific view for an audience who likely already knew the artists well.

## A thumbnail history

According to Barry Keith Grant, '... the first rock documentary, Wolf Koenig and Ralph Kroiter's *Lonely Boy* about Paul Anka, in 1962'.[14] Generally speaking, rock documentaries follow the fortunes of the music industry. In the 1960s, when there were a number of groundbreaking and counterculture-oriented festivals, films documented them. In the 1970s, there was a boom in rockumentaries which reflected the boom in record sales and proliferation of more serious and sometimes visually interesting 'progressive rock'.[15] By the 1980s, there was a slump in record sales and rockumentaries – particularly ones getting released in cinemas – became few and far between. This was compounded by VHS allowing cheap rockumentary films to avoid cinema release, while music video became a different option for musicians. By the millennium, it was a rarity for a rock documentary to receive a cinema release, while home DVD releases were ubiquitous, catering for cult bands with extremely small consumer numbers as well as more mainstream artists. Simon Reynolds noted the recent boom in rock documentaries, although he declared that they are 'Rarely inspired and often less than enthralling, they nevertheless have a curious quality of watchability. Low key verging on the ambient, they seem made for TV.'[16] This fails to register the fact that those of the 1960s and 1970s were made for the big screen and indeed are highly impressive in a cinema rather than idly consumed on a TV in a home living room. However, current rock documentaries are indeed rarely viewed on the big screen. Historically speaking, the relationship between the big and small screen was important for rock documentary. Once television had adapted its music shows to assimilate pop and watered-down rock'n'roll, it remained fairly stable in the 1960s but had difficulty in dealing with the counterculture. More serious 'rock' music was shown little on television and while the domestic space remained cossetted from aggressively novel culture, cinema took advantage of its more 'adult' consumer space.[17] At the end of the 1960s, the sheer scale of the musical events, as well as their perceived importance, meant that they needed the grandiosity and immersive experience of cinema rather than merely being integrated with the everyday on television.

Early rock documentaries included *Ladies and Gentlemen ... Mr. Leonard Cohen* (1965) and the already-mentioned *Don't Look Back* (1967), directed by D. A. Pennebaker and focusing on Bob Dylan's UK tour of 1965. The late 1960s, with its counterculture and explosion of interesting bands led to Granada TV documentary *The Doors: The Doors are Open* (1968) and *Elvis: '68 Comeback Special* (1968). Event-based films included Pennebaker's *Monterey Pop* (1968), which remains well known for the sequence where Jimi Hendrix sets fire to his guitar on stage,[18] although it also features a number of startling acts including Big Brother and the Holding Company (with Janis Joplin). Similarly, *Woodstock* (1970), based on a larger festival, embraced techniques such as split screens and perhaps concentrates more on the audience than the music, showcasing countercultural hippie dress and behaviour in an almost anthropological manner. The third notable festival film from this period is *Gimme Shelter* (1970) directed by the Maysles brothers with Charlotte Zwerin. This documented what was proposed to be the west-coast counterpart to the Woodstock festival, which collapsed into violence and is topped by the remarkable spectacle of the Rolling Stones having their performance halted by people sharing their stage and violence taking place in the audience in front of them. Events remained of interest into the following decade, with the Beatles' disintegration charted in *Let It Be* (1970), which also includes the famous impromptu concert on the rooftop of the Apple building in London. Similarly, a large charity event became *Concert for Bangladesh* (1972) featuring ex-Beatle George Harrison, Bob Dylan and Eric Clapton, amongst others, with the film release a few months after the triple album's release.

The 1970s saw a number of concert films focusing on particular bands and aimed decidedly at their fans. For instance, *Born to Boogie* (1972) showcased Marc Bolan and T. Rex in concert and was directed by Ringo Starr, while D. A. Pennebaker documented David Bowie in *Ziggy Stardust and the Spiders from Mars*, which was shot in 1973 but had its release held up until 1982, while notable films of concerts included *Led Zeppelin: The Song Remains the Same* (1976) and *Bob Marley and the Wailers: Live at the Rainbow* (1977). One of the most celebrated of all rock documentaries is Martin Scorsese's *The Last Waltz* (1977), which recorded The Band's final concert at Winterland in San Francisco in 1976. As a special four-hour event, the concert included many guests who had worked with The Band, Bob Dylan, Neil Young, Eric Clapton, Van Morrison, Joni Mitchell, Emmylou Harris, Muddy Waters, Dr. John and Paul Butterfield. This extensive concert was collapsed into a film of nearly two hours' length and also released as a triple-album. Scorsese's careful direction included interview segments while also capturing notable performances and an essence of the event and its emotional tone.

Punk rock was a cultural outburst that reacted against conventional dominant popular music and, in particular, against so-called 'rock dinosaurs' who had become remote and self-indulgent. Initially developed in the UK between 1976 and 1979, this confrontational movement was spearheaded by the Sex Pistols, the Damned and the Clash, later joined by the Stranglers, Buzzcocks and Siouxsie and Banshees.[19] This London scene was documented in Wolfgang Büld's *Punk in London* (1977) and Don Letts' *The Punk Rock Movie* (1978). The movement's leaders, the Sex Pistols, had their own documentary to tell their story. However, *The Great Rock 'n' Roll Swindle* (1980), directed by Julien Temple, is more of a mockumentary in that it mixes reality with comedy and very much projects a 'story' that seems some way from the truth. Indeed, Temple later directed a 'response' to this film, *The Filth and the Fury* (2000) which aimed to tell the truth and dispel some of the myths propagated by *The Great Rock'n'Roll Swindle*.[20] A reassessment of sorts also took place for the Clash, who had made the documentary-drama *Rude Boy* (1980) but received a full documentary with *Westway to the World* (2000). American punk rock also inspired documentary films, most notably *The Decline of Western Civilization, Part One* (1981), Penelope Spheeris' study of the Los Angeles punk rock scene of the late 1970s; featuring Black Flag, the Circle Jerks, X, and the Germs, while similarly the new development of hip hop culture was documented in *Wild Style* (1982).

The 1980s saw some significant developments: the advent of MTV made music and images more prominent but rendered films less important for musicians, and the widespread use of VHS videotape allowed not only for a re-release of old rock documentaries but also meant that new ones could have a video release rather than needing a cinematic release. In some ways, 1984 was a remarkable year for rock documentary, producing two outstanding films. The first was Jonathan Demme's concert film of Talking Heads, *Stop Making Sense* (1984), which carefully planned and choreographed a concert for the camera. The film begins with singer David Byrne alone on the stage for the first song and then adding a band member for each successive songs while stage construction takes place simultaneously. Demme's hand as director is evident and although the film is visually distinct from other rockumentaries, a case might be made that these aspects detract from direct recording of the music. However, such a thoughtful approach befitted the 'art rock' band Talking Heads, who clearly did not simply want to document one of their live performances. The other notable film is *This is Spinal Tap* (1984), a 'mockumentary' about an English heavy rock band, which lampoons the standardized aspects of rock documentaries as much as parodying the stereotypical issues and concerns of an ageing rock band.[21] It is ironic that *This is Spinal Tap* is probably one of the most widely recognized rock documentaries despite being a parody of the genre. Yet, one reason for its success is that it has strong song performance sequences, an aspect that can be forgotten in the mixture of strong characterization and consistent comedy. The film's success led to the band touring, releasing albums and a sequel, *The Return of Spinal Tap* (1992).

Rock documentaries that merely showcased concerts were far less on the ground, although new pop phenomenon Culture Club were accorded their own concert film, *Culture Club: A Kiss Across the Ocean* (1984). Older, well-established artists still made films with cinematic releases, such as *Chuck Berry: Hail, Hail Rock "n' Roll* (1987), and there were new, more 'serious' artists making concert films such as *Sign 'O' the Times* (1987) with Prince and *U2: Rattle and Hum* (1988). This latter film, directed by music video director Phil Joanou, was a sign of the international superstar status achieved by U2 in the wake of the international success of their album *The Joshua Tree* (1997) and also depicts them going to America and visiting Elvis's Graceland home and performing with artists such as Muddy Waters. Indeed, at this point for bands to have their own rockumentary with a cinematic release, this was something of a prestige project and sign of their status.

The 1990s saw the broadcast of regular slot *MTV Unplugged*, where musicians such as Nirvana, Alice in Chains, Neil Young and The Cure performed hour-long acoustic sets live. Beginning in 1989, this constituted something of a mixture of the 'event' film and the concert film and was rapidly made available for home consumption on video. In some ways, the show reflected the music industry's situation of 'reformatting', where products were resold to audiences on a new digital platform (CD and DVD), while emphasizing the authenticity of rock music and the validity of established artists alongside newer ones. Rock documentaries in the 1990s included historical stories or concert-based films. The former included *Hype!* (1996) on the Seattle grunge scene and *Stepping Razor Red X: The Peter Tosh Story* (1993) about the reggae singer. A notable concert film was *Year of the Horse: Neil Young and Crazy Horse Live* (1997), directed by independent film director Jim Jarmusch, who specialized in offbeat narrative films, sometimes in black and white and often showing an aficionado's interest in rock music.[22]

Informative documentaries had a short boom of sorts after the Millennium. D. A. Pennebaker made a documentary about soul singers, *Only the Strong Survive* (2003), while *Tom Dowd and the Language of Music* (2003), focused on the unheralded recording engineer and producer who had a hand in classic albums by artists including Ray Charles, Eric Clapton and John Coltrane. This early noughties burst of rock documentaries was notable in that all the films received cinematic releases and a certain amount of acclaim. Although lacking music, *The Mayor of Sunset Strip* (2003) concerned music impresario Rodney Bingenheimer and featured artists such as David Bowie, Tori Amos, Beck, Neil Young, Mick Jagger, Paul McCartney and Noel Gallagher amongst others. *Tupac: Resurrection* (2003) was about the controversial rapper whose career had been cut short by his assassination. *End of the Century: The Story of the Ramones* (2003) charted the development of one of the United States' most enduring bands, while *Metallica: Some Kind of Monster* (2004) followed internal wrangles in the heavy metal group as they record and replace their bass guitarist. A crew followed them for over a year filming and recording, and they were present for some extraordinary arguments between band members. Another film which has highly memorable interviews with band members is *DiG!* (2004), which focuses on Portland bands, the Dandy Warhols and the Brian Jonestown Massacre. These last two films illustrate a situation where rock documentaries do not have to rely on the audience being fans to gain success and acclaim. If they contain interesting material, they can attract a wider audience. Another notable film from this period is Tim Irwin's *We Jam Econo: The Story of the Minutemen* (2005), which compiled old material and included new interviews concerning a cult Californian punk band, whose career had been foreshortened by the tragic death of their singer and guitarist D. Boon in a car crash. While such films may receive a degree of acclaim, *Anvil! The Story of Anvil* (2007) was also a box office success. Concerning the comeback of a Canadian heavy metal band who had been an ace away from massive success in the early 1980s, despite the film's sincerity at times it seemed curiously close to *This is Spinal Tap*. Although the film is funny at times, it is never fully at Anvil's expense, and *Anvil! The Story of Anvil* provides insight into a growing cultural trope, that of the problems facing an ageing band. A further example of failing to age gracefully was emphasized in Jay Bolger's *Beware of Mr. Baker* (2012). The film is subtitled: 'the devil takes care of its own' and is a historical narrative and extended and illustrated interview with drummer Ginger Baker, who perhaps most famously played in the 'supergroup' Cream. It includes animated sections, still images, people sitting in chairs talking, archive footage, but little sustained music sequences. *Beware of Mr. Baker* is more 'telling the story' of his life and is not a film based on live performance, and indeed, it only shows a handful of performance excerpts but based on looking back on a remarkable career. However, this film is defined by its difference from the many self-congratulatory historical accounts on other documentaries and revels in Baker's abrasive character.

# Conclusion

For each documentary about a new artist, such as *Never Say Never* (2009, about Justin Bieber) and *Demi Lovato: Stay Strong* (2012), there seems at present to be more about artists from the 'golden era' of rock. Martin Scorsese, no stranger to the rock documentary having directed *The Last Waltz* in 1977, made a concert-based film about the Rolling Stones, *Shine A Light* (2008), while *Lou Reed: Berlin* (2007), directed by Julian Schnabel, documented a concert at St. Anne's Warehouse of the whole of Reed's iconic 1970s album. Rock documentaries have been buoyed by an interest in rock history and the possibility of gaining rights to archive footage that can be assembled into a film made of disparate elements. It is worth noting that in parallel to rockumentaries, the drama-documentary format has had a degree of vigour and success, including film such as *Sid and Nancy* (1986, about Sid Vicious), *Superstar: The Karen Carpenter Story* (1987), *The Doors* (1991), *What's Love Got to Do with It* (1993, about Tina Turner) and *24 Hour Party People* (2002, about Factory Records).

Trends in rock documentary are more easily understood when approached from the point of view of the music industry rather than the film industry. Edgar, Fairclough-Isaacs and Halligan ask: '... how can it be that documentary, operating in the field of popular music, has strayed so far from ideas of objectivity and reportage – ideas that represent the fundamentals of documentary form – and become pure promotion?'[23] First, many of these films have a genealogy which might be better understood in relation to fan club products in the 1960s and 1970s rather than in relation to the noble documentary tradition, Indeed, while rock documentaries are nominally 'films', in some ways they make more sense as 'music'. Indeed, their relationship with other areas of cinema is often minimal. In terms of aesthetics, films based on live concert clearly appear more 'music' than 'film'. For instance, in the 1970s, distribution could sometimes be through 'roadshowing' – making a succession of appearances at different locations rather like a rock band on tour. Exploiting late-night bills, double-bills and special showings, these were more a special event than an everyday visit to the cinema. For example, in January 1972, the celebrated Jimi Hendrix film *Jimi Plays Berkeley* (1971) was screened in the UK as a touring event, accompanied by two American rock groups that had some sort of connection with Hendrix.[24] Whilst in the film industry special films might occasionally be roadshown, this process is far closer to a musical group tour than conventional film distribution.

Furthermore, rock documentaries remain firmly minority interest films, often not pandering to a wider audience and lacking the aspiration to be 'mainstream films' with a general release. Indeed, these days very few rock documentary films receive wide cinematic releases. However, a visit to any large record shop will illustrate just how healthy the genre remains as there are shelves of DVDs ranging from mainstream musicians with Hollywood-level production values to obscure artists working on a shoestring budget.

# 6

# Blaxploitation: Singing Across 110th Street

**B**laxploitation marks a point where film-makers, instead of looking to film convention and traditions of film scoring, aimed at procuring popular musicians to produce highly dramatic music which could then be used as a frame onto which to place the film images. In the majority of cases, rather than follow the Hollywood convention, where music would be written to accompany the precise requirements of a 'nearly finished' film, here the music was a semi-independent item, also released on disc, which would often have the images of the film to some degree cut to its requirements. As Lawrence Novotny notes, music is one of the key elements of Blaxploitation films: 'many black exploitation films include contemporary rhythm-and-blues soundtracks that match the filmic images in theme and content. Significantly, both well-known and up-and-coming artists such as Curtis Mayfield, Earth Wind and Fire, and Isaac Hayes composed the soundtracks. The films often feature extended montages that are enhanced by the funky, upbeat songs.'[1] In some cases, the soundtrack records for these films eclipsed the popularity or longevity of the films themselves.

The 1970s phenomenon of 'Blaxploitation' films, premised upon depictions of black American urban culture, tended to have strong input from popular music. For instance, Isaac Hayes produced the iconic title music for *Shaft* (1971), Earth, Wind and Fire supplied the whole score for *Sweet Sweetback's Baadasssss Song* (1971) and Curtis Mayfield produced both songs and incidental music for *Super fly* (1972) and Bobby Womack produced music for *Across 110th Street* (1972). Many of these films exploited black popular music, sometimes to the point where the character of the films almost verged on being film musicals. Indeed, the music as much as the distinctive imagery forms an essential 'landscape' for Blaxploitation films. This aesthetic landscape not only involves primarily urban settings but distinct stereotypes connected to American black communities and narratives involving crime and violence. In terms of music, the sound embraces American soul songs and instrumental music based on sounds derived from soul, funk and jazz.

Blaxploitation films were strident in terms of representation and featured violence, sex and action. Although often quite crude in conception and execution and cheaply made, these films now have something of a cult status and are considered remarkable. The genre's significance is summed up well by Walker, Rausch and Watson:

> Blaxploitation films changed how black men and women were portrayed in films. Gone were the old negative stereotypes that had dominated films for over 70 years. Replacing them were new archetypes, including drug dealers, pimps, and hardened criminals. The new images were initially a welcome change for audiences, and the studios were more than happy to be making money, but the constant barrage of morally ambiguous anti-heroes soon led to a backlash.[2]

The cinema screen appeared to offer freedoms that were not yet widely available to African-Americans in US society. In contrast with many mainstream Hollywood films of this period, these films are not overshadowed by anxiety and fear but exude a sense of positive outlook and confidence.[3]

Concurrently, African-American musicians were producing confident and novel popular music, running from developments in mixing jazz and rock led by musicians such as Miles Davis and Herbie Hancock, while soul and funk music were developing different forms that would go on to have a dominating influence on dance music in the following decades. Black musicians were also producing strident music that mixed soul traditions with rock and extremely pronounced beats to produce 'funk'. James Brown, Sly and the Family Stone and Funkadelic were particularly eclectic. James Brown excelled live in concert but also produced imaginative and complex studio recordings. Their musical style at least fed into Blaxploitation film soundtracks. It was striking that among the artists producing music for films, Sly and the Family Stone and Funkadelic did not provide soundtracks to any Blaxploitation films, although the leader of the latter, George Clinton, later wrote some successful film music. Some of this soul and funk music that fed into Blaxploitation films conveyed a serious political message, which was evident in some of the films' music, while there was also a connection to proto-rap culture.[4]

Blaxploitation films evince a high degree of what might be called 'rhythmic scoring', where the beat of the music dominates and the film follows. The most common strategy in these films is the use of a 'groove', a repetitive rhythmic continuity which is particularly effective in accompanying action sequences or scenes without dialogue. For instance, in *Super Fly* (1972), foregrounded music usually of the character of a 'groove' accompanies the many scenes of walking or driving through the streets of New York. Such music has the character of being soul or funk music often without any singing to remain as a so-called 'backing track', dominated by a bass guitar riff and drum beat, which also is similar to the basic rhythmic foundation for improvisation evident in some fusion or jazz rock. A groove might be defined as arguably the successor to jazz's sense of 'swing'. A repetitive rhythm comprising a meshing of instruments, often cohered around the drum kit and bass guitar, which has particular emphases and nuances that give it a particular 'feel' or sense of movement.[5]

The overwhelming majority of the musicians producing scores for Blaxploitation films had no experience of scoring films in the traditional sense. The assumption from the point of view of film-makers was that musicians did not need to know the 'craft' of writing music for films, and that assuming they were good at making music, any music they produced could then be edited into the film and would be effective in itself. In many cases, the musicians involved would supply a handful of songs and instrumental versions of those songs, sometimes as extended instrumental workouts. These were usually written to fit the general character of the film in question and not written to fit a rough cut of the film, as had been the convention for film music production during the Hollywood studio era.

## Genre and industry

The genre began in 1970 with *Cotton Comes to Harlem* and then *Sweet Sweetback's Baadasssss Song* (1971), followed quickly by *Shaft* (1971).[6] The first was a studio production, while the second was an independent production with Melvin Van Peebles starring, directing and producing. It costs only $450,000 but had made $12 million after a year.[7] Many Blaxploitation films were made outside the mainstream, with independent productions, such as AIP's *Black Caesar* (1973). Hollywood was quick to take advantage (certainly in distribution). In 1974 and 1975, Blaxploitation films buoyed the US film industry to its highest domestic box office in 28 years according to *Variety*.[8] The films were almost all commercially aimed and aimed primarily at black audiences through representing the black urban experience. However, there was a certain ambiguity about whether these films offered a positive and culturally specific version of African-American life, or whether they continued a tradition of black American representation in pejorative terms. The films tended certainly to be filled with stereotypes, often celebrating crime and misogyny. However, they usually depicted extremely strong black characters, often striving against negative white characters. Josiah Howard offers a tentative definition of Blaxploitation films as '... 1970s black-cast or black-themed films ... created, developed, and most importantly heavily promoted to young, inner-city, black audiences'.[9] Lawrence Novotny's study defines Blaxploitation films as 'movies made between 1970 and 1975, by both black and white film directors alike, to exploit the black film audience.'[10] According to Mikel Koven, the term 'Blaxploitation' was coined by the *Variety* reviewer of *Cotton Comes to Harlem* (1970).[11] Combing 'black' and 'exploitation', the term was clearly intended to be pejorative, suggesting the low-budget sensationalism of exploitation cinema. However, others suggest it came as a critical term from black culture. The term was possibly coined by Julian Griffin, the head of the Los Angeles branch of the NAACP (the National Association for the Advancement of Colored People), who were campaigning against films which they thought demeaned black people.[12] Blaxploitation films initially were aimed at and consumed by black urban audiences in the United States. They were part of the 'Coalition Against Blaxploitation' (along with other groups of moral guardians) and this pressure among other things led to the petering out of this film cycle by the end of the 1970s.

Whilst on the one hand, these films catered specifically for black audiences, on the other, they offered an exotic vision of urban African-American culture for white audiences. Part of their impetus came from exploiting a specific, even 'ghetto-ized' audience, while some film-makers approached such film-making as a 'separatist' enterprise, refusing 'integration' into mainstream cinema on the terms of the dominant Hollywood studios. However, the Hollywood studios had been through something of a crisis in the 1960s. Overseas investment, particularly in British film production, had impoverished American film-making but buoyed independent production companies such as AIP (American International Pictures). The return of investment to American films focused on relatively cheaply made films such as *Bonnie and Clyde* (1967) and *Easy Rider* (1968). Blaxploitation films similarly offered rapid and cheap production with rough and ready production values for an industry that was looking to narrower margins and more fragmented audiences.

Although Blaxploitation was seemingly a coherent film genre, it hybridized easily with other genres, and this worked in a manner as if films could be 'blackened' through the substitution of black characters and concerns. Examples include distinctive runs of Westerns and horror films (such as *Blacula* [1972]), as well as comedies and kung fu films (such as *Black Belt Jones* [1974] starring Gloria Hendry). The exception was derivations of the Hollywood gangster and crime genre, which cut out a character all of its own with particular urban settings and flamboyant characters.[13] While women were presented as objects of desire, they also appeared as confident action stars, in films including *Cleopatra Jones* (1973) with Tamara Dobson, *T.N.T. Jackson* (1974) with Jean Bell, *Black Belt Jones* (1974) with Gloria Hendry, and *Coffy* (1973), *Foxy Brown* (1974), *Friday Foster* (1975) and *Sheba Baby* (1975) with Pam Grier. Despite the diversity and variations across the Blaxploitation genre, music tended to be fairly constant in style. In terms of setting, these were overwhelmingly urban films, and many were set in New York's Harlem (literally 'across 110th Street' as the film proclaims), although not exclusively, as, for example, *The Mack* (1973) was set in Oakland, *Detroit 9000* (1973) in Detroit, *Together Brothers* (1974) in Galveston and *Sugar Hill* (1974) in Houston.

# Music

Many of these films were notable for their music, and indeed, Blaxploitation films often took advantage of black popular music to give a contemporary urban flavour to the films. This was a bold move, and well beyond the possibilities for music in film evident for popular musicians desiring to work in mainstream film production. A principal attraction of these films was the depiction of colourful characters from contemporary American urban life, while another clear attraction was the constant appearance of the contemporary sounds of black popular music. Indeed, African-American popular music had become one of the main areas of pride and signifiers of black identity, so it was no surprise that Blaxploitation films relied upon it so heavily.

Music was a central defining characteristic of these films, using a sound palette for non-diegetic music that later filtered into mainstream use. This embraced drum kit and bass guitar grooves, choppy rhythmic wah wah guitar and bass guitar lines as ostinato melodies, among other aspects. In the overwhelming majority of cases, these films were not 'scored' as such in the traditional sense, but rather pieces of music were written to fit general situations in the film. The popular musicians involved simply imported the modes of soul and funk music to film. Indeed, the 'scores' produced by many soul and funk artists bear direct resemblance to their regular musical output. Rather than attempting to produce something approaching a conventional film score, they clearly produced music the way they knew how. This, of course, would mean that the 'soundtrack album' would not be a radical departure from the rest of their recordings and thus had a readymade clientele in the artist's existing fans and record buyers.

Much of the music in Blaxploitation films is song-based, either being songs or instrumental music that derives broadly from song structures. Sometimes the incidental music consists simply of 'grooves', which could easily being made into songs. Indeed, rather than follow the traditions of film scoring, Blaxploitation films readily imported musical fabric and techniques from black popular music, with a strong emphasis on the rhythmic impetus of the music and its structure based on 4-bar units. In relation to the traditions of film scoring, the process was closer to existing library music being 'tracked', simply cut-in over a piece of film footage, and controlled by means of either being cut (stopped suddenly) or being faded with a volume control knob.

Certain timbres tend to dominate and provide a characteristic 'sound' of Blaxploitation scores. The music regularly is based on a muscular 'rhythm section' of electric guitar, bass guitar and drum kit, often playing a repetitive riff-based groove. The electric guitar is played almost as a percussion instrument. Played as chopped chords or heavily palm-muted notes, this has a particularly distinctive sound which appears in film scores since at time but often with a desire to connote something approaching a black urban 1970s milieu. Perhaps the most iconic form of this is the choppy guitar played with a wah wah effects footpedal that is perhaps the defining aspect of Isaac Hayes's opening theme to *Shaft*. Similarly, Gene Page's instrumental main theme for *Blacula* (1972) is based on a wah wah guitar groove alongside some less common wah wah bass guitar.

Another featured instrument, or rather series of instruments, would be percussion. Most commonly bongos and congas, which supply a repetitive pattern of alternating drum pitches higher than the drum kit. A good example is the chase music from *Willie Dynamite* (1974) by J. J. Johnson. Hand-played drums, most obviously the congas, which are played rapidly for action such as in the pool hall sequence in *Black Belt Jones* (1974), which adds then big band brass to the fast-beat kinesis. Latin percussion was also evident, such as the wooden stroking sound of the guiro in the running music from *Sweet Sweetback's Baadasssss Song*.

Perhaps one of the most characteristic musical aspects of many Blaxploitation film scores is the use of bass guitar to produce a repetitive ostinato upon which the rest of the music is built. These can be part of a full song, rhythm section activity as a 'groove' or carrying on their own as part of a so-called 'drop out' where instruments stop playing for a period, leaving one to carry the music during a more quiet passage. This is evident, among other places, in Curtis Mayfield's music for *Super Fly* (1972). Other common musical elements included closely co-ordinate horn sections, playing supporting melodies and often punctuating rhythmically off the beat. An occasional but notable timbre was the use of breathy solo flute, which was something of a fashion in the late 1960s and early 1970s in film scores more generally. This appears in the quiet opening to the song *Brother's Gonna Work It Out* by Willie Hutch, from *The Mack* (1973) and at the start of the main theme by Isaac

Hayes in *Truck Turner* (1973), in which he also starred. Flute (by Jimmy Vinson) is also prominent in guitarist Don Julian's score for *Savage!* (1973), which consists of a number of ensemble pieces broadly characterized as fusion but with a strong funk beat.

One effect of popular music appearing in films was that certain aspects of popular music sounds were more prominent and noticeable, such as the emphasis of an open high hat cymbal beat, which often on records simply became a norm, in films could become a defining part of a groove to accompany action. Indeed, aspects such as this, which were merely a conventional passing element in a pop song, could become more significant for music in films, defining the sort of minimal texture that was a rarity in popular music but could unify a long-scale piece of music. The use of the drum kit was almost universal in the non-diegetic music of Blaxploitation films.

For black American audiences, Blaxploitation films must have sounded rather familiar. The distinctive rhythmic character and timbres were derived directly from developments in wider African-American popular music. Although instruments such as electric pianos (primarily Fender Rhodes or Wurlitzer) had become a more widely available instrument from the late 1960s onwards, they were a staple of soul and funk music and its cousin jazz-rock. The importing of these musical aspects created a distinguishing 'sound' for Blaxploitation films, which almost never contained mainstream-sounding orchestral scores.[14] Indeed, evident in many of these scores is an influence from fusion or jazz-rock, which emerged from jazz musicians embracing rock rhythms and electric instruments. However, this is not to suggest that there is a direct confluence into these scores from fusion music, it is more that the black popular musicians who were making this music adopted techniques to sustain music without singing, such as extended solos or changes in texture that were the sort of musical strategy common in jazz and related music. Influential figures in fusion included keyboard players such as Herbie Hancock and Chick Corea, guitarists John McLaughlin and Larry Coryell, bass player Ron Carter and drummer Billy Cobham. Miles Davis was a catalyst in developments, assembling crossover musicians for albums such as *In a Silent Way* (1969) and *Bitches Brew* (1970), while one of his collaborators, Herbie Hancock, later produced a landmark funk-influenced album, *Head Hunters* (1973).

Elsewhere, urban-set films followed suit with action underscored by drum kit beats and electric bass guitar ostinato forming flowing 'grooves'. In 1971, Lalo Schifrin's score for *Dirty Harry* (1971) exploited the sort of jazz rock sound evident on Miles Davis's recent *Bitches Brew* double album. Having a similar musical palette to many of the later Blaxploitation films, the score incorporates drum kit, bass guitar, a wordless female vocal, with energetic exotic percussion keeping the score and the film's action moving. However, it also used orchestral strings, sometimes inspired by modernist art music with resonating cluster chords. The sequel, *Magnum Force* (1973), was also scored by Schifrin, and although in many ways it sounds like a continuity, it in fact sounds notably similar to Gordon Parks's score for *Shaft's Big Score*, which was released a year earlier. It is in effect energetic funk-inspired jazz rock. I am not suggesting a direct influence, merely noting that there is a similarity. Schifrin also used a similar musical language in *Enter the Dragon* (1973), which, although it was a Bruce Lee vehicle, also had a black character played by Jim Kelly who went on to star in a handful of Blaxploitation films.[15]

Musicians of distinction were attracted to these films. Roy Ayers had been in demand as a specialist jazz vibraphone player. Starting as a jazz musician in the US West Coast jazz scene of the early 1960s, he later began to mix jazz with other forms, notably funk in the 1970s and hip hop in the 1990s. As a highly influential musician and composer, Ayers's career has involved a massive variety of recordings with a great many different musicians. Indeed, to the point where his scores for Blaxploitation films only get the barest mention in summaries of his career. In 1973, Ayers recorded the memorable and effective score for *Coffy*, which starred Pam Grier and was about a nurse who became a vigilante to fight drug dealers. While jazz musicians such as Ayers and J. J. Johnson produced Blaxploitation film music, there were many more soul or rhythm and blues musicians who made music for these films. Examples include Willie Hutch (*The Mack* [1973]), Osibisa (*Super fly T.N.T.* [1973]) *Foxy Brown* [1974]), Marvin Gaye (*Trouble Man* [1972]), Bobby Womack (*Across 110th Street* [197] with J. J. Johnson) and Barry White (*Together Brothers* [1974]).

# Defining films

*Sweet Sweetback's Baadasssss Song* remains a startlingly original film, following .... It starred, was written and directed by Melvin Van Peebles. *Sweet Sweetback's Baadasssss Song* also has a score credited as 'written and composed by Melvin Van Peebles' and 'featuring Earth, Wind and Fire'. Van Peebles had a background which had included recording music. He had recorded an album for A&M, called *Ain't Supposed to Die a Natural Death* which included a version of the song *Come On Feet Do Your Thing* which appears in the film. Van Peebles provided musical ideas and some melodies, which were then developed by the musicians.[16] Earth, Wind and Fire were not famous at this point, before they had achieved a number of big hit records in the mid and late 1970s, although they had already released their self-titled debut album immediately before working on the film. A wholly independent production, the film initially had trouble getting distribution,[17] although ended up making a lot of money for Van Peebles.

The film's music involves the constant use of musical 'grooves', repetitive rhythmic backing tracks and a few songs. The memorable repeated organ-based theme accompanies a running montage as Sweetback escapes from the white police. Beginning with some startling colour effects on the image, he runs through hills in a semi-urban location as the continuous musical piece develops from an extended saxophone solo to an electric piano solo. The same music appears for shots of cars driving in the street. The music is built around a brisk beat and a repeated two-bar organ motif of three major chords (I-mIII-mVII). This is supported by a leading bass riff and forms the foundation for sustained improvisation by saxophone and horns, and later electric piano. Although the music initially sounds like a soul backing track, its lack of singing and instrumental solos bears a stronger resemblance to jazz. The music's continuous structure and dynamics makes an effective and energetic accompaniment to the chase on screen. Indeed, variations on this appear for other dialogue-free moments in the film particularly if they include movement. One arrangement has some prominent electric piano, one of the key instrumental sounds in later Blaxploitation films and in 1970s soul and funk music. The melody is related to the chant which appears at the conclusion of the film ('they bled your brother'), which is sung in a call and response pattern reminiscent of a religious song. There is a looseness to the relation of sound and image in *Sweet Sweetback's Baadasssss* Song, which comes from much of the film having been shot silent, meaning that the soundtrack was mostly built in post-production, which allowed for more prominent music.[18]

The concluding section of the film underlines the film's singular aesthetic strategy. The music involves a strange vocal chorus which addresses the character Sweetback, alongside 'vox pop'-style images where people (who seemingly are not actors) declare that they have not seen him. This is a means of expressing the police hunt for him and includes some startling repeated footage and dialogue (such as where a woman asks, 'Did I have a LeRoy?').[19] This extensive flight sequence has run most of the way through with the three-chord riff appearing on and off, concluding with Sweetback arriving in Mexico. It contained no sustained dialogue and almost constant music, giving it a perpetual pace and purposefulness.

*Shaft* (1971) was produced by Hollywood studio MGM, who had bought the rights cheaply and expended a low production budget on the film. Isaac Hayes supplied the iconic title song and some instrumental pieces for the music, although the music was a collaboration with Johnny Allen, who was a highly successful arranger for records, specializing in string and brass arrangements. Hayes's theme has a long instrumental introduction, premised upon a choppy guitar rhythm played through an opening and closing wah wah pedal. The key was the combination of the defining guitar with orchestral forces, which worked a rhythmic arrangement around the guitar's central and continuous position in the arrangement. Amid muscular orchestral stabs, Hayes's gravelly baritone voice half sings and half speaks the words with interjections from a chorus of female backing vocalists. The lengthy title track accompanies an extended opening/title sequence, which depicts John Shaft (Richard Rowntree) walking through the streets of New York. *Shaft* won an Oscar for Hayes's theme song and an Oscar nomination for the score. The sequel was *Shaft's Big Score* (1972), which was made with a larger budget. The score was by the director, Gordon Parkes, although it included songs sung by O. C. Smith and one by Isaac Hayes. The score embodies Blaxploitation film music's mixture of jazzy orchestra and muscular rhythmic grooves dominated by drum kit and electric bass guitar. The music draws on eclectic sources. For instance, there is a swinging jazz piece for the funeral (replacing diegetic sound), while the sex scene which is obscured by special lens effects is accompanied by a smooth song sung by O. C. Smith. This slow love ballad (Don't Misunderstand) obliterates diegetic sound and works anempathetically with the images, first showing an exotic dancer in a club where this appears to be diegetic music, but then introducing parallel editing cuts away to a violent attack.[20] The third film in the series, *Shaft in Africa* (1973) had an even larger budget and was directed by experienced English film director John Guillermin, who went on to direct *The Towering Inferno* (1974). On this occasion, the score was by Johnny Pate and it featured three songs by the Four Tops, who were a perennially successful musical act by this point. The score exhibited key characteristics of most Blaxploitation scores, matching dense drumming with wah wah guitar semiquaver pulse and close-playing 'big band'-style horns.

The director of *Shaft*, Gordon Parks Snr, was a veteran film-maker, photographer and musician, and one of his sons, Gordon Parks Jnr, went on to direct another of the canonical Blaxploitation films, *Super Fly* (1972), less than a year after his father had directed *Shaft*.

*Super Fly* encountered many difficulties during the shoot; the studio stopped the money supply and producer Sig Shore managed to raise finance to finish the film from black businesspeople.[21] While *Shaft* made the genre popular, *Super Fly* developed and set the style, iconography and terms of representation.[22] The film also showcased an outstanding Blaxploitation score. The music by Curtis Mayfield is highly impressive including a number of songs which comment on the film's action, such as *Pusher Man* and *Freddy's Dead*. Although the film appears to glorify drug dealer Priest (Ron O'Neal), Mayfield's songs provide a more critical commentary which does not directly tally with the film's tone. This is not to suggest a disjunction. The music fits the film well but has a far more critical tone than the rest of the film.

*Pusherman* is sung from the point of view of the drug dealer, although it mostly appears in the film without singing. It includes exotic percussion, tuned drums (possibly rototoms), alongside Mayfield's high-pitched and intimate voice, the use of the male falsetto voice of which is not uncommon in soul music. The music is riff-based – on bass guitar with electric guitar support – augmented by busy varied percussion played across a steady drum kit beat. The beat being slightly 'pushed' – the first beat of the bar arriving slightly early – helps generate the 'groove' and sense of rhythmic energy. As a song, *Pusherman* appears as non-diegetic music when the car drives through the street at night after the heist. When protagonist Priest enters a club and meets people, Curtis Mayfield is performing on stage, singing *Pusherman*, with a predominance of medium close-up shots of him. The song also appears for the remarkable sequence which represents a montage of making drug deals, making drugs and taking drugs but through a succession of still images. This surprising aesthetic move includes split screens but significantly also includes some cutting to beat, which retains continuity with the *Super Fly*'s use of rhythmic music as a central structural tenet of the film. Indeed, *Super Fly* regularly exploits the rhythmic impetus of the music, with Priest's arrest near the end of the film involving a groove of percussion, featuring congas heavily, alongside percussively clicking wah wah guitar, leading to a few horn punctuations. Earlier in the film, Priest and his woman walk on a bridge and by the river in the snow accompanied by a bossa nova rhythm-based cue which fades out quite crudely when they talk and then back in again once they finish. This illustrates how the music was not written to fit the action but has been edited and faded to fit the final cut of the film.

*Super Fly* and *Freddy's Dead* both made an impact on the singles charts at the time of release. The title song appears a few times as instrumental versions in the film, including opening the film, but the existence of an instrumental version (as 'score') and a sung version illustrates the dual function of much Blaxploitation music: as score providing an essential character for the film, but also as output from musicians whose main area of production was as music artists rather than in the film industry. This marks a form of synergy where the music's primary function is as music in itself rather than tied directly to the film. These two songs, along with Pusherman, dominate the film's soundtrack. The pretitle sequence follows two junkies walking through the streets accompanied by *Super Fly* as non-diegetic music with diegetic sound pushed to the margins. The onset of the titles is accompanied by an instrumental arrangement of the song *Freddie's Dead*. Later sequences, including one of streets beginning with a close-up of the front of a car use this instrumental version of *Freddy's Dead*. The sung version of *Super Fly* accompanies Priest dealing with white men in a restaurant, replacing diegetic sound fully to occupy the foreground of the film. *Super Fly* was Mayfield's first score. He went on to score *Claudine* (1974, with Gladys Knight and the Pips), *Let's Do It Again* (1975, with the Staple Singers), *Sparkle* (1976, with Aretha Franklin), *A Piece of the Action* (1977, with Mavis Staples) and prison film *Short Eyes* (1977), where he appeared as a prisoner singing the song *Doo Wop is Strong in Here*.

*Black Caesar* (1973) had a certain moral ambiguity, following the rise of a black criminal in Harlem. It starred Fred Williamson (who had originally been a football player) and Gloria Hendry and had music by James Brown. Written, produced and directed by Larry Cohen for AIP (American Independent Pictures), *Black Caesar* was an iconic and successful gangster film that owes something to Warner Brothers gangster films of the 1930s *Little Caesar* (1931) and *Angels with Dirty Faces* (1938).

The score and diegetic music for the film was written and performed by James Brown, often dubbed 'the Godfather of Soul'. This is proclaimed at the start of the film and one of the final credits lists the availability of the soundtrack album on Polydor Records. On the end titles, the film credits the song *Big Daddy* to the writing team of Lenny Stule and Joelle Cohen. Although he had a rough cut of the film to work from, Brown and his band did not produce music that followed traditional patterns of musical underscores. Instead, they produced pieces of music that they thought fitted the mood of the scenes that were deemed to need music. Director Larry Cohen noted:

> James did a fantastic job but unfortunately the music he submitted wasn't timed out to fit the actual scenes in the film. I called up his manager and told him that James had not done what he had been contracted to do and his manager just said, 'So, he gave you more than you paid for!' I said, 'Unfortunately, that's not the way it works. We need the music to fit the scenes exactly – that's why we gave you a copy of the film.' In the end, I made it work but AIP was furious. James had done the same thing with another of their films, *Slaughter's Big Rip-Off*. Consequently, when it came time to do a sequel, James had to do his music on spec. When AIP refused it, he released it as a solo effort called *The Payback* and it became the biggest album of his career.[23]

Cohen's description of Brown supplying 'too much music' which did not 'fit' illustrates how many inexperienced film composers worked: through simply providing music that fitted the character of the film rather than to fit specific dramatic moments or precise dynamic developments. In some cases, such musicians simply supplied songs. There are a few songs in *Black Caesar*. The film opens with Brown singing *Down and Out in New York City*, which was written by Bidie Chandler and Barry DeVorzon. The soul funk character forms a suitable homology with the images of urban America, despite the action on screen having been set in the early 1950s and the music sounding distinctly something from two decades later. Inaugurated by a brutal shooting, the song is crudely silenced by a rapid fade rather than dovetailing with the film's action.

The incidental music in the film consists of 'grooves', repetitive rhythmic pieces that have little dynamic development and merely provide a background for the images. These are simply cut-in and provide a strong atmosphere and energy to the sequences where they are used. Songs are used in a similar manner, with one appearing for a traditional montage sequence. In each case, music tends to appear when there is little or no dialogue. Another song, *Mom's Dead*, appears at his mother's funeral and reappears slightly later, on both occasions continuing under dialogue.

# Conclusion

Although in recent years Blaxploitation films have been generally celebrated, it has been to a degree at the expense of their controversial status in the 1970s. *Shaft*'s title song tells of priorities of the film (and the genre following in its wake). The opening line is: 'Who's the black dick who's a sex machine to all the chicks.' Strong gender division is reinforced by the song's use of popular music, especially soul, tradition of a male lead singer and female backing singers. (As if the singer is the protagonist and the backing female singers are 'all the chicks'.) While this might, perhaps unconvincingly, be dismissed these days as steeped in irony, or the whole might be received by current audiences in a sophisticated 'ironic' mode, criticisms cannot easily be dissipated. The NAACP (National Association for the Advancement of Colored People) and Rev. Jesse Jackson denounced *Super fly*, stating that the films made audience feel momentarily powerful but at the expense of not only failing to help the cause of African-American empowerment but also through denigrating black culture. Indeed, Blaxploitation films almost uniformly showed African-Americans in relation to crime, drugs, pimps and prostitution. Picketers outside cinemas held placards reading: 'Black Shame, White Profits'.[24] Indeed, they were uniformly cheaply made films usually made by white producers and investors but significantly they primarily targeted young black audiences.[25] Black TV producer Tony Brown stated:

> The 'blaxploitation' films are a phenomenon of self-hate. Just look at the image of *Super Fly*. Going to see yourself as a drug dealer when you're oppressed is sick. Not only are blacks identifying with him, they're paying for the identification. It's sort of like a Jew paying to get into Auschwitz. Blacks who contribute to the making of these films are guilty of nothing less than treason.[26]

These sentiments indicate the vehemence of opposition that Blaxploitation films received. Yet, they were popular with urban black audiences because they represented the community's locations and represented blacks as heroic and powerful. Despite the well-founded criticisms, these films gave opportunities to African-American film-makers and musicians. For instance, a number of black film directors, such as Gordon Parks Snr, Melvin Van Peebles, Oscar Williams, Gordon Parkes Jnr, Bill Crain, Michael Schultz and Ivan Dixon, came to the fore working on Blaxploitation films. Furthermore, Blaxploitation films moved music to the centre of dramatic films. Not only giving score for black American musicians to work in film, the type of music that graced Blaxploitation films became evident elsewhere in other films and television programmes, and the use of repetitive rhythmic 'grooves' as a backing of musical continuity for action sequences became prevalent in mainstream films.

# 7

# Falling to Earth: Bowie's Failed Film Soundtrack

This chapter is an investigation of the notion of the 'film soundtrack' through events and their potential outcomes in the mid-1970s, surrounding *The Man Who Fell to Earth* (1976) and David Bowie's unrealized score for the film. In the 7 June 1975 issue of *Melody Maker*, it announces under the heading 'Bowie Moves into Films' that for *The Man Who Fell to Earth* there would be a soundtrack album featuring at least two new Bowie songs.[1] This was a comedown from earlier statements that he would provide the whole score, and on the way to the reality that he would provide no music at all.

David Bowie was a successful music star with a show that played upon the persona of the alien-like 'Ziggy Stardust' when he was chosen by Nic Roeg to star in *The Man Who Fell to Earth* as an alien marooned on the earth. What is less well known is that Bowie originally was to supply the film's music. Bowie set to work writing during the shoot, but his score was never used. However, some of the music he produced ended up on his *Low* album in 1975, which subsequently and ironically became influential on later ambient and film music. This chapter will outline the events and reasons for the collaboration failing to come to fruition, as well as addressing the assumptions of the time about what film music should do for a film and how it might be produced by 'inspired musicians' rather than 'industry hacks'.

*The Man Who Fell to Earth* was an Anglo-American film vehicle for English pop star David Bowie. As a science fiction film, it was literally light years away from the sort of pop star vehicles that had been made a decade earlier (such as *Summer Holiday* [1963] or *A Hard Day's Night* [1964]). Its serious tone was characteristic of developments in the 1970s whereby 1960s pop stars endeavoured to reinvent themselves in order to sustain careers that had surpassed initial life expectancy. Director Nic Roeg had already dealt effectively with a pop star in his debut film (*Performance* [1970] with Mick

Jagger) and again successfully blurred the division between reality and on-screen. In *The Man Who Fell to Earth*, though, this is taken further. The film plays so heavily upon Bowie's star image that by the conclusion of the film, Bowie is basically the 'Thin White Duke' character that he projected for the 1975 album *Station to Station*. Bowie's persona seemingly converged with that of Newton, with images from the film being used as his album covers of the time, and stranded alien Newton ending up recording an album of music in the film. During production, Bowie set about recording a musical score for *The Man Who Fell to Earth*. This was never used in the film or released commercially but had a not insignificant effect on Bowie's musical future. This paper will investigate this elusive and complex saga of music and film, looking to *The Man Who Fell to Earth* as a nexus point between music and film as converging aesthetics at a time of experiment and possibility.

## Bowie vehicle

This chapter is concerned with an event that never happened: David Bowie's musical score for *The Man Who Fell to Earth*, in which he starred. This music was never completed and not used. In its place, the film had a composite assemblage of pieces put together by John Phillips (once of the Mamas and Papas[2]) that mostly involved album tracks by Japanese percussionist Stomu Yamashta and a diverse array of existing musical pieces and songs. It is hard not to be interested in what *might have been*. This allows us to see cultural history as a nexus of possibilities rather than monolithic (and inevitable), and unproblematically describable. As such, this chapter includes a focus perhaps less on the film and more on the film's lumber room.

Although shot in the United States, *The Man Who Fell to Earth* was a highly singular British film. It is about an alien (called 'Newton' and played by David Bowie) who lands on Earth from a planet doomed by drought. He becomes rich and makes a rocket, is incarcerated and examined by the authorities and then drifts into obscurity as an alcoholic. *The Man Who Fell to Earth* is ripe with allusions to Icarus, Howard Hughes, Jesus Christ and (perhaps most clearly) to Bowie himself.

One important development in the relationship of music and film in the 1960s and 70s was the move from pop musicals to using pop stars as straight actors in mainstream dramatic films. In the UK, this embraced actors such as Adam Faith, John Leyton, Jess Conrad, David Essex and Ringo Starr, amongst others. Before *The Man Who Fell to Earth*, David Bowie had appeared in a few acting roles, including an ice cream advertisement directed by Ridley Scott in 1969.[3] *The Man Who Fell to Earth* is a pop star vehicle of sorts, and therefore, it is not unreasonable to expect the soundtrack record to have reflected this and comprised an integral component of the project. The official soundtrack album was not a success and unlike Bowie's albums of the period has not remained available.[4] Thus, it might be possible to see a parthenogenesis as having taken place, dividing the film from its spiritual soundtrack album: Bowie's contemporaneous album. *Station to Station* was released in January 1976 and therefore was on release concurrently with *The Man Who Fell to Earth*. It looks precisely like a soundtrack album for the film, not least through sporting a still image from the film on the front of the record sleeve. Bowie's subsequent album, *Low* (1977), also had a cover still from *The Man Who Fell to Earth*. Indeed, there is a fairly widespread misnomer that *Low* was derived from Bowie's unused (and perhaps rejected) soundtrack for the film. Some of this album sounds like it could have been a film soundtrack, certainly more so than the diverse collection of songs that comprised the overwhelming majority of pop LPs of the time. The album's final track, *Subterraneans*, indeed began life as a theme that Bowie had written for the score of *The Man Who Fell to Earth*, although it was never used in the film.[5] However, there is much in the way of contradictory information about the score. Interviews with Bowie and director Nic Roeg are far from reliable. However, it seems sure that Bowie wrote and recorded some music for the film.

## Events of film's production

As a pop star, David Bowie consistently proved himself a successful chameleon figure, reinventing himself consistently in terms of image and musical style in order to prolong and renew his musical career.[6] For example, in the early 1970s, he had transmogrified from the 'Ziggy Stardust' character, a stereotypical but defining glam rock icon, to the 'white soul boy' figure of the *Young Americans* album and tour.[7] Later in the decade, his 'Berlin period' saw him espouse a certain sartorial austerity[8] while by the early 1980s, for the *Let's Dance* album, he had assumed a more conservative white-suited image not far removed from crooners like Frank Sinatra. Bowie's first LP had been released in 1967, followed by his defining *Space Oddity* single in 1969 which coincided with the Apollo moon landing. *The Rise and Fall of Ziggy Stardust and the Spiders from Mars* was released in 1972, followed by other 'glam rock' albums *Aladdin Sane* (1973) and *Diamond Dogs* (1974). In April of that year, Bowie moved to the United States to live in Los Angeles. He renamed the *Diamond Dogs* tour 'the Philly Dogs tour' in tribute to American soul music.[9] At this point, Bowie was taking large amounts of cocaine and was filmed by Alan Yentob for the documentary *Cracked Actor* (part of the BBC's *Omnibus* series). Bowie's appearance in this documentary directly inspired director Nic Roeg to ask him to star in *The Man Who Fell to Earth*.[10] Director Roeg's original desire was to have the very tall and thin Michael Crichton play the lead role and then Peter O'Toole. Both turned it down,[11] and Bowie's evident cocaine-fuelled paranoia and disconnection from his surroundings in the documentary recommended him as the archetypal 'outsider' figure for the film.

In March of 1975, Bowie's album *Young Americans* was released and attained a top ten position in both Britain and the United States, evincing a much more 'American' style than his previous recordings. In June, *The Man Who Fell to Earth* was being shot in New Mexico, with Bowie off cocaine during its filming. In August, he achieved his first chart-topping single in the United States with *Fame*, co-written with John Lennon. By September, the filming was over, and Bowie's re-released single of *Space Oddity* became his first chart-topping single in the UK. In the wake of these hit records, Bowie's trajectory turned. In February of 1976, his album *Station to Station* was released, and the film went on wide release in May.[12] In January of 1977, Bowie released his following album, *Low*, having moved from Los Angeles to Berlin. His involvement with the film bridges two distinct periods in Bowie's career, that of his American 'Plastic Soul' period and his more serious (certainly more self-serious) 'Berlin period'. These were not merely discrete fashions and looks but highly differentiated styles of music. One might go further and say that the film changes Bowie's career trajectory, while perhaps even marking a notable historical moment in youth/pop culture more generally.

In culture terms at least, 1975 was a crisis year: the oldest members of the baby boom generation reached the age of 30. This seeming end to youth might well have precipitated the beginning of a 'cultural neurosis' of sorts. With hindsight, it appears that rock music did not know where to go. This is illustrated vividly by British rock dinosaurs discovering funk and producing albums that diverge radically from their earlier recordings (for instance, Led Zeppelin's *Physical Graffiti*, Deep Purple's *Come Taste the Band* and Hawkwind's *Astounding Sounds, Amazing Music*, all released in 1975). In an interview during the film's shoot, Bowie laconically told a journalist that 'rock'n'roll is dead',[13] while John Savage wrote of 1975 as a point of 'cultural inertia' that precipitated the nihilism of punk rock in Britain.[14] At this moment, and in a manner more pronounced than before, Bowie reinvented himself. His involvement with *The Man Who Fell to Earth* is crucial. The film sees Bowie in a pupa stage: after the film, his public persona was notably more like the film's principal character Newton than beforehand. It might be argued more generally that popular music's renewal process partially took place in relation to other areas of culture – art and film, for example – rather than coming from within musical culture.

This historical moment is an important development in the move away from an essential disposability associated with popular culture, towards a more sustained sense of continuous value. The pop music industry had been premised upon short careers and a quick turn over of stars, in perpetual pursuit of novelty. The more serious intentions of popular music in the late 1960s, under the influence of the counterculture meant that pop musicians did not wish to simply fade away. One avenue of career longevity for pop musicians was that of writing and performing film soundtracks. In Britain, John Barry was the first to make the transition (with *Beat Girl* [1961]) and the James Bond films later in the decade. Paul McCartney scored *The Family Way* (1966) and provided the song and main theme for the James Bond film *Live and Let Die* (1973). This path was followed by many, an increasingly attractive and viable option for musicians who were ageing and had uncertain futures. Indeed, there was a concerted move from the pop music world into film scoring, increasing the degree of pop music techniques evident in contemporary film music, as well as giving further impetus to the use of pop music as non-diegetic music in films (see discussion in later chapter 'New Careers').

At around the same time, popular music evinced a notable interest in 'art' and particularly the status accorded to art and 'legitimate' culture. Groups like The Nice, King Crimson, Emerson, Lake and Palmer and Manfred Mann integrated classical music into their albums and live set, while rock operas were emblematic of the whole process of equating popular and classical music, as clearly embodies in Ken Russell's *Lisztomania* (1975), a biopic of composer Franz Liszt, who was played by rock singer Roger Daltrey. Rhetoric of the time often endeavoured to relate popular music to more respected areas of culture. In interviews at the time of *The Man Who Fell to Earth*, Bowie talks about his music as an 'art form' and alludes to Man Ray, William Burroughs, Dada and Surrealism.[15] By 1977, he was talking about making a film with Marc Bolan where they would have collaborated on the score, and he was in negotiation with producers about making a film about artist Egon Schiele.

It is round about this point where Bowie's assumed surname begins to be pronounced differently. At first, the opening syllable was pronounced to rhyme with 'plough' making for the rhyming naming of his son as Zowie Bowie.[16] Since the mid-1970s, the opening syllable has more commonly been pronounced to rhyme with 'glow', thus producing a more conventional surname, and one that possibly was less associated with his 'immature' glam rock manifestation. The mid-1970s may seem like a significant moment in the collapse of the High Art/Popular Culture divide, yet in the wake of *The Man Who Fell to Earth*, Bowie's activities confounded critics. He played the Elephant Man on Broadway, starred in Bertolt Brecht's *Baal* (1982, BBC) on television, directed by Alan Clarke, and worked with Japanese film director Nagisa Oshima. However, in stark contrast to these 'artistic' pursuits, there was the naked commercialism of his *Let's Dance* (1983) album and his appearance as the King of the Fairies in children's film *Labyrinth* (1986). In December of 1977, he counterposed recording the narration for Prokoviev's *Peter and the Wolf* with duetting with Bing Crosby on the aged crooner's TV Christmas special. In a sense, Bowie's work encompassed the spectrum of popular and art culture more than perhaps any other individual at the time. His films should be approached as rapprochements between art and commercial culture. Bowie later appeared in Tony Scott's *The Hunger* (1983), where art constantly is referenced yet within a commercial film genre format. One might approach this as characteristic of Nic Roeg's films, which have artistic pretensions yet retain a commercial edge. This period demonstrates how far Bowie had become a 'renaissance man', and film had an important role in opening the door to other activities for him. It aids one aim: becoming more accepted as an 'artistic' person, elevating his cultural value through being involved in more than simply pop music.

As I have noted, the 1970s is an interesting moment for culture generally and pop and rock music in particular. In the mid- and late 1970s, notable developments are afoot. Bowie's 'Berlin Trilogy' was part of a general trend but also highly influential. *Low* and *Heroes* mark a move away to moody instrumentals, a reconsideration of pop, not simply as conventional pop *songs*. David Toop commented: '...the Berlin LP ...' collaborations (*Low*, *Heroes* and *Lodger*) between David Bowie and Brian Eno suggested a torrent of visual images which only needed an imaginative director to respond to them.[17] These albums are singular hybrids of songs and atmospheres, marking converging platforms between music and film, but less in terms of technology or sales, and more in terms of aesthetics.

# Aesthetic convergence

In 1968, Mark Edwards, a film and record producer, noted that,

> People are becoming far more interested in film – not so much a bit of film to go with a record for TV, but something complete in itself. I think films could eventually be marketed with records. It is already happening to an extent in France and there have been experiments in America, too. It would be perfectly possible for people to show these films together with records in their own homes.[18]

From a vantage point of nearly fifty years later, this seems to suggest either great foresight on behalf of Edwards or that technology was already indicating a trajectory that has been slower to arrive than expected. This is a clear statement of the perceived convergence of film and music; however, we should keep in mind that soundtrack discs have been available since the 1940s and that the earliest impetus of synchronizing disc and film projection often involved songs.

In the above statement, Edwards sees films and musical albums as equivalent. This is less convergence and perhaps more 'synaesthesia', where images have a correspondence with sounds on some level, whether it is illustrative, literal or abstract, including dynamic and spatial. Mark Sinker has pointed to something similar, although in a different form than many. He notes the 'cinematic' elements and influences that can be identified in pop music.[19] Bowie has a number of songs about films, most obviously *Life on Mars* and *Drive In Saturday*, although there were other indications of cross-pollination of film and music on a conceptual level. Pink Floyd's *Dark Side of the Moon* was released in 1973 and managed to mix film's impression of 'reality' with aestheticized aspects of music. The album included both songs and instrumental pieces, special sound effects, brand new synthesizer technology, snatches of film-like dialogue, a gatefold sleeve with lyrics and posters and a vague overall unifying concept. *Dark Side of the Moon* sold by the million, breaking the record for time spent in the LP charts (there is some discussion of this in the earlier chapter 'Obscured by Pink Floyd'). The cinematic influence on the extraordinary sounds of that album manifested itself most tangibly in the use of speaking voices, tape sound effects of different places and the overall (LP-wide) extra-musical logic; the album clearly manifested something of 'the cinematic' on record. By 1976, Bowie was following suit. The title track on his *Station to Station* album begins with over a minute of stereo train noise and then over two more minutes until the singing starts. The song is over ten minutes long and nearly five minutes into it, there is a segue into a more up-tempo part of the song that bears no resemblance to the earlier part of the song. As this description suggests, this is a long way from standardized popular song form evident in most pop songs. One might add that it also does not follow the format of many progressive rock songs, with extended instrumental passage and solos, instead it is more like a 'montage' of different musical and song ideas that only really add up to a whole by their contiguity rather than any organic relationship of parts.

The title song, which starts the album, begins with a stereo effect of a train moving from one speaker side to the other, while the song includes some lyrics which reference the Jewish esoteric tradition of the Kabbala. With hindsight, this may not seem as strikingly original as it must have in 1976.

Bowie's stage show for his tour which started in March 1976 was also 'cinematic', beginning with a screening of Bunuel and Dali's surrealist film *Un Chien Andalou* (1928), leading into *Station to Station*'s train noise. A review noted: 'The entire production – from the [pre-performance tape of] Kraftwerk to *Un Chien Andalou*, to the black and white [projections and design] – is like a film David's directed himself.'[20] In a 1975 *Creem* interview, Bowie stated that his concept albums had been soundtracks without movies.[21] While this idea may now be commonplace, in 1975, it was an early example of this sort of activity, and an indication of early attempts to bring rock/pop and film together on a genetic level rather than simply adding one to the other.

## What could have been and what was

In a *Creem* interview on set during the film's shoot, Bowie claims that he is doing all the music for the film. 'Yeah, all of it. That'll be the next album, the soundtrack. I'm working on it now, doing some writing. But we won't record until all the shooting's finished. I expect the film should be released around March, and we want the album out ahead of that, so I should say maybe January or February.'[22] As it turned out, nothing appeared. What would Bowie's score have sounded like? It certainly would not have been 'scored' in the traditional sense. Indeed, we should remember that there was something of a 'British Film Music Tradition' where art music composers not able (or willing) to score to precise momentary developments of action would instead write semi-autonomous pieces, which could often be made into suites for the concert hall.[23] These thus could stand up as music in their own right rather than being tied intimately and fatally to their film. Bowie's score doubtless would have followed similar lines.

In 1993, composer Philip Glass completed his 'Symphony no. 1', which is also known as the 'Low Symphony'. This is an orchestral piece based on a number of variations on pieces from the *Low* album, and credited by Glass to Bowie and Eno. One of the main movements is based on *Subterraneans* from the *Low* album. This is the piece that likely started life as possible incidental music for *The Man Who Fell to Earth*. Indeed, a fairly reliable source, Bowie's long-time producer Tony Visconti, stated that the music Bowie had written during the film's shoot ended up partly as *Subterraneans*.[24]

An interesting aspect of Glass' developments of the music is that it brings out a slight resemblance in the melody to the famous 'Nimrod' section from Edward Elgar's Enigma Variations. This section of Elgar's piece is inspired by a German living in England, and thus an 'alien' foreigner not unlike Newton in the film, and indeed, not unlike Bowie in the United States.

Perhaps Bowie's music for film (would have) had a higher cultural status than mere 'pop music', and this was confirmed as being closer to art music by Glass' reorientation in a kind of 'double translation'. Does this mean there is something 'cinematic' about the music, something conductive to its use as accompanying music? Certainly some of the music from Bowie's *Low* album has had an influence on an area of rock music that has, to some degree, later fed into producing music for films. It is as if Bowie wanted to make a direct connection between *The Man Who Fell to Earth* and *Low* through the choice of a photograph for the album cover of himself in the film despite the passage of time between the film's release and album's release.

The actual soundtrack to the film, although nominally was scored by John Philips, once of the pop group the Mamas and the Papas, was a compilation of existing recordings from various sources. No soundtrack album was released. It seems that RCA were going to release it, but contractual problems and clearly the difficulty of obtaining the rights for all the music scotched the plan. John Philips wrote and recorded original music in London, with a group of session musicians which included the ex-Rolling Stones guitar player Mick Taylor.[25] He only features on one song, *Hello Mary Lou*, the original song of which was sung by Ricky Nelson and written by Gene Pitney.[26] There are pieces by Japanese percussionist Stomu Yamashta: *Poker Dice and One Way* (from the LP Floating Music), *Thirty-Three and a Third* (from the LP Raindog), *Wind Words* (from the LP Freedom is Frightening) and *Mandala and Memory of Hiroshima* (from the LP The Man from the East). Yamashta's music is used for atmosphere but also as underscore for dramatic moments, such as the 'landing' at the beginning of the film, the love scene and when Newton reveals his true form to Mary Lou (Candy Clark). Like a Kubrick soundtrack, there is a diversity of existing recording used, including *Songs of the Humpback Whale* (recorded by Frank Watlington), 'Mars, the Bringer of War' and 'Venus, the Bringer of Peace' from Gustav Holst's Op.32 *The Planets* Suite, but also some natural sound recorded by the Woods Hole Oceanographic Institute, and special electronic sound and ocean effects by Desmond Briscoe, who had been a mainstay of the BBC Radiophonic Workshop, who increasingly are accepted as important sonic experimentalists. In addition to these pieces, there was also a selection of middle-of-the-road popular songs, including *Blueberry Hill* (Louis Armstrong), *Enfantillages Pittoresques* (Frank Glazer), *A Fool such as I* (Hank Snow), *Make the World Go Away* (Jim Reeves), *Try to Remember* (The Kingston Trio), *Blue Bayou* (Roy Orbison), *True Love* (Bing Crosby and Grace Kelly, written by Cole Porter), *Love is Coming Back*

(Genevieve Waite), *Stardust* (Artie Shaw, written by Hoagy Carmichael) and the hymn *Silent Night* (the Robert Farnon arrangement). The film is full of short excerpts and fragments of music, and indeed, it includes much that it fails to credit.

# Conclusion

The overwhelming volume of literature concerning Bowie is aimed at fan consumption, and most of it is lightweight material.[27] In this zone of writing, rumour and myth manifest a form of popular history. There are a number of uncorroborated notions that circulate concerning the soundtrack for *The Man Who Fell to Earth*: that Bowie recorded a soundtrack which was unused, that the editor wanted to use all of Pink Floyd's *Dark Side of the Moon* as the film's soundtrack, that existing songs by Bowie were to be used on the soundtrack and that the original screenplay included Bowie's *Changes* and *Space Oddity*, as well as Elton John's *Rocket Man*.[28] While some of these are unlikely, there is a difficulty in achieving definitive answers. As I have already noted, interviews with Bowie and Roeg have yielded contradictory and inconsistent answers. Indeed, with some questions there is such a difficulty of reaching any 'real' answers that it has precipitated a situation where history has to become less about simple answers and more about possibilities and diverse connections. The para-historical offers some interesting answers. After some sustained searching on the internet and among peer-to-peer file sharing, a soundtrack by Bowie for *The Man Who Fell to Earth* can be found in different forms.[29] However, it is a counterfeit. This new archive on the internet includes red herrings among its many cultural clues, while occupying an uncertain space between popular notion and evidence. This is a powerful zone, where myth subsists on a mixture of definitive evidence and cultural imagination or simply desire.

In fact, this is the very territory that *The Man Who Fell to Earth* attempts to inhabit. The film exploits a point of union between the cinematic and real worlds, a point beyond the film, and beyond the real, making it a particularly strong, mythic piece of culture. In the film, Bowie as Newton has recorded an LP called *The Visitor*, which was going to be the title of Bowie's soundtrack album for the film. The film is a charged site for the confusion of commodity, star and fantasy. Part of this is achieved through the intersection of the music and film worlds, allowing the reality of one to confuse the fantasy of the other, and vice versa. This is less traditional 'life-as-art' aestheticism and more that *The Man Who Fell to Earth* is interested in figuring a relation of culture and 'reality'. This concern perhaps is in the DNA of the film rather than being 'discussed' as a theme in the film.

The sequence in the film of what appears to be Newton's 'memory' of his desertified home planet and travelling with his mate and child was startling in its prescience. The film's release across the UK coincided with the unprecedented drought in the Summer of 1976. This is one of the engaging 'confusions' connecting the film very directly to the world outside the screen. At heart, *The Man Who Fell to Earth* plays upon the relationship of culture and 'reality'. The film features astronaut James Lovell, appearing as himself, while Newton records an album in the manner of Bowie. In fact, *The Man Who Fell to Earth* arguably is not science fiction at all, but rather a mediation on the relationship of 'the real' and culture (indeed, on the problematic status of our mediated perception of 'reality' anyway). Indeed, the film's intermittent images of the alien planet might be approached as an imagined 'recovered memory', perhaps, and Bowie/Newton not construed as an alien at all, but as a deluded yet brilliant recluse of obscure origin.[30] We might think of him as a confused genius, rather like 'The Piano Man', a mute who mysteriously appeared in England in 2005 and was unable to communicate yet was able to play the piano immaculately.[31] Given that Bowie was very much disorientated at this point, was an alien living in the United States and had consistently used imaginative imagery relating to alien visitors, such a perspective suggests that *The Man Who Fell to Earth* could easily be taken as a Bowie biopic.

This 'alien' image that Bowie had propounded was evident in songs like *Space Oddity* and *Starman* and suggested that *The Man Who Fell to Earth* might simply be an implementation of Bowie's earlier propositions. Indeed, he had already been offered parts in a number of films playing an alien.[32] His singing had, quite justifiably, been seen as deriving a good deal from Anthony Newley; however, his acting in *The Man Who Fell to Earth* owes more than a little to Michael Rennie (as Klaatu) in *The Day the Earth Stood Still* (1951). Rennie, of course, was not only another alien figure abroad on earth but was also another soft-spoken Englishman adrift in the United States.

*The Man Who Fell to Earth* does not evince the traditional relationship of 'mutual publicity' between film and popular music. Instead, the interaction is at a conceptual level, leading to a 'genetic fusion' of material. Rather merely than using Bowie's pop songs in the film, *The Man Who Fell to Earth* integrates their concerns and representations at a micro-level. This is a reaction to the way that some popular music, Bowie's work included, had integrated filmic aspects on an aesthetic level. For example, not only do Bowie's albums *Station to Station* and *Low* both include moody film-inspired music, but the former also finishes with a song from an Anthony Quinn film (*Wild is the Wind*). *The Man Who Fell to Earth* might be approached as a pop star vehicle without the songs, while we might also approach *Station to Station* and *Low* as soundtrack albums that have become fully uncoupled from the film, certainly if we follow the clue of the album cover images from *The Man Who Fell to Earth*.

The soundtrack album industry has become one of the main ways to repackage existing music as well as showcase new music, and the expansion of the film soundtrack market has matched the contraction of the pop music market since the early 1970s. It is clear why there would be a desire for a Bowie soundtrack for the film, but its non-materialization must have been for good reasons. On the Criterion DVD commentary, Bowie says he was labouring under the idea that it had been contracted when in fact it had not. Producer Si Litvinoff suggests that the film people '... tried to outsmart David on the music rights. David turned [them] down'.[33] Director Nic Roeg suggested another reason to interviewer Neil Spencer: 'The soundtrack he'd been contracted to write never materialised – or was rejected. Roeg remains vague about the subject even now.'[34] So, the music either was written or it was not, and either was rejected or withheld for copyright reasons. Finding an ultimate answer may be impossible, after all of the players involved have an axe to grind. Perhaps it is more important that there is an ambiguity about it, which holds in suspension the notion that Bowie was highly creative in this matter as elsewhere, and that Roeg and the film people ran their own show.

# 8

# Cohabitation? The Resurgent Classical Film Score and Songs in the Batman Films

**M**usic was and continues to be an integral part of the multimedia phenomenon of Hollywood blockbuster films. This is highly evident in the Batman series of films. Danny Elfman wrote the musical scores for *Batman* (1989) and *Batman Returns* (1992), and they provide a continuity across the films along with director Tim Burton and Michael Keaton as Batman. Elfman's music had a significant impact and elevated his reputation for engaging and effective film scores. Both films also illustrate how dramatic musical scores are forced to work alongside popular songs. This is also highly evident in Joel Schumacher's *Batman Forever* (1995) and *Batman and Robin* (1997). Although not discussed here, Christopher Nolan's subsequent 'Dark Knight Trilogy' (*Batman Begins* [2005], *The Dark Knight* [2008] and *The Dark Knight Rises* [2012]) avoid use of popular music, allowing full license to their orchestral scores. This chapter asks how films negotiate songs as well as score. There are narrative, aesthetic and financial concerns which compete and together determine how music that mixes songs and score finally appears.

## Classical and neoclassical film music

In some ways, Batman films are representative of the contemporary trends in expensively produced Hollywood blockbuster films – although they have interesting and unusual aesthetic strategies. While, superficially, films have changed a great deal since the 1930s, in some ways, their underlying structures and assumptions are similar. In terms of film scores, what Claudia

Gorbman refers to 'classical film scoring' and Kathryn Kalinak to 'the classical film score' dominated mainstream Hollywood films and its principles may have persisted although some went out of fashion.[1] The use of a loud orchestral score, especially written as fragments and appearing as an almost continuous ('wall-to-wall') musical fabric, became less dominant in the 1960s, although it became resurgent from the late 1970s.

The assumption of the classical film score was that music should 'underscore' the visuals, creating emotional and dynamic effects, homologizing visual activity and providing information and atmosphere for the film's narrative development. Kathryn Kalinak, in *Settling the Score*, suggests that contemporary Hollywood film music proves the persistence of the musical blueprint established by classical cinema,[2] suggesting that the style and assumptions behind film music have changed little. Her declaration of the seeming permanence of Hollywood film music's form directly matches Bordwell, Staiger and Thompson's claim for the persistence of the classical mode of film production.[3] Kalinak points to the prevalence of pop songs as scores in the late 1960s and early 1970s as a something of an aberration, indeed an opposition to classical principles through which the process of 'classical scoring' has managed to endure.[4] Yet, although many contemporary scores bear some resemblance to studio era film music, industrial imperatives and aesthetic concerns have not remained static, mitigating against the notion of a direct continuity between contemporary film music and that of classical cinema.

While films like *Easy Rider* (1969) and *American Graffiti* (1973) forewent especially written musical scores in favour of a succession of pop songs, many contemporary Hollywood films use both in some way. In addition to this, instrumental forces changed. The sound of the romantic large-scale orchestra, which had been introduced to films from the classical concert hall and was ubiquitous from the early 1930s onwards, declined in the 1960s and 1970s. There were more sparse scores, both in terms of the amount of music and in terms of the number of instruments used. Also evident was the use of a more discordant musical language imported from more recent concert music. Prime examples of these styles are Richard Rodney Bennett's score for *Figures in a Landscape* (1970), Jerry Fielding's music for *Straw Dogs* (1971) and Jerry Goldsmith's score for *Chinatown* (1974). In 1970, composer Ron Goodwin declared:

> I think there was once an attitude, very firmly adopted, that 'if it's film music, it's got to be big', but that has certainly changed in the last couple of years ... the main thing [now] is that 'wall to wall' music isn't necessary. You must give the film room.[5]

Kalinak points out an explicit return to the style and sound of the classical film score in the wake of John Williams' music for George Lucas's Star Wars trilogy (*Star Wars* [1977], *The Empire Strikes Back* [1980] and *Return of the Jedi* [1983]). These films use a lot of music, and the Batman series of films includes scores of more than an hour's duration, marking a returning to the wall-to-wall *bravura* orchestral music that had seemingly drifted out of fashion.

In industrial terms, the mode of production for film music in contemporary cinema is very different from that of classical cinema. There is no more film music 'production line',[6] where there were rosters of composers, arrangers and musicians all under one roof and on the permanent payroll. This has meant that there is undoubtedly less of the standardization that characterizes the music of classical cinema. Now, there are even a few film composer superstars with names known by the general public, figures like Ennio Morricone, Jerry Goldsmith and Hans Zimmer. Some musicians producing music for films have also had an eye on commercial success outside films. Indeed, there are significantly different imperatives, most notably tied-in musical products – namely singles but more importantly soundtrack albums of both orchestral scores and pop songs. In fact, there have been musical tie-ins with films since silent days, for example, 'Fats' Waller's *The Sheik of Araby* was sold as a sheet music tie-in for the Rudolph Valentino film *The Son of the Sheik* (1926), while the development of the film musical gave great opportunities to the sheet music industry. Yet, since the late 1950s, with the advent of rock'n'roll and the saturation development of the record market, there has been a proliferation of tied-in songs films. Batman's high-profile release in 1989 was complemented by the release of two soundtrack albums: Danny Elfman's large-scale orchestral score and Prince's song cycle. The second one gave a large profile to the film through association with one of the world's top music stars of the time.

## *Batman*

Incidental music in the Batman films certainly draws on the classical Hollywood tradition, yet rather than being simply a return to the styles of studio era scores, it manifests explicit allusions to particular aspects of studio era film music. Kalinak's use of the term 'persistence' presupposes direct continuity, 'revival' might be a more appropriate description. After all, contemporary Hollywood films differ in many ways from those of the studio era.

At this point, Elfman was a relatively minor name on the film composing circuit, having scored Tim Burton's previous films *Pee Wee's Big Adventure* (1985) and *Beetlejuice* (1988). Prince, on the other hand, had become one of the bestselling pop artists of the 1980s with albums such as *Around the World in a Day* (1983) and *Sign '0' the Times* (1987), as well as writing the music for and starring in the film *Purple Rain* (1984) and providing music, starring in and directing *Under the Cherry Moon* (1986).

*Batman* involves an uneasy cohabitation of Elfman's score with Prince's songs. Although the songs are marginalized and indeed much of Prince's album does not grace the film, it manifests an extension of the text beyond its traditional boundaries to include intersecting aesthetic products. During the 1980s, the term 'synergy' gained currency as a description of the simultaneous promotion of a 'franchise' product,[7] tying-in products from the music industry with the film industry to create a compound package. Thomas Schatz cites *Batman* as characteristic of the multimedia nature of contemporary film production.[8] The existence of two soundtrack albums for Batman, indeed the existence of Prince's music tied to the film, is an example of the synergy of Warner Brothers' recording and cinematic arms. *Batman*'s producer Jon Peters commented on the high-profile extensions of the film: 'The album and the film are separate works ... in two different media, complementing and supporting other.'[9] It seems that Peters was instrumental in the release of Elfman's album, music of which was originally to appear only as a track or two on the Prince album.[10]

Soundtrack albums provide a space for the plenitude of music; what may have been few seconds and hardly noticed in the film can be enjoyed as an aesthetic object in its own right, its own logic undiluted by the exigencies of the film. *Batman* was the first film to institute the release of two soundtrack albums, a strategy that became common in its wake, examples being *Dick Tracy* (1990) (three discs), *Addams Family Values* (1993), *The Crow* (1994) and *Forrest Gump* (1994) (two discs, one of them double). In each case, these soundtracks reveal a division of the films' music into orchestral score and song compilation. One reviewer commented about *Batman*'s dual soundtracks: 'both [albums are] excellent accessories for the further enjoyment of the biggest movie of the year' and suggested, 'Buy the Prince album to get in the mood for the movie. Then go see it and whistle Elfman's haunting theme on your way back home to Prince.'[11]

Prince's album forms an intersection with the film, aesthetically, commercially and in narrative terms. It not only includes some dialogue from the film, but is bizarrely conceptualized as a coherent narrative with dialogue apparently sung between the characters. It comprises its own narrative of sorts, with Prince singing various character parts: Batman in *The Future*, Joker in *Electric Chair*, Vicki Vale and Bruce Wayne in *Arms of Orion*, Joker in *Party Man*, Bruce Wayne in *Vicki Waiting*, Joker in *Trust*, Vicki Vale in *Lemon Crush*, Batman in *Scandalous* and all of these characters in *Batdance*. This final song is the culmination of the dynamics, and the narrative of the LP *Batdance* comprises an 'operatic' interaction between Joker, an obscure character called 'Gemini', Vicki Vale, Bruce Wayne and Batman. While Joker and Batman interject samples of dialogue from the film (such as 'I'm Batman'), the sleeve notes also ascribe voices within this song to 'choir', 'Joker's Gang', 'Bat Dancers' and even 'Prince' himself. *Batdance* was the scout single from the package, released before the film to precede it as an advertisement. It became Prince's equal most successful single in the UK and was the forerunner to two other UK Top 30 singles from his soundtrack (*Party Man* and *Arms of Orion*), with the film seemingly having driven his LP's success. *Batdance* provides an interface with the past, announcing the new *Batman* film through referencing the chorus vocals from Neal Hefti's theme for the camp 1960s television show. This provided a musical bridge between the previous representation of the character and the oncoming film. *Batman* presents all the songs as diegetic music, that is, it grounds them all as appearing 'realistically' within the filmic world. *Party Man* is foregrounded, played on a ghetto-blaster by Joker when he indulges in some art terrorism, while *Trust* materializes at the carnival, and some Prince songs appear as ambient music at Bruce Wayne's party (*The Future*, *Vicki Waiting* and *Electric Chair*). Thus, the film ties the songs to the mundane everyday 'reality' of the film, while Elfman's more prominent orchestral score functions as the film's 'heavenly voice', appearing from nowhere. Despite the bipartite nature of the music in the film, there is one point of union between the two. The Prince song *Scandalous* appears for a portion of the end credits while some of its music, rearranged by Elfman, appears earlier in the film, albeit fleetingly. Generally, Prince's music appears obtrusively but only occasionally, while Elfman's orchestral music is virtually continuous throughout the film. The music as a whole is constantly foregrounded in a non-classical fashion, with musical logic often overriding narrative logic.

Reviewers noted the film's musical strategy, that of Elfman's wall-to-wall studio era-styled score plus the foregrounding of Prince's music in the fringes of the film: 'Prince's songs, which interrupt an outstandingly old-fashioned score by Danny Elfman ... only get gratuitously in the way during two scenes.'[12] Prince visited the set during production and was inspired. He reportedly said, 'I can hear the music.'[13] But sadly for him, the final product turned out to have Danny Elfman's music rather than his own.

Elfman's orchestral score dominates, but is not as well integrated with the film as it initially appears. This is at least partly accounted for not only by Elfman's relative lack of experience in film music but also by his lack of experience in orchestral music. Elfman is from a rock background, having been the singer in experimental rock band Oingo Boingo in the 1980s. At times, his *Batman* score is obscured by sound effects rather than take them into account, and the internal musical logic of many pieces outweighs their logic in the filmic environment. For example, when Joker first sees a picture of Vicki Vale, the refrain of *Beautiful Dreamer* appears, and dialogue continues, the music lacking any direct interface with the action. At this point, the music does not bow to the image track through matching the momentary dynamics of the action; rather, its time scheme carries on regardless of the film. Much in the same way that pop songs are often forced to in films, here the music retains its own full integrity rather than being forced to bend itself to fit momentary changes in the action. Songs usually have their own regular rhythmic and standardized temporal structure (set by tempo and repeating structures like verse and chorus), which means that when they are foregrounded, action must be cut to their requirements, unlike the flexible orchestral underscores which have traditionally been built around the requirements of the processes of filmic narration. So, while there are songs by Prince, Elfman's score also adapts an older form of popular song, which follows similar patterns in its relationship with moving image events.

Elfman's music distinctly resembles scores from classical Hollywood films.[14] His score not only uses an extremely large orchestra, up to 110 instrumentalists, but also *leitmotifs*, musical themes associated with characters or other things, a central strategy of musical scores in classical cinema. There is a repeated Batman theme, while Joker has a foregrounded musical theme associated with him, the melody from the old Stephen Foster song *Beautiful Dreamer*. In addition to these, a rearrangement of Prince's *Scandalous* appears twice, associated with the love of Wayne and Vale. These themes interact at times, forming a direct union between musical and narrative processes. At the film's conclusion, for example, the *Batman* theme and the *Scandalous* melody (the love theme) alternate in quick succession, suggesting a union of Batman and Wayne's love for Vale, the two halves of the protagonist's schizoid character. Yet, the film's climactic triumphant fanfare, which owes more than a little to Richard Strauss' *Also Sprach Zarathustra*, immediately supersedes them and asserts the superhero himself as we then see Batman alone on the rooftops.

The theme for Batman himself codes the Gothic at its opening, with deep strings and brass, and then the martial, where it leads to a pounding march with snare drum and brass punctuation. It functions directly as a fanfare for Batman, announcing his presence while being associated solidly with both film and character.

Elfman's music in *Batman* is pure Gothic melodrama, using a large, dark and Wagnerian orchestral sound. A key characteristic of Elfman's score is the use of massed and strident brass instruments. The score for *Batman* is characterized by parallel harmonies, chords that move up and down by a semi-tone, a staple of music in the horror genre. Like pop, rock or dance music, Elfman's score is underlined consistently by a strong rhythmic impetus, a pulse or beat that is at the heart of many of the film's pieces of orchestral music. This beat gives the music a highly purposeful edge as well as propelling the action. For instance, when Batman with Vicki Vale drives the Batmobile to the Bat Cave, the music is portentous and compensates for the lack of dialogue. A vocal chorus provides stabbing rhythmic notes, reminiscent of Carl Orff's *Carmina Burana*. The choir keeps a regular rhythm in operation, which builds and paves the way from the *Batman* theme's climactic entrance, and while this provides an aural zenith for the sequence, it is surmounted by the visual *coup de grace* of the Batmobile not slowing to enter a hatch in a sheer rock wall.

At times, *Batman* uses music as a direct communication. The Flugelheim art gallery sequence is explicit in its use of the audience's mental library of musical styles and genres. It contains in succession Mozart's *Eine kleine Nachtmusik* (a token of high art culture), Prince's *Party Man* (pop song) and the theme from *A Summer Place* (cheap Mantovani-style arrangement of a worn-out romance tune, originally a film theme by Max Steiner). Audiences are extremely musically literate, and the music in the film gears itself precisely towards this. Also, while Joker and his gang perform their art terrorism in the gallery, the foregrounded song *Party Man* flaunts its self-consciousness through being explicitly about Joker and indirectly about Prince. ('All hail, new king in town. Young and old, gather round. Black and white, red and green, the funkiest man you've ever seen.')

In the *Party Man* sequence, the beat of the music is the central temporal process, underlined by some cuts taking place on emphasized beats (the first beat of the bar). Joker and his gang's actions directly reflect the rhythmic impetus of the song through their dancing. Musical logic dominates visual and narrative logic. This bears out Kalinak's point about pop songs disregarding the dynamics of films,[15] yet in this case, the song is articulating and creating the dynamics of the action in a way reminiscent of song sequences in film musicals. In any case, the aesthetic evident in this sequence is certainly an anomaly in the dominant form of mainstream narrative cinema, where music regularly takes a back seat to other elements of the film, and traditionally is rarely foregrounded in this manner.

Prince's songs are notably associated with Joker: *Party Man* at the Flugelheim and *Trust* at the Gotham carnival. These and *Beautiful Dreamer* tend to keep their integrity, their musical logic – one could almost say that Joker represents the triumph of musical logic over cinematic logic, while Batman represents the subordination of musical logic to cinematic logic, his image consistently invoking his musical theme.

# Batman Returns

If *Batman* demonstrates a situation where commercial logic has foregrounded aspects of the film's music, the first sequel displays a qualitatively different scenario – or at least a development from the musical strategy of the original film. *Batman Returns* has a similarly large-scale orchestral score using a language derived from classical cinema, while relegating pop music's role to some short-lived music at a party and an end titles song. It has one featured song, *Face to Face* (performed by Siouxsie and the Banshees), although it briefly uses Rick James' *Super Freak*. *Face to Face* was co-written by Elfman and attains a degree of continuity with the orchestral score through using musical elements from the film's character themes (*Leitmotifs*). It appears for the end titles and as diegetic ambient music in the party sequence where, literally face to face, Bruce Wayne (Batman) and Selina Kyle (Catwoman) recognize each other's alter egos. *Batman Returns* certainly contains less in the way of pop music than its predecessor, with the film's soundtrack album consisting of Elfman's score and the one featured song. According to Elfman, 'Tim Burton was very clear that there wouldn't be Top 40 songs dropped in at random.'[16] Recorded by Siouxsie and the Banshees, who had been most prominent at the end of the 1970s and start of the 1980s, the song was merely used by the film sufficiently to justify its tied-in status while in conventional fashion the music video for the single incorporated images from the film.

*Batman Returns*' preponderance of scored orchestral music demonstrates film logic dictating musical logic, following the modes of the prestige orchestral scores of the 1930s and 1940s. The music is tethered directly to the screen action. So, the film's principal characters all elicit the appearance of their respective musical themes: Batman has his own heroic theme that survives from the first film, a four-note figure and a deep plodding melody represent The Penguin, while Catwoman has scratchy string glissandi and a full string melody. My rudimentary descriptions of the respective musical themes (scratchy' like a cat, 'plodding' like a penguin) bear out the use of musical clichés. Elfman confirms this: 'whenever he walked on the stage, I saw the Penguin as an opera singer who was about to deliver an aria. I gave his melodies a grand, overblown quality'.[17] All three Leitmotifs appear in quick succession when Batman accosts The Penguin 'surveying the riot scene', which intercuts with Catwoman's acquisition of a whip in a department store. Here the music moves from one character theme to the next, subordinating itself to the film's action. Classical Hollywood composer Max Steiner said of his score for *The Informer* (1935): 'A blind man could have sat in a theatre and known when Gypo was on the screen.'[18] Steiner means that whenever the film's protagonist appeared, he was doubled by the appearance of his own *Leitmotif*, much like sections of *Batman Returns*. Elfman's orchestral score is, however, paradoxical in that it follows very precisely the modes of classical scores, using thematic techniques to build a wall-to-wall fabric in the same way that Steiner and Erich Wolfgang Korngold constructed their scores in the 1930s and 1940s. It is paradox in that it copies explicitly the musical techniques of classical cinema, yet the effect is overblown and parodic. Elfman's distension of classical principles led to a startling score that provided a very large and antiquated texture for the film. This ties obliquely to the notion of 'retrofuturism' which is event in Batman Returns' design, perhaps more so than in the first film. The film appears to be representing a different time trajectory, as if things had developed differently in the 1940s, and the music is an integral part of this.

Elfman's *Batman* scores contain a degree of parody corresponding with the generally hyperbolic and self-conscious character of the films themselves. We could see the score's 'revivalism' in terms of the art music (and art history) concept of the neoclassical, where composers 'revived the balanced forms and,: clearly perceptible thematic processes of earlier styles . . . [while] the prefix of "neo-" often carries the implication of parody, or distortion, of truly Classical traits'.[19] The *Batman Returns* score is certainly excessive in comparison with the scores in classical cinema despite its obvious referencing of that style. It uses the principles and form, the surface of studio era scores, yet these appear distorted by the music's distinctive character and its conspicuousness in the film. Elfman verifies this process: 'Though I try to reflect the spirit of Korngold and Rózsa when I write traditionally, the music still goes through some funny circus mirrors in my head. So it comes out far more twisted than those great old scores.'[20]

John Williams's film music is also an essential reference point (in fact the *Batman* music bears a passing resemblance to Williams's music for Brian De Palma's *The Fury* [1978]), yet Elfman's music is much more arch and based more upon exaggerating the tenets of musical style in classical cinema. However, both composers could to some degree be dubbed neoclassical in that they value the classical and use it as a model while also differentiating their music from it. The architectural resonance of the term neoclassical ties the music of the *Batman* films with the startling set designs of Anton Furst (*Batman*) and Bo Welch (*Batman Returns*). Both music and set design situate the films in what seems to be an alternative present, one projected to now from a 1940s past. This resonates with Jameson's description of earlier representations of the future having 'turned out to have been merely the future of one moment of our past'.[21]

Elfman's music, then, seems to be a future version of the Classical Hollywood film score, but one that has followed a different and more direct line of development, although not quite the same one as John Williams's film music. While both composers' music could be characterized as neoclassical, John Williams's work is best described as a pastiche of classical film scoring, and Danny Elfman's music for the Batman films is best described as a parody of the film music of the past. However, Williams was instrumental in the renewal of classical Hollywood-inspired film scores. Kathryn Kalinak writes that 'Through Williams' example, the epic sound established in the thirties once again became a viable choice for composers in contemporary Hollywood.'[22] Williams's music for *Superman* (1978) and *Raiders of the Lost Ark* (1981) is the characteristic of this style, as is Alan Silvestri's for *Back to the Future* (1985). The epic sound and style of the studio era classical score is clearly evident in *Batman Returns*. Elfman is plain about his admiration for the scores of classical cinema, particularly Hugo Friedhofer's score for *The Best Years of Our Lives* (1946) and decries modern film music. He said: 'To me, contemporary film scoring doesn't enhance the action, all it does is provide pretty wallpaper. Old-fashioned film scores were much more dynamic.'[23] Although shortly afterwards Elfman went on to provide (and sing!) songs for Tim Burton's *A Nightmare Before Christmas* (1993), he eschews the dramatic potential of songs in favour of a return to the big orchestra sound of the past, that since the release of *Batman Returns* has again become ubiquitous.

In the wake of the two films, one-time Elfman orchestrator and conductor of the Batman score, Shirley Walker, wrote the music for the film derived from the animated television series, *Batman: Mask of the Phantasm* (1993), and declined to use Elfman's *Batman* theme, although it retained the distinctive flavour and style of Elfman's music which was so strongly associated Batman.

## *Batman Forever* (1995)

After Burton's *Batman* and *Batman Returns*, the franchise changed direction. Director Joel Schumacher, who had made *St. Elmo's Fire* (1985) and *The Lost Boys* (1987) was brought in as Burton's replacement as director (he remained as producer) and Schumacher wanted to assert the novelty of the new film, *Batman Forever* (1995), through instilling many differences from the previous two films. Not only was there a new Batman (Val Kilmer replacing Michael Keaton) but there was also a significant change in tone, from the gothic style of the first two films to a more psychedelic, colourful and comic-book inspired approach to design and visual aspects. Music was also an important part of this reorientation. Elfman's highly characteristic music was erased, with new music by Elliot Goldenthal, which refused to retain the highly identifiable theme for Burton's Batman. Despite the wide usage of the theme, *Batman Forever* and its sequel *Batman and Robin* (1997), in keeping with many other changes from the previous films, instituted a new theme for Batman.

*Batman Forever* feels rather overloaded, not only including the adversary Two-Face (Tommy Lee Wallace) but also The Riddler (Jim Carrey). It also spends screen time developing a romance between Batman/Bruce Wayne and Chase Meridian (Nicole Kidman) as well as detailing Dick Grayson/Robin's (Chris O'Donnell) trajectory from the circus to fighting crime alongside Batman. Set pieces allow little room for careful narrative development. The change in tone is immediately apparent in the opening shots, where Alfred the butler asks Batman, 'Can I persuade you to take a sandwich with you, sir?' to which Batman answers, 'I'll get drive-through.' *Batman Forever* has a rather uncertain tone, moving rapidly from comedy to more serious drama, giving a fairly fragmented effect. Indeed, the first street scene uses a Dutch tilt on the camera as a direct reference to the 1960s television serial *Batman*, but that programme's jokey and ironic approach is not duplicated in the film. As a further reference, there is an almost 'psychedelic' sense of colour and lighting in the film, perhaps obliquely inspired by the 1966 television show's startling design and hyperbolic comic villains. This appears some distance from the understated humour and dark, serious (although ironic) tone in Burton's first two films.

Goldenthal's score does little to mediate the comedy and drama. It is certainly a striking orchestral score, running wall-to-wall and providing much energy for the film. The opening title sequence showcases Goldenthal's new theme for Batman, which in many ways is similar to Elfman's.[24] Based on a more sustained melody, it presents the highly memorable and fanfare-like melodic theme as loud, self-important brass. Goldenthal's invention across the score is impressive indeed. It tends towards a complexity and subtlety that is beyond Elfman's range in his Batman scores. It appears unremittingly loud, with the orchestra often at full tilt, but also uses dynamics effectively. For example, in the scene where Bruce and Chase are getting closer and closer to kissing, Goldenthal uses a quiet but highly distinctive string cue which directs the action and, despite being mixed quite high, does not pull attention away from the love scene.

Goldenthal's score offers little space or scope to pop songs being used in the film. There are only three songs which appear in the film. The first is The Flaming Lips' *Bad Days*, which appears (possibly diegetically) in Edward Nygma's (Carrey) apartment. The words to the song state audibly 'You hate your boss. In your dreams you blow his head off.' This is a very crude use of song words as a commentary on screen narrative, after Nygma's disappointing meeting with Wayne, which includes volume lowering to allow Nygma to converse with his riddler manikin. The second is when Dick steals the Batmobile and accosts a street gang threatening a woman. The song here is *Smash It Up* by The Offspring. Again, the song is ambiguous about whether it is diegetic or non-diegetic, although it certainly provides a marginal and 'punky' soundtrack to complement the garish mock-punk costumes of the gang and their skull-face-painted leader. The Offspring were a 1990s, radio-friendly US punk band, and they were covering a song by The Damned, the British band who were at the forefront of the punk explosion in London in the mid-to-late 1970s. *Smash It Up* was one of their later songs, at a point where they were becoming less 'punk rock' perhaps, and reasserted their credentials by being a point in their stage show where they smashed up their instruments. The nihilism of the song is not immediately apparent in The Offspring's version, although the energy of the song is succeeded by a short almost inaudible excerpt from Brandy's *Where Are You Now?*, which is overrun by Goldenthal's energetic score of frantic percussion and thrash metal guitars.[25]

Two songs appear (almost in full) on *Batman Forever*'s end titles: First, U2's *Hold Me, Thrill Me, Kiss Me, Kill Me*, followed by Seal's *Kiss from a Rose*. The first was a collaboration between the internationally successful rock group and producer Nellee Hooper, who had been successful with more electronic dance-based music. This was released as a single and was a hit, as was Seal's *Kiss from a Rose*. The U2 and Seal songs were nominated for MTV Movie awards, while Seal's won a Grammy. Seal's song, an R&B-inflected slow ballad was produced by innovative record producer Trevor Horn (who had once been one of The Buggles). It topped the US charts and became a massive international hit.

As these two songs appear 'in the film' but not as part of the film, i.e. on the end credits, the songs' bearing on *Batman Forever* is virtually nothing. However, the success of the hit single associated with the film provided a certain public persona for the film. Indeed, the film's director Joel Schumacher directed the film-connected music video. This 'disconnected' form of relating pop songs and film became a dominant strategy in the later 1990s. It would matter little for the character of a song if it was not going to have to appear in the film but merely grace its end titles – however, on some level there should be a consonance between the perceived character of the film and the associated songs. The rest of the songs on the *Batman Forever* soundtrack album include artists such as P. J. Harvey, Brandy (Norwood), Massive Attack (with Tracey Thorn from Everything But the Girl), Eddi Reader (from Fairground

Attraction), Mazzy Star, Nick Cave, Method Man, Michael Hutchence (from INXS), The Devlins and Sunny Day Real Estate. It is worth noting that there are only four tracks by American artists on the disc, which is surprising as it is an American film (four are from the UK, two are from Ireland and two from Australia). They are also not new artists needing to be 'broken' through publicity tied to the film. For instance, Reader, Cave and Thorn had been prominent in the previous decade. However, there may well have been a strategy to attempt to secure success for these European artists in the United States. The soundtrack album even includes a piece of Goldenthal's score, although later a whole disc of Goldenthal's score was released as the film's second soundtrack album.

While the film was successful, interestingly the Seal record was a massive international success. It is almost as if the film was overshadowed by the song. Many audience members going to see the film would have known the song and indeed expected it to appear at some point in the film.

## *Batman and Robin* (1997)

Despite having a new Batman (George Clooney), *Batman and Robin* is in many ways a continuity with *Batman Returns*. It retains a very similar look and sound, directed by Joel Schumacher again, and was again scored by Elliot Goldenthal, and with a number of returning actors. Again, the film's narrative is heavily laden. Batman not only has to deal with two new adversaries, Mr. Freeze (Arnold Schwartzenegger) and Poison Ivy (Uma Thurman), but he also has to negotiate conflict with his sidekick Robin (Chris O'Donnell) and acquires another sidekick, Batgirl (Alicia Silverstone).

Again, songs are marginalized by Goldenthal's loud and energetic orchestral score. The sound palette used is very similar to *Batman Returns*, and indeed, Goldenthal reuses some of the same cues, and although there are many newly recorded ones, his score sounds remarkably similar to that of the earlier film. Variations include thematic use of trumpet for Mr. Freeze and more exotic music and jazz saxophone for Poison Ivy. Indeed, there is an edge of 1950s and 1960s 'exotica' to the score most notably for some scenes with Poison Ivy, which matches the film's visual décor. The score contains more in the way of fast, clattering percussion cues than the previous film, and again there are some memorable cues, such as the sumptuous choral cue for Mr. Freeze getting his massive freezing gun working.

The narrative, textural and emotional work is completed by the score with only a couple of spots for songs. Despite a full album of songs, there are merely a couple of snatches of them which appear in the film. The auction sequence, where Poison Ivy is first unveiled, uses the song *Poison Ivy* sung by American singer Meshell Ndegeocello, the original having been originally recorded by The Coasters in 1959. When Poison Ivy and Bane evict a garishly face-painted gang from an old Turkish bath, we hear some rock music on the soundtrack which clearly is intended to express something of the gang. It is *Lazy Eye* by the Goo Goo Dolls but is the instrumental section and does not include any singing. When Batgirl and Robin both attend a place for motorcycle racing, Moloko's *Fun for Me* appears. This again appears to communicate the unruly and lawless social elements, with a selection of gangs including one based precisely in dress and demeanour on Alex's droogs in Stanley Kubrick's *A Clockwork Orange* (1971). Singer Coolio makes a very brief cameo appearance just before the race ensues and has a line of dialogue.

This is the sum of the songs' activity in the film, although two more songs appear (and more extensively) on *Batman and Robin*'s end titles. The end credits begin with The Smashing Pumpkins song *The End is the Beginning is the End*, while the song has its sequel in a different version called *The Beginning Is the End Is the Beginning*, which appears on the soundtrack album only. These were both new songs and would likely have been enough for fans of the group to have bought the soundtrack album. The first version was released as single and became a minor hit. Other songs on the soundtrack album that were released as singles and became hits included Bone Thugs-N-Harmony's *Look into My Eyes*, R. Kelly's *Gotham City* (which also appears on the end titles) and Jewel's *Foolish Game*.

*Batman and Robin*'s soundtrack album as a separate entity that was almost wholly disconnected from the film, and indeed it was titled 'Music from and Inspired by the Motion Picture'. The album appeared conceived as a disc that would attract maximum audiences through having something for everyone rather than courting a specific music consumer. Apart from having two Smashing Pumpkins songs, which doubtless furnished a degree of 'hipness' to the film, there are two R&B songs (R. Kelly and Eric Benet), Gangsta rap (Bone Thugs-N-Harmony), 'indie rock' (R.E.M., Soul Coughing, Arcarna, Goo Goo Dolls), electronic dance music (Underworld, Moloko), country ballad (Jewel).

It is tempting to suggest that the album was heavily contrived as a general product and it made no different which film it was tied to, or indeed, if it was tied to a film at all. It was a top ten album, partly through 'hedging bets' and including something likely to pique the interest of most pop and rock record buyers. But then, does it matter about the film? Goldenthal's impressive score, however, received no accompanying CD release (at least not officially).

# Conclusion

In summary, the first two Batman films demonstrate two strata of contemporary Hollywood's musical strategies. *Batman* exhibits a cohabitation of orchestral score and tied-in pop songs, while *Batman Returns* uses only one tied-in song and has a large-scale score inspired more directly by the music of classical cinema. They both use classically inspired forms recast by more recent procedures. The fragmenting of the Hollywood studio system had a significant effect upon the production of music for films, and there have also been important changes in film music due to cultural developments outside the cinema. With film production becoming a component of multimedia industries, films themselves have increasingly become vehicles for tied-in pop music, as can be verified by any visit to a CD retailer. Musical tie-ins were important for film production during the studio era and they directly affected film form: they spawned the musical film. With the recession of the musical genre, this impetus has moved into dramatic films, as witnessed by the use of Prince in *Batman*.

Yet, tie-ins can equally include the film's orchestral score as well as songs. The mere existence of two soundtrack LPs suggests that music has a more important position in films than it had in the past. It is not unreasonable to suggest that the dual function of music – as both film element and object in its own right – has had an effect upon the character of the music itself. Music's status in films has become elevated[26] and this has removed the orchestral music from the alleged position of 'unobtrusiveness' which it occupied in classical cinema and into a more conspicuous position.

Although it initially seems to resemble the film music of the 1930s and 1940s, the orchestral music in the two films signifies in a fundamentally *different* way from classical film scores. Both of the films are premised upon the existence of a sophisticated cultural literacy among the audience. This assumes that the unprecedented access to images and narratives has supplied a knowledge of the Batman figure, Gothic imagery, and so forth, largely made available through contemporary audiovisual culture's principle of recycling. The music works in exactly the same way, relying on the audience's musical literacy for its signification. Particularly in *Batman Returns*, the music goes beyond the generic music and forms used in classical cinema. It works through the use of archetypal sounds and musical styles, burlesquing certain musical forms under the umbrella of its parody of the classical film score. The orchestral music in the *Batman* films matches the mixed construction of period in the films, blending both the historical (1940s design, the classical score with parodic and contemporary aspects. Post-classical cinema seems to display a proliferation of music that is unified at the point of the film as both text and as commodity. Indeed, Tim Burton, director of the first two *Batman* films allegedly asked, 'Is there a movie here, or just something that goes along with the merchandising?'[27] Yet *Batman* and *Batman Returns* can hardly be accused of being fully determined by the requirements of tie-ins. The music in the films is testament not only to the pressure to use marketable pop music in films, but also to the ongoing significance of several aesthetic traditions and strategies which incorporate such music in a variety of ways.

Batman went on to a further rethought trajectory with Christopher Nolan's *Batman Begins* (2005), *The Dark Knight* (2008) and *The Dark Knight Rises* (2012). Again, while there was a new Batman (Christian Bale), musical score was used to help change character and texture, this time with music provided by Hans Zimmer and James Newton Howard and with no purchase for tied-in songs.[28]

# 9

# New Careers in New Towns: Rock Musicians Become Film Composers

Film scores have been envisaged by the overwhelming majority of mainstream narrative films, particularly in the United States and Britain, as essentially orchestral (or chamber ensemble) in nature. Traditionally, this has favoured the musician from a 'classically trained' background in art music. Indeed, while many orchestral film composers were trained in musical conservatoires, popular musicians have always become writers of orchestral music for films as well. Many of the key composers from the era of classical film came from songwriting and providing music for theatre or silent film. There has been a misnomer that film scores have been produced by musicians who have been though classical training rather than being self-taught 'amateurs'. This does not stand up to too much scrutiny.

In recent years, there has been a more insistent flow from rock and pop musicians into film music, even though in some cases only as isolated forays. While most have to adapt to the conventional musical modes of orchestral film scores, they also often import certain aesthetics from rock and pop music along the way. This chapter will provide some historical perspective on these developments. The examination of rock and pop musicians creating film soundtracks invites questions concerning the traditions of scholarly approaches to film scoring, including assumptions about the nature of incidental music, the semiotic and narrative status of music in film, as well as the shifting cultural value assigned to music in films.

There has always been a strong connection between film and music – not simply as industries but as aesthetics. At times, music has been inspired by or aspired to the condition of film, while equally film has been inspired by music. On some level, there is a sense of similarity nearing equivalence. Such a notion certainly helps movement across borders between film and music. Actors making records was once an everyday idea, while many pop singers try their hands at screen acting. But in recent years, digital technology has been particularly helpful in allowing popular musicians to become composers for films, as well as television programmes and video games. It is almost as if a 'classical training' in the abilities of the orchestra has now been replaced with familiarity with digital audio workstations, as testified to by the proliferation of such programming courses. Fine examples of this are Charlie Clouser and Atticus Ross. Before creating music for films, Clouser, although performing keyboards on many recordings also was often credited as programmer, while Ross had forged a successful career as a musician often involved in digital programming for other rock musicians.

## Career swapping

Career swapping had been something of a tradition in the cinema, most clearly with singers becoming actors but also actors becoming singers. Frank Sinatra's progress in the 1940s sums up the attraction of singers to film producers: Sinatra achieved fame as a singer which then ensured a certain audience for any film in which he featured. Sinatra started with a film musical then continued with mainstream dramatic film productions, paralleling his film career with a musical career. Pop music followed the same path in the late 1950s, initially given impetus by Elvis Presley's successful films. However, by the late 1960s, pop stars went beyond simply acting in pop musicals. John Lennon appeared in a dramatic role in Richard Lester's *How I Won the War* (1967) and fellow Beatle, Ringo Starr, appeared in *The Magic Christian* (1969) along with Peter Sellers. In some cases, but by no means all, this was an excuse for the use of pop music in films. Other high-profile pop singers acting included Mick Jagger in *Performance* (1970) and Tony Richardson's *Ned Kelly* (1970), while Donovan starred in Jacques Demy's *The Pied Piper* (1971), virtually re-enacting his folk and psychedelic star image and singing a number of songs. David Bowie started his screen career with a prominent acting role, as the star of Nic Roeg's *The Man Who Fell to Earth* (1976) as discussed in an earlier chapter in this book. Roeg's film, scripted by Paul Mayersberg, plays directly upon Bowie's star image and even has his character 'Newton' becoming a pop star at the film's conclusion. Bowie also starred in the BBC television production of Brecht's *Baal* in the early 1980s and developed his film acting career with starring roles in *Just a Gigolo* (1978) with Marlene Dietrich, *The Hunger* (1983), Nagisa Oshima's *Merry Christmas, Mr. Lawrence* (1983), alongside another pop musician, Ryuichi Sakamoto, and the extremely expensive British musical *Absolute Beginners*

(1985). Another following this path was Roger Daltrey, the singer of the Who, was more active as an actor than a pop star in the second half of the decade of the 1970s. He had the lead role in Ken Russell's realization of the Who's 'rock opera' *Tommy* (1975) while also starring as Franz Liszt in Russell's *Lisztomania* (1975). In 1980, he played the protagonist of *McVicar* (1980), a mainstream dramatic production that included a few of the Who's songs, and had a leading role in *Buddy's Song* (1990). Similarly Sting, the singer in the Police and later a successful solo artist, made a brief appearance in Christopher Petit's art film *Radio On* (1979), then went on to star in *Brimstone and Treacle* (1981) and the television movie *Artemis '81* (1981) after which he attempted a fitful career as an actor in films like David Lynch's *Dune* (1984), *Plenty* (1985) with Meryl Streep and Mike Figgis' *Stormy Monday* (1988) with Melanie Griffith.[1] Some have managed almost parallel careers, such as Madonna, whose films include *Desperately Seeking Susan* (1985), *Who's That Girl* (1987), *Dick Tracy* (1990) and *Evita* (1996), and Cantopop superstar Jacky Cheung (known as 'God of Songs') who appeared in *As Tears Go By* (1988), *Swordsman* (1990), *July Rhapsody* (2002) and *Crossing Hennessy* (2010) among other films. Also, the door has opened the other way, with numerous actors producing isolated music discs. Richard Harris had a massive hit with *McArthur Park*, while albums by William Shatner, Leonard Nimoy, Peter Wyngarde and David Hemmings have become cult items. Other actors and actresses making music include Dennis Waterman, Rupert Everett, Don Johnson, Kylie Minogue, Bruce Willis, Crispin Glover, Will Smith, Jared Leto (in the band Thirty Seconds to Mars), Juliette Lewis, Scarlett Johansson and Jamie Foxx. Indeed, if I wished to list these it would take up a significant amount of space. Some actors have a strong interest in music, while others can be convinced of a musical project to make a little extra money.

## Popular musicians scoring films

'Popular' musicians have always been involved in writing music for films and not only generating songs but also full scores. In the mid-1950s, rock'n'roll (and skiffle in Britain) marked a significant change in its dominance by 'untrained' musicians: rough and ready 'folk' basics rather than polished musicians with years behind them in the 'biz'. To some degree, rock'n'roll was assimilated into established popular music in late 1950s. The 'Beat Boom' of the mid-1960s led to a massive rise in the number of pop music bands and records being made and sold. In some ways, pop and rock at this point were more like folk music culture, with the overwhelming majority of musicians being self-taught rather than carefully schooled in a particular manner and educated into what was 'good' and 'bad' practice.[2] When these musicians turn their hands to other activities, such as scoring films, there is thus a tendency for them less to follow convention and more to adapt their existing techniques to the new context. The lack of a general musical training and lack of awareness of the accrued conventions for scoring films led in some cases to more experimental approaches to film music.

Traditionally, many film composers were from a 'Light Music' background but by the 1960s, increasing numbers of self-taught rock musicians were becoming involved with films. There were some notable pioneers in the early 1960s, for instance Hammer composer Harry Robinson had been a member of Lord Rockingham's XI, who had a significant UK hit with *There's a Moose Loose Aboot This Hoose*. His contemporary, John Barry, is probably the best example. The leader of the John Barry Seven, who often produced instrumental records although Barry himself even sang lead vocals on some. He was self-taught as a composer, learning composition from a correspondence course. This was the perhaps controversial Schillinger Method, which used a number of architectural and mathematical principles for orchestral music composition. Barry worked as orchestrator for Monty Norman's music for *Dr No* (1962) but quickly established himself as the Bond composer supplying a distinctive musical palette that mixed traditional orchestral film scoring with aspects from jazz and rock music.[3] Other rock musicians who dared to score films at this time were Paul McCartney scoring *The Family Way* (1966, help from George Martin), Brian Jones (from the Rolling Stones) scoring Volker Schloendorff's *A Degree of Murder* (1966), George Harrison scoring *Wonderwall* (1968), Manfred Mann and Mike Hugg scoring *Up the Junction* (1968) and Mike Vickers scoring *My Lover, My Son* (1969) and later *Dracula AD 1972* (1973).

In the late 1960s and 1970s, some musicians were 'early adopters' of the option of writing music for films, while the 1980s became dominated by the cross-industry 'synergy' of aesthetic interaction on the back of mutual sales publicity. While this was hastened by crises in both the music and film industries, with conglomeration encouraging collaboration, this also opened the door wide for musicians to write and record music for whole films, too. By the 1990s, it was unremarkable for a popular musician to produce the score for a film. This trajectory built upon an established closeness between music and film, not only on an industry level (musicians make films, visual aspect of music fully developed) but on an aesthetic level (where films inspire songs and songs inspire films).

In the 1970s, some pop stars of the 1960s desired to 'grow up', to show a maturing of their status as musicians. Consequently, they consistently told the press that they were writing film soundtracks, as Mark Sinker noted.[4] This was the logical conclusion of the trajectory of legitimization for pop musicians, another way that they could promote themselves as 'artists'. Wootton and

Romney noted that translocation from pop music to films was a 'natural progression' for some 'mood producing' musicians.[5] It was an increasingly attractive and viable option for musicians who were ageing. Bill Wyman, the Rolling Stones bass player declared: 'I think it's a natural progression from playing popular music. You can experiment more.'[6] Ironically, his score for *Green Ice* (1981) was not only to prove his first but his last. Yet there was a concerted move from the pop music world into film scoring, increasing the degree of pop music techniques evident in contemporary film music, as well as giving further impetus to the use of pop songs as non-diegetic music.

David Toop suggests that the entry to film scoring is as a result of the adventurousness of pop musicians themselves,[7] and indeed, the bounds of pop music had become very wide since the late 1960s, if not altogether untenable as a distinct musical genre. Indeed, a proportion of the experimentation that had grown up in rock music from the end of the 1960s onwards ended up gracing film soundtracks. Pink Floyd are perhaps the most obvious example in this period, as discussed in Chapter 4.[8] While music might be provided by full bands, scoring films was also commonly an option for 'solo' projects for individual musicians. For instance, progressive rock musicians had a propensity for making solo albums, as outlets for their creativity beyond the strictures of their collective. For these musicians, films as projects were usually isolated forays, although in some cases they functioned as career stepping stones, facilitating a career move into a new profession. Many were 'amateurs', dipping their toes into a different musical activity, and some approached their brief with little regard for the received wisdom about how film music should work. Indeed, some appeared to see what they were doing as a way of aggrandizing themselves and proving their creative status. Almost all of them bypassed the 'apprenticeship' of orchestrating and assisting composers that is still a common route to writing music for film and television today. Indeed, many have felt no need to spend years learning the traditional craft of music for film and have been successful enough through adapting their existing musical techniques which have proved more versatile than film music composers of years past would have imagined.

# 'Classical training'

In musical circles, 'classical training' refers to formal training in traditional aspects of art music. This often is run by a conservatoire-type institution (these days often within universities). It includes aspects such as musicology, composition, orchestration, harmony and counterpoint, conducting and ensemble playing. As film music since the time of classical Hollywood has tended to be dominated by orchestral music, there has been an assumption that musicians had to be conservatoire trained in order to write film scores. There are (and were) many composers who came to film music from a background of classical training at a specialist music college. Miklós Rózsa, for example, trained at the Leipzig conservatoire, Max Steiner at the Imperial Academy of Music in Vienna, Franz Waxman at the Dresden Music Academy and Daniele Amfiteatrof at the Royal Conservatory Saint Cecilia in Rome as well as having private tuition with different composers. Famously, Hollywood managed to attract acclaimed classical composer Erich Wolfgang Korngold to score a handful of films in the late 1930s and 1940s.

Yet many classical Hollywood composers were from more popular music backgrounds, although they certainly were not self-taught or 'untrained'. Indeed, Conservatory-trained composers were not common during Hollywood's studio era.[9] For instance, Roy Webb, Alfred Newman and Adolph Deutsch (who had been a silent film pianist) came from writing music for Broadway shows, Victor Young from songwriting and radio work, Bronislau Kaper and Frederick Hollander were songwriters, while David Raksin was a jazz arranger and Dimitri Tiomkin had been a concert pianist. The music industry has changed. In recent years, many film music composers have originated from 'untrained' backgrounds in popular music. Indeed, among the most successful Hollywood composers at present, Hans Zimmer and Danny Elfman, came from a popular music rather than conservatoire background. However, today there are few from a highly specialized musical training. Elliot Goldenthal is one from a classical background, attending the Manhattan School of Music, while British composers Harry Gregson-Williams and Edward Shearmur attended the Royal College of Music and Debbie Wiseman attended the Guildhall School of Music. Jerry Goldsmith was taught by Rózsa at USC (the University of Southern California) before going on to work for CBS Television, while John Williams attended UCLA (University of California, Los Angeles) and the Julliard School. Don Davis was trained at UCLA, while Basil Poledouris and John Ottman both attended USC and James Horner attended UCLA and the Royal College of Music in London. However, there are many composers now working in Hollywood who do not come from a classically trained background. There has been a strong tradition of orchestral music in Hollywood, written by composers who in some cases came from art music backgrounds but in other cases came from musical backgrounds that involved writing popular music for small orchestras or similar ensembles. The influx of musicians from pop and rock backgrounds to film scoring was likely to change the procedure and the final product.

# Three cases

From the 1990s, there are some particularly good examples of the process of transmuting pop and rock musicians into suppliers of incidental music for films. The French band Air, consisting of Nicolas Godin (who had studied architecture) and Jean-Benoit Dunckel (who had studied mathematics) had made an interesting hit album in 1998 called *Moon Safari*. This included hit singles *Sexy Boy* and *Kelly Watch the Stars* and contained interesting sounds derived from the musicians being aficionados of old electronic instruments, in particular 1970s keyboards and voice-changing vocoders. Sophia Coppola asked Air to produce a score for her film *The Virgin Suicides* (1999) and they produced some highly effective music, which not only adds immeasurably to the film but has also been used many times as library music on television since that time. However, the music is not 'scored' to fit the film precisely but has more of the character of mood pieces that fit the situations but are part of the general assemblage, being cut to fit scenes. Coppola was happy with their music and indeed has used it in her later film *Lost in Translation* (2003) and *Marie Antionette* (2006). However, she did not feel the need to have them score the whole film, as her films have had close musical supervision by Brian Reitzell, who has compiled diverse recordings to make up a score. For Air, *The Virgin Suicides* was an isolated project and did not lead to a career change for the group.

For some musicians, however, career changes were dramatic. For instance, Cliff Martinez was originally the drummer in rock group the Red Hot Chili Peppers in the early 1990s. He had already played with many other bands and even produced a small amount of music for television show *Pee Wee's Play House* (1986–90) in the late 1980s and upon exiting the band pursued a career in film scoring. Martinez formed a close relationship with Steven Soderbergh, indeed scoring all of his films, including *Sex. Lies and Videotape* (1989), *Traffic* (2000) and *Solaris* (2002). Other films Martinez has scored include *Wonderland* (2003), *Havoc* (2005), *Arbitrage* (2012) and *Only God Forgives* (2013), as well as television programmes *Gray's Anatomy* (1996) and *The Knick* (2014) as well as some video game music. His transition has been enabled by his use of electronics and, in particular, computer-based music making. This is evident in his characteristically highly subtle but insistent film scores and in his anachronistic but defining music for television costume drama *The Knick*.

Charlie Clouser had come to prominence as the keyboard player in extremely successful industrial rock band Nine Inch Nails. He had been involved in remixing other artists, electronics programming (including work for TV composers), produced a Howard Stern album and worked with rock singer Marilyn Manson. Clouser's film scoring began with *Saw* in 2004 and he then went on to score the rest of the series (*Saw II* [2005], *Saw III* [2006], *Saw IV* [2007], *Saw V* [2008], *Saw VI* [2009], *Saw 3D* [2010]), as well as *Dead Silence* (2007), *Resident Evil: Extinction* (2007) and *The Stepfather* (2009). He scored the first *Saw* film at the age of 41, which suggests that it might be a career move brought on by increasing maturity. Indeed, this is not uncommon. Pop and rock musicians traditionally had short shelf lives, although since the turn of the millennium rock has arguably become the preserve of the older generation. Ageing musicians traditionally went 'behind the scenes', working for record companies, becoming songwriters or producers. Adventurousness in film making and the expansion of television production from the 1960s onwards increasingly offered new career options to these musicians and by the year 2000, it was common to find film and television music produced by pop and rock musicians.

Another fine example of this is Clint Mansell, whose first film score was written at the age of 35. Previous to this, he had been the singer in rock-rap band Pop Will Eat Itself.[10] After the breakup of the group, he forged a close relationship with film director Darren Aronofsky on both their feature debuts with *Pi* (1998). He then collaborated with Aronofsky on *Requiem for A Dream* (2000) [usable elsewhere (trailers, The Apprentice)], *The Fountain* (2006), *The Wrestler* (2008), *Black Swan* (2010) and *Noah* (2014). He also provided the music for *The Hole* (2001), *Murder by Numbers* (2002), *Doom* (2005), *Definitely, Maybe* (2008), *Moon* (2009) and Park Chan-Wook's *Stoker* (2013), amongst others.

Trevor Rabin came to prominence as the guitarist for Yes in the early 1980s, at about the time they had a massive international hit record with *Owner of a Lonely Heart*. Later, he became a prolific film composer, specializing in scores for action films. Rabin briefly attended university in South Africa and did some study of orchestration but came to film scoring in his early forties, providing music for *Con Air* (1997 with Mark Mancina), *Armageddon* (1998) and *Enemy of the State* (1998 with Harry Gregson-Williams). He then went on to score films including *Deep Blue Sea* (1999), *Gone in 60 Seconds* (2000), *National Treasure* (2004), *Snakes on a Plane* (2006), *Race to Witch Mountain* (2009) and *I am Number Four* (2011).

## Popular musicians score films

Composers who are not known for coming from a popular music background include Hans Zimmer (once in the Buggles), James Newton Howard (who played with Elton John), Carter Burwell (who collaborated with members of

New Order in Thick Pigeon), Clint Mansell (Pop Will East Itself), George Clinton (Parliament/Funkadelic), Keith Emerson (Emerson, Lake and Palmer and The Nice), Danny Elfman (Oingo Boingo), Cliff Martinez (Red Hot Chilli Peppers), Graeme Revell (SPK), Colin Towns (Gillan), David Arnold and songwriters Randy Newman and Randy Edelman. This is by no means an exhaustive list. While keyboard players are well represented (Howard, Towns, Hans Zimmer, Mark Mancina, Stanislas Syrewicz, Giorgio Moroder, Mark Mothersbaugh (of Devo), Tony Banks (of Genesis), Vangelis, Ryuichi Sakamoto and Nick Glennie-Smith[11]), guitar players are less so. However, over the past two decades scores have been written (and often performed) by guitarists such as Ry Cooder, Trevor Rabin, Jimmy Page, Eric Clapton, Mark Knopfler, David Arnold, W. G. 'Snuffy' Walden, David A. Stewart and Neil Young.[12] Bass guitarists are perhaps more rare. Apart from Barry Adamson, Marcus Miller and John Cale, jazz-rock bassist Stanley Clarke has produced some startling incidental music for *Romeo Must Die!* (2000), which mixes rap songs with Clarke's funky groove-based underscore.[13] Drummers are rarer still, with only Brian Bennett, Stewart Copeland and Cliff Martinez immediately coming to mind.[14] This suggests, if only obliquely, that rhythmic impetus is still of less importance to screen music than texture and melody.

Some interesting isolated examples of popular musicians 'dipping their toe' into film music might include *The Killing Fields* (1984), which had a musical score by Mike Oldfield, almost exclusively using synthesizers. Oldfield had produced a number of albums since his initial success with *Tubular Bells* (an excerpt of which had been used effectively in *The Exorcist* [1973]), many of which comprised extended instrumental pieces. His score for *The Killing Fields* included an electronic rearrangement of Tarrega's *Etude*, a classical guitar piece, thus giving an electronic frame to high culture. *Lamb* (1985) is about a priest (Liam Neeson) and a young boy who run away from Northern Ireland to London. Northern Irish singer Van Morrison wrote the music for the film, while *Restless Natives* (1985) boldly assigned the task of music entirely to the very successful Scottish pop group Big Country (who had evolved from punk band the Skids). The group retained their distinctive sound and instrumentation for the music, a rock electric guitar(s), bass and drum kit format allied to Celtic-inflected melodies and a sturdy rock rhythm. Big Country's vigorous music is highly effective as non-diegetic music in the film's montage and action sequences which document a succession of robberies by the film's protagonists but is forced into the background at other times.

I would argue that rock and pop music style has had an impact on recent orchestral film music, adding significant aesthetic developments to Kathryn Kalinak's description of the established Classical film scoring traditional mainstream cinema.[15] It is of course not the only development that has overtaken the Classical film score. Both modernist art music, inspiration for music in the *Alien* films and much horror film music, and jazz, as appearing in *Lift to the Scaffold* (*Ascenseur pour l'échafaud*, 1958), performed and written by Miles Davis, and *The Man with the Golden Arm* (1955), evince significant stylistic development from the traditions of Hollywood (and other mainstream) film music. Jeff Smith points to the impact of popular music on film music composition in the 1950s and 60s,[16] and since that time there has been an increased influence from other musical areas and genre, not least this has come from the significant amount of composers coming to film music from a background in rock and pop music.

# Changing aesthetics

As the basic blueprint of film music established by the Hollywood studio system, the Classical film score is a heavily dated language. Some these days are only too ready to laugh at the unsubtle underscore in romances such as *Now, Voyager* (1942). Pop music speaks in a very current and direct emotional language, allowing films to register an emotional impact with audiences accustomed to pop music rather than orchestral art music. This cannot be underestimated. In the past couple of decades, the two languages have been mixing increasingly. For example, Bill Conti's music for the James Bond film *For Your Eyes Only* (1981) includes drum backbeats for car chase sequences. Similarly, David Arnold's incidental music for the underwater action and the break-in in Hamburg in *Tomorrow Never Dies* (1997) constantly exhibits the direct mixing of pop music and traditional film music aspects. In fact, the way more generally that the James Bond theme itself is cut into films without being matched to screen dynamics is a most obvious example.

As an ongoing process, film scores increasingly have taken on aspects of other music. While modernist art music has been influential in scores for horror and science fiction films, jazz increasingly had an impact on the style of non-diegetic music in films, followed by pop, rock and then electronic dance music. The so-called pop score was a hybrid of the traditional approach to scoring (the classical film score) and elements of popular song dominant in the music industry from the late 1950s onwards. Jeff Smith notes that it

> often adapted popular musical forms to the particular needs of the film it accompanied. Traditional devices such as ostinatos, pedal points and sustained chords, were written in pop idioms and combined with sixteen- and thirty-two-bar song forms. Through this process of adaptation, pop song forms were sometimes shortened, fragmented, and varied to fit the

temporal constraints of the scenes they accompanied. This adaptation enabled the pop score to serve both dramatic functions within the film and commercial functions within the record industry in the somewhat different format of the soundtrack album.[17]

An accommodation was reached between the traditional flexible format of the film score and the quite rigid structures of the popular song. Indeed, the whole nature of pop music is very different from traditional underscore, primarily in the way that it rarely matches the dynamics on the screen directly. This is due to its own strong rhythmic and temporal schemes, which mean that it is often foregrounded when used as non-diegetic music in a sequence. So while pop songs work best in sequences of loose visual dynamics (e.g. long travelling shots) or fast rhythmic editing (montage sequences), the use of pop music as non-diegetic music regularly energizes the filmic narration. It provides kinetic forward movement for the image track and in the absence of anchoring diegetic sound converts the image track to an energetic play of shape, texture and movement. Music's sense of movement supplies a vector to the image, while the regularity of the beat provides a degree of expectation.

In 1979, Philip Tagg pointed out that pop was 'still mainly confined to usage in sequences that require clear geographical, social and historical denotation of environment and mood, being seldom utilized consistently as codes for illustrating changes in affective message throughout and entire film'.[18] In 1984, Simon Frith noted, 'Rock has often been taken to be problematic for film scorers – its very *presence* can swamp surrounding visual images.'[19] However, now audiences are used to different aesthetic norms and a wider range of aesthetic options. Songs are regularly used as non-diegetic 'score', particularly in montage or action sequences and pop and rock aesthetics are highly evident in scores more generally. Jeff Smith describes the merging of styles in the 1960s that '... enabled the pop score to serve both dramatic functions within the film and commercial functions within the record industry in the somewhat different format of the soundtrack album'.[20] Composers such as Mancini and Morricone combined pop appeal with traditional structural coherence, merging commercial opportunity with aesthetic functions. In recent years, this has developed further. Film music often runs to 4/4 time, which is utterly dominant in popular music. There is a stronger sense of rhythm and beat (sometimes drum beats), there is more evidence of pop or rock instrumentation (electric guitars, bass guitars, drums) and arguably more simple melodic and harmonic structures as evinced by popular music.[21] Harmonic movement (chord progression) can be extremely basic, while simpler and more lyrical melodies abound. John Williams' scores are a fine example. Similarly, 32-bar and 8-bar temporal structures, a staple of the popular song, are also apparent, despite film music's requirement for temporal flexibility dictated by the activity of the image track.

In 2000, film music composer Graeme Revell observed that: 'With a few exceptions, producers and directors no longer want the old-style film scoring.'[22] In the past few decades, the two languages, that of traditional film scoring and popular music, have been mixing more than in earlier years. For example, John Debney's *The Scorpion King* (2002) uses shredding heavy metal guitar solos mixed into orchestral scoring, while John Powell's *The Bourne Identity* (2002) features 'techno' programmed beats integrated with an essentially orchestral score. John Carpenter's *Ghosts of Mars* (2001) had a score which was a collaboration between John Carpenter, who usually wrote and recorded electronic music for his own films, and thrash metal group Slayer and other rock musicians. The end result is a kinetic musical accompaniment that takes advantage of the energy central to the performers from 'outside' film scoring. Indeed, electronic dance music has had a significant impact upon film scores, with an especially written techno score proving effective for *Lola Rennt* (*Run Lola Run*, 1998), while dance music artists the Chemical Brothers scored *Hanna* (2011) and Daft Punk scored *Tron Legacy* (2010).

The whole nature of pop music is very different from traditional underscore, primarily in the way that it rarely matches the dynamics on the screen directly. This is due to its own strong rhythmic and temporal schemes, which mean that it is often foregrounded when used as non-diegetic music in a sequence. So while pop songs work best in sequences of loose visual dynamics (e.g. long travelling shots) or fast rhythmic editing (montage sequences), the use of pop music as non-diegetic music regularly energizes the filmic narration. Yet many 'popular music' devices have been assimilated into the current language of film scores. One effective development in more recent film scores is the insistent use of beats for dramatic purposes but clearly derived from the dominant use of beat in popular music. This is most evident in scores that take some inspiration from electronic dance music, with beats usually having a mechanical character, being programmed and produced electronically. Such beats can provide a sense of kinetic forward movement, like a vector, as well as providing expectation and anticipation, as well as transferring the music's energy to the depicted events on screen. Stronger beats also became evident in scores such as John Barry's for the James Bond films, which included some elements apparent in earlier John Barry Seven hit records, such as Vic Flick's trebly lead guitar. As pop music became more influential, and pop musicians began to score films, more in the way of 32 bar structures and 4 bar strophes became discernible. In Danny Elfman's score for *Batman* (1989) the music often keeps up a busy pulse that remains almost solidly in 4/4 time. Such techniques betray a certain autonomy of film scores in relation to the film they accompany where it is less dictated by the momentary dynamics of action, as was regularly the case with the subordinated music in classical Hollywood cinema. Arguably, this is down to the fragmentation of cinema into a number of attractions, where music can be a featured element as much as any other and indeed often becomes a foregrounded component of cinema's effects.

Increasingly the musicians producing music have included guitarists, drummers and untrained keyboard players. This has partly been due to technological developments. Since the mid-1990s, the development of software to allow the production of music through digital signal processing has revolutionized music production and 'democratized' music making through allowing people with little traditional musical knowledge to produce music on their home computers. The software is normally known as a 'soft studio', making for a 'DAW' (a 'digital audio workstation'). Although an understanding of music and sound is definitely useful, music can be made with little need for an understanding of music theory and certainly no need for any musical training, indeed perhaps no need for 'musical knowledge' in the traditional sense. Not so long ago, to be a film composer, one had to go through specialist training, either through specialist musical training or an apprenticeship learning on the job, where the score needed to be written out on manuscript paper, it needed orchestrating, had to be written to match precise film event timings decided on before composition and perhaps even needed to be conducted by the same musician. Recent developments certainly have freed musicians to produce music more easily, producing music more cheaply than before and allowing different approaches to musical creativity.

# Conclusion

With the advent of rock'n'roll in the mid-1950s, it did not take long for rock musicians to 'cross over' to scoring films. The first high-profile case was Paul McCartney's score for *The Family Way* (1966), but musicians such as John Barry had already moved from top ten songs to providing the music for the James Bond films. From the 1970s onwards, this has become an increasingly common route for ageing musicians. In most cases, these musicians have brought something (indeed, sometimes everything) from popular music into their film scores. In the 1990s, a handful of films experimented with their soundtracks, asking rock musicians with no background in film to supply the music (examples include Craig Armstrong for *Plunkett and Macleane* [1999] and Gavin Friday and Maurice Seezer for *The Boxer* [1997] and later Pop Will Eat Itself's Clint Mansell for *Pi* [1998] and Radiohead's Jonny Greenwood for

*There Will Be Blood* [2007]). The logic of such 'experimental' collaborations is that the film score has a ready commercial value irrespective of the film. For film producers, the promise of ready-selling music and characteristic sonic style seems little risk. In some cases, the scores are more successful than the films but in others the naivete of the musician is evident.

In many cases, it seems likely that the move towards film music comes at a certain point in the musician's career and at a point where middle-age is encroaching. According to Ian MacDonald:

> Pop/rock is essentially young people's music and the eventual encroachment of home-making usually ensures the gang-mentality of a group proves impossible to sustain beyond its members' late twenties. Something new has to take over: a switch to other pursuits – management, production, TV presentation, acting (in [George] Harrison's case, gardening) – or solo careers based on more inward music befitting growing maturity, supposing this to be the case.[23]

This certainly appears to be the case in the 1970s and 1980s, but in more recent years rock musicians have sustained careers, perhaps in the wake of rock's most senior citizens the Rolling Stones. It is also worth noting that over the last couple of decades, there has been more opportunities, particularly with the expansion of television channels and a place for cheaply made films and budget TV shows.

Some of the music being produced is perhaps not as context-specific as film scores were traditionally conceived. Air's highly effective score for *The Virgin Suicides* (2000), for example. Director Sofia Coppola clearly cut-in the music at certain points and the volume control is used to negotiate other sound, betraying the fact that the music was not written to fit precise events on screen. However, the integrity of some of the musical pieces has allowed them to be reused constantly as library music on television. The same goes for Mansell's score for *Requiem for a Dream*, where the main theme has become one of the most heard pieces of music accompanying images, on television and perhaps most famously on one of the *Lord of the Rings* film trailers, in a revamped form.

A case might be made that film music or scores are a branch of popular music rather than having a direct antecedence in orchestral 'classical' music. Orchestras did not always perform art music and the twentieth century saw popular music ensembles producing so-called 'light music'. Mantovani was perhaps the most famous purveyor of orchestral music for the masses, and in recent years this has been successfully sustained by Dutch violinist André Rieu. The 'easy listening' and 'lounge' music, which was prominent in the second half of the last century had a notable crossover with film music. Prominent film composers such as Jerry Fielding in the United States and Stanley Black in Britain released many light music albums, as a complementary career to scoring films. Furthermore, many current film composers also produce popular music beyond film. Famously, John Williams conducts the Boston Pops Orchestra as well as writing music for events outside film, while Craig Armstrong has scored films, been a string arranger on other people's records and released his own recordings and numerous others also retaining careers as popular music artists in combination with scoring films.

# 10

# Golden Years: 1980s and 1990s Hip Song Compilation Films

**W**hile popular music in the wake of rock'n'roll had started out on the margins of film and wider culture, by the late 1980s it had become fully assimilated into mainstream cinema.[1] As both an aesthetic strategy and an industrial procedure, pop and rock music increasingly marked a norm in Hollywood and mainstream films from many other countries. Increasingly it appeared as ambient diegetic or non-diegetic music rather than as song sequences using the performance mode or the lip-synch mode. This meant that rather than requiring a club scene or the film being a musical, songs could be integrated more easily and with less of a sense of being disruptive for narrative and more easily integrated in mainstream dramatic films. The 1980s and 1990s increasingly saw the use of compilation scores for films, where a group of existing songs would be compiled together as the musical soundtrack to a film. This process was nothing new. In the 1930s, Hollywood musicals were often built around a grouping of pre-existing diverse songs that had been compiled into a folio, after which a script would be woven around them. Perhaps the best example of this is *Singin' in the Rain* (1952). Similarly, there was a tradition of creating a musical score using library or stock music, which would then be 'tracked' into a film by an editor rather than being written to fit already edited scenes.

It is not difficult to see the musical logic of these films as having been inherited from the film musical, and it is notable that the songs tend to appear for set-piece spectacles where dialogue is forced into the background to allow music to take at least something of the foreground. Furthermore, the songs are embedded and sold, much as they were in the classical Hollywood film musical. Indeed, at times, these films seem less interested in devising a scenario than they are in other things, such as articulating pop music as an internal momentary logic of the film.

In the 1970s, films such as *American Graffiti* (1973) made a significant profit from having a soundtrack album of songs that had appeared in the film. By the early 1980s, this was a strategy that dominated the marketing logic of the conglomerating film and music companies. Films like *Footloose* (1984) and *Flashdance* (1983) emblematized the strategy of 'synergy', whereby films could almost be built around a selection of pop songs by diverse musicians but on the same record label, which then not only would be sold as a soundtrack album but also would allow for the staggered release on songs as singles. Since the 1980s, the concepts of synergy and connecting compilation albums to films had been an established cross-platform commercial strategy for mainstream films and the floundering music industry. While this was often an artless affair, dictated by record label executives, it reached something of an artistic apogee with *Trainspotting* (1994) and *Pulp Fiction* (1994).[2] These films, rather than merely try to sell songs exploited the potential for diverse music as a driver of film narrative and aesthetics, with Quentin Tarantino, the director of the latter claiming that he compiled songs as the starting point of his films.[3]

There is something highly distinctive about many films in the 1980s and 1990s that is evident in their reliance upon rock and pop songs. For instance, films such as *Manhunter* (1986) and *Natural Born Killers* (1994) illustrate a form of cinema where music functions as a central aspect, in a similar manner to film musicals. In films that are not musicals, music usually is conceived and theorized as an afterthought to what are usually seen as the 'primary' aspects (the film's images, dialogue and narrative development or the diegetic world on screen). Yet plenty of films seem to contradict this notion to a greater or lesser extent.

## Selling pop songs

The development of MTV and the frantic exploitation of record label back catalogues in the late 1980s and 1990s are both vividly inscribed across *Hardware* and *Trainspotting*. MTV started broadcasting in the United States in August 1981, Euro-MTV started six years later, although European terrestrial television shows were already showing pop videos and exhibiting the 'MTV style'. What was identified as style derived from MTV, loud pop songs, glossy images and rapid editing was decried by film critics as an embodiment of style over substance. Pop promo videos became increasingly important throughout the 1980s, both as marketing tools and as cultural objects in their own right. Many commentators have proclaimed their influence on film negative, yet they have been part of the influence of the film musical format in mainstream dramatic films, where the urge to music can erupt in films without their being musicals in the traditional sense.[4] If dramatic film structures traditionally are built around a strong narrative drive, then films that have a weakened narrative allow other elements of the film to adopt the foreground, as was the case in the classical film musical. In some films, aspects such as spectacle and music as semi-independent attractions have partially replaced the idea of developmental narrative.[5] Kathryn Kalinak notes the way that the enduring principle of the film score has been in some films thrust aside by the use of songs:

> the pop score represents the most serious challenge to the classical score Among the various attempts to update it in the fifties and sixties. Specifically, the pop score's insistence on the integrity and marketability of the nondiegetic song frequently brought it into conflict with some of the basic principles of the classical model. Unlike earlier innovations which added new idiomatic possibilities, like jazz, or demonstrated the adaptability of the leitmotif, like the theme score, the pop score often ignored structural principles at the centre of the classical score: musical illustration of narrative content, especially the direct synchronization between music and narrative action; music as a form of structural unity; and music as an inaudible component of the drama.[6]

As an option, this marked an industrial, financial, cultural and aesthetic change. The late 1960s saw the highly successful use of compilation scores in *The Graduate* (1967) and *Easy Rider* (1969), while the early 1970s set the format for such a musical strategy in films. The most successful use of a compilation score came shortly afterwards with George Lucas' influential and highly successful *American Graffiti* (1973). According to Jon Lewis: 'Virtually the entire film is narrated by the music track, the stack of 45s spun by "the crude disc jockey", Wolfman Jack .... in *American Graffiti* as in so many teenfilms since its release in 1973, the soundtrack is designed to articulate precisely what the teenagers feel they themselves can never express.'[7] This illustrates a 'functional approach', seeing elements as all working together well for the purposes of narrative information for the audience, no matter how subtle their additions to the most obvious points of narrative and character development. However, the songs also appear as signifiers of era and as attractions in themselves. They are also able to be sold as a compilation album. *That'll Be the Day* (1973) was, if you like, the British version released in the same year. British producer David Puttnam made a deal with record label Ronco, whereby if they put up finance for the film, it would feature a certain amount of rock classics on the soundtrack, which Ronco could then release on a double-album. Puttnam and screenwriter Ray Connolly went through the script, noting where they could have a radio or a record player in an attempt to cram in a large number of songs.[8] S.W.A.L.K. (1971), which retained its original title Melody in the United States, was in a similar vein. It was written by Alan Parker and David Puttnam, who built the story around the songs which had been acquired. The story concerned two children who meet at school and elope. S.W.A.L.K. was less successful than That'll Be the Day, both in cinematic and musical terms. Despite squeezing in many excerpts from songs, the British films lack the impact of the American in that they are unable to provide a regular, rapid and sustained succession of foregrounded 'golden oldie' records as cultural coordinate points and attractions in their own right, following the procedure of including almost all the songs as ambient diegetic music.[9] That'll Be the Day also used the Buddy Holly hit which provided the film's title for its end titles. Like American Graffiti, That'll Be the Day repackages as nostalgia the tentative stirrings of rock'n'roll, as well as dealing heavily in self-conscious reference.[10] Both of these films provide blueprints for founding a film upon a collection of old songs from different artists that would be sold simultaneously on a soundtrack LP.

## Eighties synergy

The increasing use of existing recordings led to an expansion of the traditional film credit of music supervisor. As Denisoff and Romanowski note, '... filmmakers increasingly sought out contemporary soundtracks. With few exceptions, most knew little about the uses of rock in cinema. They were, however, dissatisfied in the knowledge that albums frequently earned more than their pictures. This gave rise to a poorly specified occupational role ...'[11] Many of the music supervisors in the 1980s were record company executives or producers of some sort. In some cases, their focus was more clearly on what they had to sell and how the film could help, and indeed many of the films during this period reflect notions about the record-buying public as an important part of their overall character.[12]

In the 1980s, nostalgia culture developed apace beyond its immediate stirrings in the 1970s. Pop star Sting starred in Brimstone and Treacle (1981), although this was before his group The Police reached their peak of success. Based on a controversial BBC television play by Dennis Potter, the film had a successful tied-in single.[13] Sting sang a cover version of an old (pre-Second World War) song, Spread a Little Happiness. It was arranged in the original manner rather than updated, although it was of obvious attraction to older record buyers. *Spread A Little Happiness* appears in its full length over the film's end titles, an increasingly common space for tied-in songs by this point.

*The Big Chill* (1983) was a highly successful comedy-drama with an ensemble cast depicting a group of college friends reuniting after fifteen years after the death of a friend. The film soundtrack is dominated by songs from the time when this group of people were student friends, songs from the mid-1960s up until the start of the 1970s. Indeed, Melissa Carey and Michael Hannan argue that the compilation of songs that comprise the soundtrack are unified in terms of period (1963–71), tone, sense of nostalgia and origin (five songs are from Motown Records.[14] *The Big Chill* uses many songs as short excerpts, although a memorable moment in the film is when The Temptations' *Ain't Too Proud to Beg* is put on the record player and the friends enliven washing up by dancing. The range of songs is reminiscent of the earlier repertoire of songs used by American Graffiti and likewise was made available as a tied-in product. Two soundtrack albums were released at the time, both selling well. The initial disc's popularity was buoyed by the inclusion of classic songs like Marvin Gaye's *I Heard It Through the Grapevine*, The Temptations' *My Girl*, Smokey Robinson and the Miracles' *The Tracks of My Tears* and Procol Harum's *A Whiter Shade of Pale*. One of the songs featured in *The Big Chill*, the Rolling Stones' *You Can't Always Get What You Want*, failed to make either soundtrack album after securing the rights for use in the film only. The music tapped very directly into the growing cultural nostalgia of the 'baby boomer' generation who had come of age in the 1960s.[15] *The Big Chill* addressed this demographic grouping and although it was bittersweet and philosophical nevertheless ultimately celebrated the character of the generation. Despite some negativity, the film finishes with the cast laughing and Three Dog Night's version of *Joy to the World*.[16]

A further example of the nostalgia that was gripping pop music and culture more generally was *Withnail and I* (1986). It used a number of well-known songs as period signifiers: Jimi Hendrix's *All Along the Watchtower* and *Voodoo Chile (Slight Return)* and The Beatles' *While My Guitar Gently Weeps*. *Withnail and I* established its pop music culture credentials from the outset, through the use of *A Whiter Shade of Pale* during the title sequence, although it is a jazz-inflected rearrangement rather than Procol Harum's original hit recording. The film maximizes the songs' cultural status as well-known, even canonical songs, illustrative of late 1960s culture while functioning as prime aural 'set-construction' for the era of the 1960s.

As well as starring a pop star, *Buster* (1988) demonstrated explicitly the possibilities for the inclusion of pop songs in films both as diegetic ambient and non-diegetic music. Some of the film's orchestral score even bases itself upon the film's songs, while excerpts from a number of 1960s vintage songs appear as ambient diegetic music. In addition to this, Phil Collins' recording of *Groovy Kind of Love* appears non-diegetically at the film's climax, in a sequence that is heavily reminiscent of a pop promo. As *Groovy Kind of Love* is a 1980s rearrangement of a 1960s hit, it constitutes a frame to the film's representations of the past, keeping a foot firmly in the present. This is also the case with the song *Two Hearts*, a 1960s pastiche co-written by Phil Collins and Lamont Dozier, once part of the well-known Holland, Dozier and Holland songwriting team of the 1960s. These songs dominated the soundtrack LP as well as proving to be sizeable hits in their own right.

There were three singles from the film. *Groovy Kind of Love* was released on 3 September 1988 as a scout single announcing the film, reaching Number One and staying in the charts for thirteen weeks. *Two Hearts* was released on 26 November 1988, reached Number Six and remained in the charts for eleven weeks; while the Four Tops' *Going Loco in Acapulco* was released on 3 December 1988, reached Number Seven and remained in the charts for thirteen weeks – all three reached the Top Ten in the United States.[17] The earmarking of £75,000 as music budget from the film's £3.3 million budget proved to be an excellent investment both in terms of profitability for the record company and publicity for the film.[18] Apparently the producers had wanted the Beatles and the Rolling Stones on the soundtrack but were unable to secure the rights to use them.[19] The substitutes were a great success and illustrate a common situation for pop songs' relationship to films by the late 1980s.

The saturation publicity supplied by the overlapping lifespans of these records in the charts is an excellent example of the synergy process described by Denisoff and Plasketes.[20] Bones Howe, Senior Vice President of music at Columbia Pictures, described the technique of using singles as a publicity device:

> a pop soundtrack is just another way of promoting and marketing the film. We get royalties from the record and we'll take the cheque, thank you very much, but those royalties are insignificant with what we'll get if the film is successful at the box office. ... A hit single is a great way of setting up the movie.[21]

A notable number of films in the 1980s employed this process. This process of 'synergy' would sometimes involve a succession of singles from a film, often proceeding with a 'scout' single before the film's release followed quickly by a soundtrack album. Yet the early 1980s saw the standardization of the soundtrack album compiled of pop songs as an emblem of the union between the film and music industries. The tied-in music was reformulated to fit into the requirements of music television, with pop promos for singles looking like condensed versions of their film, catalysed by the increasing ties between film and music companies. Examples of the increasing involvement of the two industries were films such as *Countryman* (1982) which was made by Island Films and predominantly used artists signed to Island Records and *Electric Dreams* (1982), which was produced by Virgin and used their own roster of music performers. This business synergy and the rise of music on video and music television indicated a fundamental shift in the organization of corporate entertainment, of which the developments it inaugurated in the audiovisual industries was only one facet. At this point, the synergetic process of tying-in record releases with films began to follow a basic pattern.

A good example of this process is *Top Gun* (1986), a highly successful film about US fighter pilots starring Tom Cruise. Its musical soundtrack involved an electronic score by Harald Faltermeyer and a number of featured songs. Berlin's *Take My Breath Away* became a massive international hit and appeared in the film when Maverick (Cruise) and Charlie (Kelly McGillis) get together. The song won an Oscar in 1987 for its writers Giorgio Moroder and Tom Whitlock. The other defining song from the film was Kenny Loggins' *Danger Zone*, which is used effectively in flying sequences. Indeed, the jet fighters aerobatics was perhaps the key aspect of *Top Gun*. In addition to this, the song *You've Lost that Loving Feeling* is sung diegetically by the pilots and Maverick in an iconic sequence, but the pairing of spectacular flying sequences with energetic songs contributed significantly to the film's success.

As a director, Michael Mann has tended to exploit the possibilities of the use of pop and rock songs allied to dialogue-free sequences usually involving spectacular action. *Manhunter* (1986) is a good illustration of this strategy. Songs in the film were not used for publicity, more for texture and aesthetics. Although nominally the film has a 'score' by Michel Rubini and The Reds, in effect Rubini supplies the main theme while The Reds supply three pieces of music which are used as accompaniment for dramatic moments in the film (as testified to by their titles on the soundtrack album: Lector's Cell, Jogger's Stakeout, and Leed's House). Like the rest of the pieces of music used in the film, these are used just the once. The other pieces are often songs and are edited to run for less than their full length, although their retention of musical dynamics within their duration means that the images are cut to fit the music. Indeed, the images are cut to exploit the emotional dynamics of each piece of music. For instance, *The Big Hush* by Shriekback is used effectively to accompany the sequence of killer Dollarhyde sleeping with the Reba (a woman from his workplace). This is an extremely dramatic moment in the film, revealing an unexpected degree of sympathy and empathy with the film's monster figure. Indeed, *Manhunter* foregrounds songs during key points in the film and, like in film musicals, tends to have a feeling of narrative stopping for time becoming static and image spectacular. Kitaro's *Seiun* and *Hikari No Sono* accompanies the blind Reba touching a sedated tiger, a sequence which revels in the tactility of the event, the crisp cinematography with bright-lit colours and the music, with its overblown pipe melody. The film's climax, where Detective Will Graham ultimately defeats serial killer Dollarhyde, exploits the Iron Butterfly song *In-a-Gadda-Da-Vida*, seemingly being played on disc diegetically although with a full stereo sound as if appearing non-diegetically. During emotionally heightened moments when Reba is on the verge of being killed and the police are converging on the house, the song's two-bar riff continues relentlessly, interrupted only by the song's chorus. As it appears diegetically, it is absent during the shots of the police but quickly takes on the high sound quality of non-diegetic music and articulates the action. At the point when Graham jumps through a plate-glass window, the images follow the music's dynamic. As he runs up in slow motion, the song has a quiet dropout, but the organ builds in intensity as there is an ostentatious slow-motion shot of Graham approaching the window (towards the camera), and then, at the precise moment when he smashes through the window, the music explodes back into the main riff with all instruments and the image track reverts to normal speed for the confrontation between investigator and serial killer. Despite the song being edited at times, it is not cut in this sequence, and the music's dynamic trajectory becomes that of the drama.

The cycle of Hollywood teen films, most associated with John Hughes, had soundtracks which consisted of contemporary pop songs. *Pretty in Pink* (1986) was produced by John Hughes although directed by Howard Deutsch. This so-called 'Brat Pack' film had a strong clutch of songs by Orchestral Manoeuvres in the Dark (*If You Leave*), Suzanne Vega (with Joe Jackson) (*Left of Center*), Jesse Johnson (*Get to Know Ya*), INXS (*Do Wot You Do*), The Psychedelic Furs (*Pretty in Pink*), New Order (*Shellshock*, *Elegia* and an instrumental version of *Thieves Like Us*), Belouis Some (*Round, Round*), Danny Hutton Hitters (*Wouldn't It Be Good*), Echo and the Bunnymen (*Bring On the Dancing Horses*); and The Smiths (*Please, Please, Please, Let Me Get What I Want*), The Association (*Cherish*) and Talk Back (*Rudy*). Some appear more prominently than others, while The Rave Ups appear in the film, performing *Rave Up/Shut Up* and *Positively Lost Me*. To compound the amount of music in the film, protagonist Andie works in a record store. What is striking is just how many of the songs are by British artists. This is the period of the so-called 'Second British Invasion', when British artists were highly attractive to American audiences evincing a notably different sound and different fashion.

*Pretty in Pink* followed the pattern of industrial synergy that was found to be effective in the early 1980s. Of the songs that appear in the film, six were released as singles with their publicity tied to the film. While all of them made an impact on the British singles charts, more importantly, some of them made an important impact on the US singles chart. The Orchestral Manoeuvres in the Dark song made the US top five records, while the New Order song made the top twenty. The other made less impact and indeed some did not chart at all. However, the publicity for *Pretty in Pink* afforded by the Orchestral Manoeuvres song's success was important, as surely was the film's publicity helpful for the success of the record. It is not surprising that the singles all charted in Britain, as the soundtrack is dominated remarkably by British musical artists. Indeed, the film itself was named after the Psychedelic Furs song, which had been released already in 1981 but was rerecorded with a more straightforward rock sound for the film. American Danny Hutton rerecorded British singer Nik Kershaw's hit record *Wouldn't It Be Good* for the film. *If You Leave* was also written and recorded for the film and appears for the concluding emotional scenes in the film. The film changed its ending after a negative reaction from test screenings, with a freshly written Orchestral Manoeuvres in the Dark song replacing an album track which had been selected to accompany the film's original ending.

## Tarantino and others

Over the past couple of decades, a handful of auteur directors have appeared who make a point of compiling songs for their films' soundtracks, and see this 'mixtape' as crucial element in the film's (and their own *oeuvre*'s) character. Claudia Gorbman describes such 'melomanes' as unlike a traditional Hollywood auteur director as for them music is a 'key thematic element and marker of authorial style'.[22] For instance, Quentin Tarantino's *Reservoir Dogs* (1992) includes a number of songs, often appearing quite prominently, although sometimes not in a sustained manner. The songs are *Little Green Bag* by the George Baker Selection, *Hooked on a Feeling* by Blue Swede, *I Gotcha* by Joe Tex, *Magic Carpet Ride* and *Harvest Moon* by Bedlam, *Fool for Love* by Sandy Rogers, *Stuck in the Middle with You* by Stealers Wheel and *Coconut* by Harry Nilsson. Following the film's opening sequence of dialogue by a group of men around a table, as they leave the diner and begin to walk in slow motion for the film's opening titles, *Little Green Bag* plays. The iconic images of the gang wearing the same formal clothes and walking jauntily in slow motion appeared to fit the George Baker Selection rhythm in a highly effective manner. Indeed, each two bars of the music there is a cut as each shot introduces an individual character while crediting the actor on screen. This combination of music and image provides a distinct character for the film, not simply exciting the audience but informing them that a highly distinctive film is to follow. Without doubt, the most memorable song in the film is *Stuck in the Middle with You*, which accompanies the torture scene where Mr. Blonde cuts off the captured policeman's ear.[23] This is one of the most startling instances of music use in film over the past half century and arguably in the whole history of the medium. The gravity of what is depicted in the sequence is in stark contrast to the song's seemingly banal lyrics and bouncy, light rhythm. This remarkable and extremely well-known sequence appears to embody Michel Chion's notion of 'anempathetic music'[24] perhaps more clearly than any other in cinema.

In 1994, three remarkable films were released all of which heavily exploited the possibilities of song compilation soundtracks. They were Quentin Tarantino's *Pulp Fiction*, Oliver Stone's *Natural Born Killers* and the massive international success *Forrest Gump*.

Tarantino's *Pulp Fiction* hails an audience knowledgeable about music as well as films.[25] While the film includes an eclectic mixture of song recordings, some of the film's musical highlights are *Misirlou* by Dick Dale and his Del-Tones, which is used at the start, Chuck Berry's *You Never Can Tell* being danced to at the competition by Mia and Vincent and the Neil Diamond song *Girl, You'll Be a Woman Soon* by Urge Overkill, which Mia dances to before overdosing. This last song became a minor hit record after the film's release, while the soundtrack album sold well, although it did not contain all the songs in the film.[26] Tarantino's friends Chuck Kelley and Laura Lovelace were credited as music consultants, and like Tarantino's other films, the choice of songs cohered not only into a memorable stratum of the film but made for a distinctive soundtrack album.[27] Tarantino has directed a highly successful succession of films: *Reservoir Dogs* (1992), *Pulp Fiction* (1994), *Jackie Brown* (1997), *Kill Bill, Volume 1* (2003), *Kill Bill, Volume 2* (2004), *Inglourious Basterds* (2009) and *Django Unchained* (2012). Each of these films cede a notable importance to music, which often involves old songs being wielded in a creative manner in the film. One might argue that these films are 'music-based' and consequently have a bestselling tied-in album while using specific music for a 'hip' effect (signification) as well as for its kinetic qualities. Tarantino's succession of songs are reminiscent of selections from someone's record collection – something that Tarantino noted himself as has been discussed by Ken Garner.[28]

Oliver Stone decided that instead of having an orchestral score for *Natural Born Killers*, its character based in montage and rapid MTV-style cutting and striking images would be suited by a more fragmented soundtrack comprising excerpts from different recordings. Most of these are rock songs. A striking sequence is in the diner where Mallory begins dancing, which excites some local men. The music played on the jukebox is Robert Gordon's version of *The Way I Walk*. A scene of killing then begins, inaugurated by one of them saying 'Meep Meep' (derived from the cartoon *Road Runner*), which kicks off the song *Shitlist* by L7. This rough and ready rock track, performed by an all-female ensemble, dominates the soundtrack although we also hear the sounds of gunfire. The loud music aestheticizes the sequence of violent action, choreographing and ameliorating the effect of the disturbing images. The sequence mixes colour and black and white footage and interspersed big close ups of Mickey's face with Mallory kicking men. It also repeats the shot of the man saying 'Meep Meep', among a melange of violent montage including a slow motion thrown spinning knife being followed by the camera and a bullet which halts inexplicably in front of a woman's forehead before cutting to a shot of a wall being splattered with blood.

*Natural Born Killers* includes a wide range of songs and pieces of music, including songs by Nine Inch Nails (*Burn*, *Something I Can Never Have* and *A Warm Place*), the singular *Drums a Go-Go* by the Hollywood Persuaders, Bob Dylan's *You Belong to Me* and a memorable version of the Velvet Underground's *Sweet Jane* by the Cowboy Junkies. In fact, the film contains so many excerpts from existing recordings that it could not include all of them on the tied-in soundtrack album.[29] However, the soundtrack album was more than simply a compilation of songs and was sequenced carefully and included some dialogue from the film to make the album into a distinct aesthetic experience.

*Forrest Gump* (1994) was a massive international success and included a large number of period songs as well as having an orchestral score by Alan Silvestri. The film was accompanied by a single and double album, totalling fifty-six songs. In the film, songs are often used to articulate a particular situation. For example, Forrest first landing in Vietnam is accompanied by Creedence Clearwater Revival's *Fortunate Son*, while his beginning of three-years of running starts with Jackson Browne's *Running on Empty*. Songs are exploited for setting the period for the film's representations, for example, Elvis Presley's *Hound Dog*, Joan Baez's version of Bob Dylan's *Blowin' in the Wind*, the Mamas and the Papas' *California Dreamin'*, all of which supply an instant idea of the period. The film was accompanied by a double album of old songs. Despite the prodigious soundtrack album, there were some important songs that due to copyright reasons were unable to be included: The Jimi Hendrix Experience's *All Along the Watchtower* and *Hey Joe* and The Doors' *Soul Kitchen*, *Hello, I Love You*, *People Are Strange* and *Love Her Madly*. However, one Doors song, *Break On Through*, was included on the tied-in album. These songs build a historical fabric for the film. The version of 'the sixties' constructed by *Forrest Gump* is a semi-sanitized 'consensual' view of the counter culture and US history. This is no scholarly history but one evident in popular culture outlets (popular films, television and classic hit songs) and therefore, crucially, recognizable to a mainstream audience.

*Trainspotting* contains many songs, obviating the need for a musical score to furnish mood and dramatize events, which in many cases is managed by the pre-existing songs and musical pieces used in the film. *Trainspotting*'s episodic form lends itself to the use of a succession of songs. The songs become an essential part of the film's system of narration, along with dialogue and action, as ways to move the film forward. A clear strategy is to match a montage of compressed time and space with the prominent appearance of a song on the soundtrack, allied with a voice over from the film's protagonist (the element that clearly holds the film's narrative together as a progressive enterprise). In *Trainspotting*, the songs regularly function in material terms to hold together diverse montage sequences and as cohesion in the face of a simultaneity of fragmented action and voice over. They also provide punctuation while emphasizing kinesis. In cultural terms they provide a vague periodization, the film plots a history of sorts, which acknowledges that music and drugs have both changed. The novel appeared to be set during the 1980s, but the film's music seems to be primarily form the mid-1970s and the mid-1990s, with a few eighties moments in between.

*Trainspotting* starts with a kinetic sequence of the main characters running down an Edinburgh street after stealing drugs from a chemist's shop, also accompanied by a voice-over and the introductory section from Iggy Pop's *Lust for Life*. The opening sequence leaves us in little doubt as to the importance music will play in the coming film. *Lust For Life* (originally released in 1977) appears over the opening sequence of running protagonists which echoes the start of the Beatles' *A Hard Days' Night* (1964).[30] The beat provides a spine for the succession of highly kinetic images and the voice over breathlessly listing the prosaic aspects of stereotypical modern life ('Choose life, choose a job, choose a career, choose a family ...'). The dynamic structure of the song largely dictates the layout of the sequence. The song is built around temporal structures of four bars, at the end of the first four bars, the bass guitar enters to join the drums and Renton's voice over enters at the same moment. At the 16-bar point, there is a chord change from what we have previously heard and at this significant moment, there is a freeze frame of Renton on screen, leaning on the front of a car and with his name emblazoned across the screen. The climactic point of this opening montage sequence has, in quick succession, Renton finish his voice over monologue, a football being kicked, in reverse shot hitting Renton on the head, which then cuts to him slowly falling down from a standing position as a result of a heroin 'hit'. This is intercut with him falling from the impact of the ball at the soccer game. The key point, where the football hits, is succeeded immediately by Iggy Pop's singing entering after the extensive introduction to the song. After the lengthy build-up, the singing enters and Renton dramatically falls backwards. The temporal format of the images is dictated by the musical structure, the regulated musical time of the song, which has provided a temporal and dynamic frame to which they have been edited.[31] In another memorable sequence, Lou Reed's *Perfect Day* runs to its full length, without fades or cuts, meaning that the action is cut to fit its requirements. The sequence proceeds from Renton injecting, through his overdose (which is rendered visually through a 'distancing' effect of what appears to be carpet obscuring Renton's point of view shots that are interspersed with his illness), until he is put into bed at home by his parents.[32]

*Trainspotting* demonstrates the path that music and film industry 'synergy' was attempting to follow in the 1990s. This development was part of the reorganization of the music industry, which included a rebranding of what had been 'independent' music as a more mainstream 'alternative' music, and the rush into repackaging old albums for sale on CD. This latter process, of reselling old music, is highly evident in *Trainspotting*'s soundtrack albums. The film had two tied-in soundtrack albums made available, both of which sold well. These albums clearly aimed to be coherent in themselves as well as being the record of music in the film. Thus they had a hybrid character in that they were not specifically a subset of the film but more an intersection with the film. Songs that had appeared all too briefly could be heard in their full plenitude and some music that had appeared in the film was not represented on the first album. The second soundtrack album (known as *Trainspotting #2*) contained a number of songs that appeared in the film but had not featured on the first album.[33]

It is noteworthy that *Trainspotting* attempted to ride the wave of 'Britpop' of the mid-1990s. Director Danny Boyle pointed out that the film connected with the Britpop explosion,[34] featuring Blur (and their singer Damon Albarn alone), Pulp and Sleeper. 'Britpop' was a loose grouping of guitar-based bands that made bestselling albums and were to some degree successful in the United States as well as in Britain. The white heat of Britpop was in the early and mid-1990s and centred upon the successes of Oasis and Blur. Other groups who headed the movement included Pulp, Cast, Ash and Primal Scream. Some of these were evident on the soundtracks of British films of the time.[35] Boyle went on to direct *A Life Less Ordinary* (1997), which included songs by Britpop band Ash as well as dance acts Underworld and Orbital.

Similar concern with popular music is evident in many other films at this time. Rather than merely trying to sell songs through films they are exploited for their aesthetic qualities and cultural references. For example, the imaginative British biography film *Bronson* (2008) is very self-conscious about its music and the way it is used, exploiting a wide range of pre-existing recordings, from Wagner's *Siegfried's Funeral March* from *Götterdämmerung* and Verdi's *Chorus of the Hebrew Slaves* from *Nabucco* to the Pet Shop Boys' song *It's a Sin*. In fact, it is so self-conscious that its aesthetic strategies appear almost too unambiguously ironic. In the sequence where Bronson is released from prison, the action is edited and staged around the New Order song *Your Silent Face*. The instrumental introduction to the song is protracted and has a regular structure that is used as the temporal foundation for the film's visual action. As the beat begins, a stylistic format takes shape where cuts or some notable visual movements on-screen take place at the important structural beats that begin each two- and four-bar strophic unit. Perhaps the most evident point is where the melodica enters as Bronson walks out into the sunlight of freedom. Thus the extremely clear structure of the song dictates the fall of the action, and the audience understands the temporal importance of these musical moments. This all seems too much, and such precise synchronization lays bare the effect and artifice of cinema.

Wes Anderson's films are characterised by the care he takes to compile a soundtrack of diverse song recordings as an important element of the film. For example, *The Royal Tenenbaums* (2001), a dark comedy about a successful family's change in fortunes, had a selection of songs as well as a score by Mark Mothersbaugh, once of the group Devo. The Nico song *These Days* appears as non-diegetic music for a dramatic point in the film where, in slow motion, Margot (Gwyneth Paltrow) gets off a bus and meets her brother Richie (Luke Wilson) at the quay. A highly dramatic moment in the film is accompanied by Elliott Smith's song *Needle in the Hay*. Here, Richie in succession cuts off his hair, his beard, slits his wrists and then is taken to the hospital. Songs are used as excerpts but usually are non-diegetic and often mixed high, sometimes with little in the way of dialogue or sound effects to obscure them. Curiously, Anderson uses music by British punk band the Clash to accompany two scenes involving drugs. Their over of Junior Murvin's *Police and Thieves* accompanies Margot and Eli (Owen Wilson) visiting a drug dealer while *Rock the Casbah* plays during a drug deal Eli makes. There was undoubtedly a great deal of care in how Anderson went about picking and placing pre-existing recordings in *The Royal Tenenbaums*.[36] There were two soundtrack albums, the first a song compilation and the second included Motherbaugh's score as well as more songs and pieces. Two Rolling Stones songs, *Ruby Tuesday* and *She Smiled Sweetly*, appeared in *The Royal Tenenbaums* but not on the tied-in soundtrack albums. They both appeared diegetically in the same scene between Margo and Richie but, as is the case with the Rolling Stones, the rights were not granted to use the songs on disc in addition to within the film.

# Conclusion

*Trainspotting* received a second soundtrack album release some time after the first. The majority of musical pieces on the disc have no direct connection with the film and thus marked an extension of the film. However, the album's sleeve notes inform us that a number of these pieces of music were under consideration for inclusion in the film. For example, David Bowie's *Golden Years* was going to be sung by Diane to Renton, although in the final film she sings New Order's *Temptation*.[37] This substitution illustrates a paramount aspect of using existing recordings in a films, that of licensing. Although film-makers often say little about it, licensing can be a significant determinant upon a film's final state. Some artists, such as the Rolling Stones, are unwilling to allow their songs to be used in films or sold on soundtrack albums.

Cultural recycling became endemic from the mid-1980s onwards, with record companies keen to exploit other markets. Denisoff and Plasketes detail the industrial strategy called synergy, involving the co-ordination of record releases from a film soundtrack as mutual publicity.[38] Since the 1990s, song collections that often predate film being produced, with film-makers often looking into what pop songs they can afford to license very early in the project. By the early 1990s, it certainly was common for films to have a number of pop songs incorporated with a view to soundtrack album publicity. Since the advent of CD, which really took off at the turn of the 1990s, the music industry's selling of old back catalogues has been big business. The relationship of the nostalgia industry and the record industry's repackaging of old songs has been mutually reinforcing. The retreading of the musical past has speeded up, allowing a nostalgia for the 1980s despite its relative historical proximity. Films such as *Peter's Friends* (1992), *Boston Kickout* (1995) and Mike Leigh's *Career Girls* (1997) were set in the 1980s and used songs of the period that were yet to achieve quite the 'classic' status accorded to older songs.

Tom Gunning notes the similarity between some contemporary cinema and the 'attractionism' of early cinema.[39] His approach sees film as a grab bag of effects and fragments of (often discrete) interest rather than a fully-integrated work. Overarching narrative is therefore of less importance and micro-narratives and incident tend to be of more interest. Other elements of the film can also take on more significance, and in the case of films like *Pulp Fiction* and *Trainspotting* most clearly, music seems to have a degree of importance in the film that has almost no direct bearing upon the film's narrative or diegetic world. Pop and rock songs are presented something like music videos,[40] functioning as discrete attractions and micro-narratives which break up the narrative elision. But looking from a different point of view, this is merely the union of music-dominated image alternating with other regimes of narration within the same films. From a more musical point of view, it illustrates the degree of fragmentation that is evident these days in the world of 'mixtape aesthetics'.

# 11

# Copyright and Musical Censorship: Gangsta Rap and *Bad Lieutenant*

Some of rock's social anxiety aspects were picked up by rap music during the 1990s. Although most rap comes from a pop genealogy, the rap music under discussion in this chapter has far more connection with rock music. The development of precise quoting in recording – in other words, direct use of previously existing recordings – seems to mark an end to popular music as a field of organic development, where direct influence and indirect quotation were the building blocks, and entering a period of 'the copyright wars' as a commercial art rather than a folk art. The last couple of decades have experienced a concentration on musical copyright to a degree never previously encountered. At the same time, debates about the merits of censorship and acceptability have also reached a degree of sophistication and polarization. Both of these cultural issues converged in Abel Ferrara's *Bad Lieutenant* (1992). This extremely controversial film about a corrupt, drug-fuelled New York cop (played in a *tour de force* performance by Harvey Keitel) encountered problems with its use of a shocking rap song by Gangsta rapper Schoolly D, which was forcibly removed from later VHS and DVD releases of the film. This chapter will discuss a single incident of seeming censorship, where a piece of music was forcibly excised from a film.

'Reimagined' in 2009 by Werner Herzog as an offbeat mainstream Hollywood movie starring Nicolas Cage, the original *Bad Lieutenant* was a far more challenging and extreme film. It was released as an independent film in 1992, directed by Abel Ferrara and written by Ferrara and Zoe Tamerlis Lund. Ferrara's early films were often highly challenging, from the extreme violence of *The Driller Killer* (1979) to harrowing but stylized rape-revenge film *Ms.45* (1981) and violent gangster film *King of New York* (1990).[1] Abel Ferrara's *Bad Lieutenant* was a single-minded and challenging film about a self-destructive and corrupt New York policeman's attempt to find redemption through dealing with a case where a Catholic nun is raped in church. Built from a series of vignettes, the film's narrative is unified by the investigation into the rape alongside the Lieutenant's impending doom as he awaits the outcome of a bet on the Mets in a baseball play-off series against the Dodgers. The film has a distinct visual and aural texture, matching uncompromising visuals with uncompromising music. Indeed, *Bad Lieutenant* is confrontational in terms of image and representation. One could argue that it revels in an aesthetic of shock. From the opening gang rape of a nun in a church to Jesus descending from the cross to the Lieutenant, who shouts at him: 'Where were you, you fucker?' The film consistently deals in extremity and what some might find difficult and offensive. Janet Maslin's *New York Times* review: 'When Abel Ferrara calls something bad, better believe it: he means business .... One condition of his cult status is that his films give as much offence as possible ...'[2] This is certainly true: we actually see the film's screenwriter Zoe Tamerlis Lund explicitly 'shooting up' heroin in the film. She was a chronic heroin addict[3] and died early, some seven years after the film's release.

Music is no less a part of the film's shock tactics. One of the key defining characteristics of the screen world is the intermittent appearance of a Gangsta rap song by the rapper Schoolly D. Yet this part of *Bad Lieutenant's* original soundtrack was removed unceremoniously after the film's initial release. The song in question is called *Signifyin' Rapper*, taken from the album *Smoke Some Kill* (1988) and containing directly offensive words. The nature of the rap means that the words are highly intelligible, and the aim is that we should register the lyrics. This is often far from the case with popular music, where sung words can often become merely part of musical texture. In *Bad Lieutenant*, *Signifyin' Rapper* is more than simply a song appearing on the soundtrack as is such an everyday thing in American films. It has something of an elevated position, featuring as non-diegetic music a number of times in the film.

## Gangsta rap

Schoolly D was one of the originators of 'Gangsta rap', with the single 'P.S.K. What Does It Mean?' in 1986 predating Ice T's debut record, which had a reputation for being the origins of this subgenre. The song's title refers to the notorious Philadelphia gang the 'Park Side Killers' and set some of the parameters for the culture in its seeming glorification of violence and gang culture, as well as sex and drug dealing.[4] Schoolly D forged a partnership with film-maker Ferrara, and later a couple of his songs appeared in *King of New York*, including *Am I Black Enough for You?* which was used for the concluding gun battle. He also co-wrote the music for *The Blackout* (1997) with Ferrara's regular composer Joe Delia and went on to more soundtrack activities later.

Gangsta rap was a notable phenomenon of the late 1980s and 1990s. It created a good degree of cultural anxiety. It inspired a hysteria corresponding to Stanley Cohen's discussion of moral panics and their attending 'folk devils'.[5] Gangsta rap centred on lyrics celebrating street violence and gang culture, revelling in an extremity of misogyny, homophobia, sexual violence and degradation, and all-round anti-social behaviour. Gangsta Rap's halcyon era was the late 1980s and early 1990s, with rappers such as NWA, Ice T, KRS-One, Ice Cube, Snoop Dogg and Cypress Hill amongst others. At the time of the film's release, it was going strong, with Dr. Dre and Death Row Records, and 'rivals' the Notorious B.I.G. and Puff Daddy's Bad Boy Records were both successful.

The PMRC (Parents' Music Resource Center) was founded in 1985, aggressively pursuing a form of censorship through pressure on the music industry. One of its innovations was the instigation of stickers on records that contained explicit lyrics. While on the one hand, this might have steered concerned parents away from such music, on the other it gave a certain cachet to records that were deemed 'dangerous' in this way. The extremity of some rap music, particularly Gangsta rap, might even to a degree be construed as a reaction to the cultural landscape and fears promulgated by the PMRC.

The choice of a rap song for the film is not straightforward. There is no relation of the song to the protagonist of the film (and his milieu). It has no ties to him and little clear ties to film world. It does not directly 'frame' the Lieutenant's world or provide us with any empathy with his character. (Indeed, if anything, the music proves anempathetic!) However, we first hear the song accompanying the rape of the nun, so perhaps the implication is that it embodies more the world of the rapists. The song exploits the controversy surrounding Gangsta rap while also being something of a 'story within a story' and – due to the high intelligibility of the words – functions almost like a voice-over narration (emphasized by its non-diegetic status). However, the film fragments the song, though, making its effect more textural than verbal communication.

This is a film that has little to do with black culture and indeed has no notable black characters. The use of such distinctly 'black' music is confounding, unless this aspect of black culture is used essentially to exploit its controversial status. As Clyde Taylor has suggested: 'Because it brashly transgresses the barriers of standardized communication, Afro oral tradition is also a magnet for those inclined to vaudevillize, minstrelize, or sensationalize it.'[6] Although being removed from its original black context, rather than being packaged for easy consumption here, the song certainly adds an extra sensational dimension to the film. It is tempting to suggest that the film uses a musical notion of black 'anxiety' for white audiences, although I suggest that would be far too simplistic an interpretation.

The whole of the US political spectrum attacked Gangsta rap. In 1992, Dan Quayle (US vice President) called Tupac's *2Pacalypse Now* album 'a disgrace' to American music, asking record label Interscope to withdraw the record. Quayle was a Republican but Democrats were also attacking Gangsta rap. Tipper Gore was testifying to a congressional committee about its negative character.[7] While there was a good degree of white anxiety about Gangsta rap, there was also a strong negative reaction to it from the African American middle-classes in America.[8] John Springhill approach Gangsta rap as one of a regular series of 'moral panics' alongside 'video nasties'.[9]

Gangsta rap certainly was confrontational. After Public Enemy's heavily politicized recordings, artists like NWA retained the political message, while other like 2 Live Crew espoused extreme sexism and misogyny. Schoolly D was no less controversial.[10] His first record was *P.S.K. What Does it Mean?* in 1985, which was referring to the 'Park Side Killas' who had been involved in drugs and shootings. His later albums had confrontational titles such as *Smoke Some Kill* (1988, which included Signifyin' Rapper) and *Am I Black Enough for You?* (1989). More recently, Schoolly D has supplied voice-over narration for Cartoon Network's *Aqua Teen Hunger Force* (an animated show which is part of the Adult Swim programs). He now appears more respectable and is not unique in these matters. Ice T had made the inflammatory record *Cop Killer* with Body Count but in recent years has had a career playing a cop in a TV show!

# Music

The music is based on a four-bar structure in common time, although the motif is more in triple time across this. Its repetition and structure of a repeated rhythmic motif and four guitar chords that rise in succession give it a fatalistic, driving inevitability. It is derived directly from the rhythm track of Led Zeppelin's *Kashmir* from *Physical Graffiti* (1975). Indeed, it is a direct performance of the main four-bar riff that is the foundation of the song. Although for Led Zeppelin and hard rock fans *Kashmir* was considered a classic track, it was more obscure to others. In recent times, it is perhaps a more iconic song than it was at the time of *Bad Lieutenant*, having more recently been used as incidental music on *X-Factor* (the British one) and wrestling on television. It is the basis of *Come with Me* by Puff Daddy which was the tied-in single theme for disaster movie remake *Godzilla* (1998). Schoolly D's version, *Signifyin' Rapper*, predates these other reuses, and the riff is not a sample but a re-recording, which sounds very similar although has a slightly more distorted rock guitar sound but updated with a little slap bass guitar. Indeed, it sound a little more conventional than Led Zeppelin's original, as guitarist Jimmy Page used an open guitar tuning which allows for more of a drone as part of the sound while it sounds like Schoolly D's guitar player did not. Nevertheless, this is considered a classic rock guitar riff, also more prominent since its original release due to reuse and changing attitudes towards Led Zeppelin. In the 1980s, such groups were often dismissed as 'dinosaurs' although more recently they are often appended with the title 'classic rock'. So, this was indeed an iconic song. It was covered by string quartet Bond on the 'Shine' album, by the London Philharmonic Orchestra on 'Kashmir: Symphonic Led Zeppelin' (surprisingly orchestrated by Jaz Coleman, singer in [post-]punk band Killing Joke), while it also managed an appearance as non-diegetic music in *Fast Times at Ridgemont High* (1982).

In hip hop, the music is often derived from the wordless 'breaks' in other records, mixing together existing recordings, using discs and turntables or digital samplers. A history of hip hop might be written that charts its kleptomaniac eclecticism's taming into integration with the wider music industry. A particularly fine example of this is Will Smith's series of hits which based each record on a lopped sample from another song recording: *Gettin' Jiggy Wit' It* (using Chic's *He's the Greatest Dancer*), *Wild West* (using Stevie Wonder's *I Wish*) and (using the Clash's *Rock the Casbah*).

The words of *Signifyin' Rapper* describe a duel in the ghetto. The principle strophe is a succession of insults – all of which are sexual and concerning family members. In fact, this bears notable similarity to the 'yo mamma ...' game, a well-known urban African-American activity. On the surface, it appears homophonic and misogynistic. However, things are not so clear cut and complexities are apparent that might be overlooked by a simple, naïve reading.

When confronting songs, there is a constant danger of the pitfalls of literalism. According to Eithne Quinn, Gangster rap '... because of its non-prescribed and offensive lyrics, coupled with its emergence in the 1980s at a time of acute focus on language and identity politics – has tended to attract determinist and polemical readings that underplay the formal and rhetorical complexities of the genre'.[11] It seems likely that simplistic and literal understandings of the words in such music miss the cultural specificity of the communication. The discourse is no doubt more complex than they might appear. Indeed, there is a prominent tradition in rock'n'roll where songs were often about sex but couched the subject matter in covert terms. Is the Beatles song really about driving cars and the Chuck Berry song about ringing bells? Serving specific purposes, this process of 'euphemism' is hardly limited to such songs and such subject matter.

Schoolly D's song title alludes directly to the procedure of *signifyin'*, the use of a hidden coded spoken language as an indirect form of communication. This dates from the era of slavery, where slaves were unable to say what they pleased and also wished to communicate in a manner that bypassed their owners.[12] In this way, something could be said that on the surface appeared to be saying something different. A similar process took place in music, where for instance, European-style dancing was burlesqued in the 'cakewalk' dance. This procedure persisted after slavery, sustaining into recent African-American culture and where: 'The apparent significance of the message differs from its real significance.'[13]

Some of the opening salvo gives a flavour of the language characteristic of the song: 'The badass pimp said, Sure I ain't heard a cocksucking word you said. You say some more, I'll be standin' on your motherfucking head.'

The words come across as fragmented series of insults:

The rapper said, mister pimp, mister pimp I got something to say
There's this mean, big bad faggot comin' your way
He talk about you so bad, turn my hair gray . . .
This what the faggot said
He said, you know your daddy and he's a faggot
And your mother's a whore
He said he seen you sellin' asshole door to door
Yeah that's what he said, listen to what else he said mister badass pimp
He said, your granny, she's a dyke
And your other brother, he's a faggot
And your little sister Loo
She's so low she sucked the dick of a little maggot
Yeah that's what he said . . .

*Signifyin' Rapper's* narrative is a clear reconfiguration of the slavery-era tale (likely earlier) about the 'signifyin' monkey'. In the principal tale, he is a folk trickster figure who insults the lion to his face, but claims that he is not insulting him at all but instead is simply repeating the words of the elephant. The upset lion subsequently visits the elephant to confront him. A fight ensues, which the lion loses and is badly hurt. So the monkey has not only managed to insult the lion to his face but also to have his enemy vanquished as part of the process. In the song, the same subject positions exist. The rapper is the monkey, the 'badass pimp' is the lion and 'big bad faggot' is the elephant.[14]

Eithne Quinn points out that although rap songs can have surface of misogyny and homophobia, there are also 'political ambiguities and semantic complexities' in pimp-inspired rap songs.[15] Rap tends to appear to be direct and speak straight, however even the song's subject position appears notably ambiguous. It includes 'he said', 'I said', 'the Pimp said', 'the Faggot said', 'the Rapper …', 'I don't know …' At a first listen, this slippage is not obvious but then appears slipshod. Upon more repeated listening it appears purposeful but ambiguous. It is not clear whether this actually is 'ironic' or not, as it is submerged in a context of irony. However, the ambiguity makes the song more semiotically rich and complex, suggesting a divergent rather than convergent meaning. Like the film itself, the song appears all the more complex when afforded closer scrutiny. After considering the lyrics a few times, they seem increasingly confusing, perhaps leading the listener to imagine that to be decoded they need a particular key that it not available.

# Song removal

The song was not removed because it was offensive but rather because of its use of uncleared music. Led Zeppelin and Atlantic records went to court in 1994. Although they were only able to get an injunction to have the song removed from the film and DVDs, it was only removed from some VHS releases internationally.[16] *Signifyin' Rapper*'s removal and replacement is not without effect. Michel Chion noted that if you change the music, you change the film.[17] Sections of Ferrara's film which used the song now are without music, and Ferrara remains upset. The song clearly was important – appearing for the end titles and on four separate occasions in the film. *Signifyin' Rapper* appeared early on just after Keitel drops off his children, 'powders his nose' and drives off at the beginning of the film. Indeed, its multiple appearances give it a thematic role. Ferrara exploited Schoolly D's song as an important modal and textural aspect of the film and indeed had used Schoolly D's *Am I Black Enough for You?* at the climax of *King of New York*, two years earlier.

Ferrara is certainly not known for compromising his artistic vision. However, he wrote a replacement song for the end titles, collaborating with Paul Hipp, who played Jesus in the film – so it has good credentials! The song was performed by Ferrara with Hipp, called *The Bad Lieutenant*, and apparently recorded on a Sony Walkman during a late night jam session.

A significant parameter of the film's semantic field was set by the song. The recut certainly changes it. The relentless character of the music and the aggressive, haranguing rap add a further layer to the series of disturbing incidents the film represents. For a film, either all elements are relevant and the song is an essential co-ordinate point setting the semantic field of the film, or only a few important elements define a film's meaning, and the rest is merely backdrop or window-dressing. Certainly, people I spoke to who had seen the original release remembered the song. The removal of the song amount to an indirect form of censorship, a rewriting of history where audiences are now unable to experience the film as it originally was. Rather than a 'hot' form of political censorship, this amounts to a 'cold' cultural-financial censorship.[18]

In fact, the film was already 'censored', although perhaps not obviously. The film has two different cuts, one five minutes shorter than the other. In the United States, *Bad Lieutenant* was rated 'NC-17' apparently with reference to explicit drug use in the film.[19] There was a video release made that allows the film an 'R' rating for home consumption (through the Blockbuster chain). In the UK, cinematic releases had over five minutes removed. The UK VHS release, by Guild video in 1995, lost over a minute and a half of heroin injection in addition to the UK cinema cuts (which cut the rape, the undressing nun in the hospital, and already a good portion of the heroin injection scene). A year earlier, the Aries Film Releasing (the film distributor) and Live Home Video were ordered to destroy their VHS copies of the film.[20]

In recent years there have been increasingly muscular attempts to enforce musical (and other cultural) copyright. Shortly before the film's release, there were a number of high-profile court cases dealing with musical copyright. Paul Hardcastle's *19* in 1985 (which was found to have copied Mike Oldfield's Tubular Bells), the KLF in 1987 (as The JAMs, the album *1987: What the Fuck is Going On?* was threatened by Abba and the Mechanical Copyright Protection Society leading to its withdrawal), Vanilla Ice in 1990 (*Ice Ice Baby* being based on a looped sample of Queen and David Bowie's *Under Pressure*, leading to an out of court settlement) and Michael Bolton in 1991 (his song *Love is a Wonderful Thing* and the 1966 song of the same name by the Isley Brothers, who were awarded a massive over $5 million). There is certainly plenty of work for 'forensic musicologists' these days. These cases are obvious 'samples' or easily argued pastiches. I spoke to a colleague a while ago and told her that I had just realized that a significant portion of a track on an album I liked was treated but taken mostly from another track. It had taken me a number of listens before it dawned on me. She told me that I should contact the original artist but I decided that it was not up to me; one could easily argue that the track was a long way from the original recording, and the original artists was far more rich than the more recent sound eclectician. However, in another incident I nearly reacted differently. I had bought a CD on the strength of an absolutely flattering review in *The Wire*. Upon listening to the CD, I realized that one track was for its full length an untreated recording, taken lock, stock and barrel from some old television incidental music. It was uncredited. Here,

I felt that it was the shortcomings of the review that were to blame. Perhaps the artist had done this on purpose, just to see if anyone is actually listening!

When hip hop involved discs being spun in the street and small clubs, there was little concern about copyright. The rhetoric about 'liberating' music from ownership was not far behind, at the point where records were being released and making money. Hip hop is now a long way from its origins as an anarchic, street-based culture, now increasingly working with music lawyers and big powerful record labels. NWA's track *100 Miles and Runnin'* sampled a brief guitar figure from Funkadelic's *Get off Your Ass and Jam*, leading to a law suit in 2005.

# Conclusion

*Bad Lieutenant* revels in its New York locations, starting at the corner of Central Park at 5th Avenue and concluding outside the Port Authority Bus Terminal on 8th Avenue. Yet the more the Lieutenant gets into debt, the more the film runs into fantasy sequences. The 1954 song Johnnie Ace track, *Pledging My Love*, appears twice in the film. Firstly, when the Lieutenant cries in the apartment with two prostitutes and secondly, when he puts the rapists on the bus out of New York. This latter instance is the film's climatic redemptive moment and the song signals an emotional release (he stands naked screaming during the first instance).

The film's narrative appears to be concerned only on the surface with the depravities of the lead character, played by Harvey Keitel, and is more interested in a deeper level about Catholicism and the possibilities of redemption under absolutely extraordinary circumstances. *Bad Lieutenant* is a startling reaction to casual violence in an age and place of despair and faithlessness. So, initial reactions of repulsion increasingly prove to be less sophisticated than the film itself. I would argue that the same might be true of the music. The song words are undoubtedly more sophisticated than might be immediately apparent. One overlooked aspect of Gangsta rap words are their importance as aural texture. Allied to the dramatic Led Zeppelin riff, it yields an effect of uncompromising music – although, and perhaps because of this, it later became heavily compromised.

Rock'n'roll was often about metaphor and dominant bourgeois culture missed the point. Perhaps such Gangsta rap was also metaphorical, making cultural guardians miss the point again. Perhaps there is enough in the surface of obscenity to allow an understanding of this 'celebration' of cultural negativity as a nihilistic outburst rather than necessarily a reactionary 'right wing' stance. Songs such as *Signifyin' Rapper* certainly know how to confront and consequently might be understood as a musical counterpart to Ferrara's films such as *Bad Lieutenant*.

However, will future generations be given the opportunity to make their minds up about the original version of the film or will they even know of its existence? It seems that copyright marks a form of censorship that is able to rewrite history, in a cold instrumental manner.[21] *Signifyin' Rapper* is removed from four points in the film, which is a significant intervention. Where do these developments leave cultural historians? Rick Altman has noted in 'Cinema as Event' that film historians discuss a specific film but without registering that different versions have been in circulation.[22] Is there any such thing as a single, unproblematic, originating object? In this case, there is a stronger idea of an original film than there is in most cases. The original is 'lost' unless the researcher is adept at accessing the 'unofficial archive' of the 'grey market', which is not quite the black market.[23] In this case, I had to scour second hand stores and eBay for a foreign copy of the VHS, as there were a few territories where it was released in the original version. My research has not been impacted much by censorship or films being absent from public scrutiny through availability.[24] I am aware of others working in areas of culture that are denied to the researcher. Despite floundering university support, perhaps it is our duty as cultural historians to go beyond the accepted gates of corporate consumerism, in the search for a truth that is not simply the truth of consumerism.

# Notes

## Chapter 1

1  The best book about popular music and film remains Jeff Smith's *The Sounds of Commerce: Marketing Popular Film Music* (New York: Columbia University Press, 1998), although there are other books that deal with more recent events, such as Ian Inglis's collection *Popular Music and Film* (London: Wallflower, 2003) and R. Serge Denisoff and William D. Romanowsi's intriguing industry study, *Risky Business: Rock on Film* (New York: Transaction, 1991). Beyond this, there is the varied and colourful collection: Jonathan Romney and Adrian Wootton, eds., *Celluloid Jukebox. Popular Music and the Movies since the Fifties* (London: BFI, 1995), and the more song-detail-based is Steve Lannin and Matthew Caley, ed., *Pop Fiction: The Song in Cinema* (Bristol: Intellect, 2005). Thankfully, there are many relevant journal articles.

2  Rock operas were the cinematic equivalent or manifestation of the concept album.

3  See, for instance, the aptly named book: Ian Conrich and Estella Tincknell, eds., *Film's Musical Moments* (Edinburgh: Edinburgh University Press, 2006).

4  K. J. Donnelly, *Pop Music in British Cinema: A Chronicle* (London: BFI, 2001), viii.

5  Rick Altman, *The American Film Musical* (London: BFI, 1987), 198.

6  Barry Keith Grant, 'The Classic Hollywood Musical and the "Problem" of Rock'n'Roll' in *Journal of Popular Film and Television*, vol. 18, part 4, 1986, 199.

7  The decline of Cliff Richard's film career is demonstrated by the performance of each soundtrack LP. *The Young Ones* (1961) stayed in the chart for forty-two weeks; *Summer Holiday* (1963) for thirty-six weeks; *Wonderful Life* (1964) for twenty-three weeks; *Finders Keepers* (1966) for eighteen weeks; and *Take Me High* (1974) for four weeks.

8  The initial attraction for making a Beatles film was publicity for the disc release. Robert Neaverson, *The Beatles Movies* (London: Cassell, 1997), 12.

9  In 1958, 25.7 per cent films registered in the UK were made by US companies. In 1966, it was 55.9 per cent. Thomas H. Guback, 'American Interests in the British Film Industry' in *Quarterly Review of Economics and Business*, no. 7, 1967, 11.

10  Edward R. Kealy, 'From Craft to Art: The Case of Sound Mixers and Popular Music' in Simon Frith and Adnrew Goodwin, eds., *On Record: Rock, Pop and the Written Word* (New York: Pantheon, 1990), 208.

11  Ian Inglis, 'Introduction: Popular Music and Film' in Ian Inglis, ed., *Popular Music and Film* (London: Wallflower, 2003), 2.

12  Andrew Caine notes that the film musical is the 'parent genre' of the rock film. Andrew Caine, 'Can Rock Movies be Musicals?' in Lincoln Geraghty and Mark Jancovich, eds., *The Shifting Definitions of Genre: Essays on Labelling Films, Television Shows and Media* (Jefferson, NC: McFarland, 2008), 133.

13  For a further, detailed discussion of punk and film, see David X. Laderman's writing: '(S)lip-Sync: Punk Rock Narrative Film and Postmodern Musical Performance' in Jay Beck and Tony Grajeda, eds., *Lowering the Boom: Critical Studies in Film Sound* (Chicago, IL: University of Illinois Press, 2008), and *Punk Slash! Musicals: Tracking Slip-Sync on Film* (Austin: University of Texas Press, 2011).

14  Jon Lewis, *The Road to Romance and Ruin: Teen Films and Youth Culture* (London: Routledge, 1992), 136.

15  Tim Pulleine, review, *Monthly Film Bulletin*, vol. 53, no. 631, August 1986, 237.

16  In recent years, there has been a distinct theoretical concern with music's relationship to diegetic status: Robynn J. Stilwell, 'The Fantastical Gap between Diegetic and Non-Diegetic' in Daniel Goldmark, Lawrence Kramer and Richard Leppert, eds., *Beyond the Soundtrack: Representing Music in Cinema* (Berkeley: University of California Press, 2007); Jeff Smith, 'Bridging the Gap: Reconsidering the Border between Diegetic and Non-Diegetic' in *Music and the Moving Image*, vol. 2, no. 1, 2009, 1–25; Ben Winters, 'The Non-Diegetic Fallacy: Film, Music and Narrative Space' in *Music and Letters*, vol. 91, no. 2, 2010, 224–244; Anahid Kassabian, 'The End of Diegesis as We Know It? (And I Feel Fine)' in Claudia Gorbman, John Richardson and Carol Vernallis, eds., *Oxford Handbook of New Audiovisual Aesthetics* (New York: Oxford University Press, 2013); Guido Heldt, *Music and Levels of Narration in Film* (Bristol: Intellect, 2014).

17  Altman, *The American Film Musical*, 11.

18  Robert Edgar, Kirsty Fairclough-Isaacs and Benjamin Halligan, 'Introduction: Music Seen: The Formats and Functions of Music Documentary' in Robert Edgar, Kirsty FaircloughIsaacs and Benjamin Halligan, eds., *The Music Documentary: From Acid Rock to Electropop* (New York: Routledge, 2013), 6.

19  Altman, *The American Film Musical*, 129.

20  Keith Grant, 'The Classic Hollywood Musical and the "Problem" of Rock'n'Roll', 199.

21  Donnelly, *Pop Music in British Cinema*, viii.

22  Altman, *The American Film Musical*, 110.

23  Ibid.

24  K. J. Donnelly, 'Performance and the Composite Film Score' in K. J. Donnelly, ed., *Film Music: Critical Approaches* (Edinburgh: Edinburgh University Press, 2001), 160.

25  Altman, *The American Film Musical*, 67.

26  See, for instance, Annabel J. Cohen, 'Congruence-Association Model and Experiments in Film Music: Toward Interdisciplinary Collaboration' and David Ireland, 'Deconstructing Incongruence: A Psycho-Semiotic Approach Towards Difference in the Film-Music Relationship' in *Music and the Moving Image*, vol. 8, no. 2, Summer 2015, 5–24; 48–59.

27  Sergei M. Eisenstein, *The Film Sense*, Jay Leyda, ed. and trans. (London: Faber and Faber, 1963), 67.

28  The strategies for the construction of pop group performances on television in the late 1950s and early 1960s are elucidated in: John Hill, 'Television and Pop: The Case of the 1950s' in John Corner, ed., *Popular Television in Britain: Studies in Cultural History* (London: BFI, 1991), 56–58.

29  Jane Feuer, *The Hollywood Musical* (London: Macmillan, 1982), 26.

30  Theodor Adorno, 'On Popular Music' in Andrew Goodwin and Simon Frith, eds., *On Record: Rock, Pop and the Written Word* (London: Routledge, 1990), 306.

31  Barry Kernfeld, ed., *The New Grove Dictionary of Jazz* (London: Macmillan, 1988), 412.

32  Alan Williams, 'The Musical Film and Recorded Popular Music' in Rick Altman, ed., *Genre: The Musical* (London: Routledge and Keegan Paul, 1981), 153.

33  Ibid., 154.

34  Songs were tied regularly to Hollywood films at around 1930. David Ewens, *All the Years of American Popular Music* (London: Prentice-Hall, 1977), 384.

35  Anon., 'Merchandising Keeps Disney Image in Sharp Focus' in *Kinematograph Weekly*, vol. 564, no. 2954, 14 May 1964, 22.

36  Altman, *The American Film Musical*, 356.

37  Tom Collins, 'Popular Music and Technology' in Mark Christopher Carnes, ed., *The Columbia History of Post-World War II America* (New York: Columbia University Press, 2007), 57.

38  In the early 1980s, the industry's rhetoric about 'home taping killing music' accompanied dwindling profits as a result of falling record sales, causing a conservative retrenchment of the international music industry, which concentrated on established artists rather than new developments. This was boosted by the coming of Compact Discs at the end of the decade, which allowed record companies to reanimate and resell all their back catalogues. To a degree, this was reflected in films like *Absolute Beginners* (1985) and *Trainspotting* (1996), both of which made extensive use of musical back catalogues. Jeremy Eckstein, ed., *Cultural Trends 19*, vol. 3, no. 3 (London: Policy Studies Institute, 1993), 45.

39  R. Serge Denisoff and George Plasketes, 'Synergy in 1980s Film and Music: Formula for Success or Industry Mythology?' in *Film History*, vol. 4, no. 3, 1990, 257.

# Chapter 2

1   Stephen Glynn, *A Hard Day's Night* (London: I.B. Tauris, 2005), 29–30. Bob Neaverson notes that producer Walter Shenson's interest in making a Beatles film was the soundtrack LP. *The Beatles Movies* (London: Cassell, 1998), 12.

2   The film was very successful. House records were broken at the London Pavilion. 'Box Office Business' in *Kinematograph Weekly*, vol. 566, no. 2963, 16 July 1964, 8.

3   John Ellis notes that: 'The star's performance in a film reveals to the viewer all those particular aspects of movement and expression . . . . The star is not performing here so much as "being". In other words, what the film performance permits is moments of pure voyeurism for the spectator, the sense of overlooking something which is not designed for the onlooker but passively allows itself to be seen.' *Visible Fictions: Cinema, Television, Video* (London: Routledge, 1982), 99.

4   There are distinct similarities between the style of *A Hard Day's Night* and the earlier documentary of the Beatles made by the Maysles brothers (*Yeah, Yeah, Yeah*). Neaverson, *The Beatles Movies*, 16.

5   The shooting schedule was brief, from 2 March to 24 April 1964, chronicled in H. V. Fulpen, *The Beatles: An Illustrated Diary* (London: Plexus, 1983), 68. Lester states that mostly first takes were used in *Hollywood, UK*, no. 2, BBC Television documentary series, first broadcast in August and September 1993.

6   Lester's career included musical shows for television like Rediffusion's *Downbeat* (a jazz and pop show) and awards for his advertisements. Nicholas Thomas, ed., *The International Dictionary of Films and Filmmakers* (London: St. James Press, 1990), 510.

7   John Hill, '*A Hard Day's Night*' in Nicholas Thomas, ed., *The International Dictionary of Films and Filmmakers* (London: St. James Press, 1990), 373–374.

8   Rick Altman notes that classical narrative is not applicable to the analysis of the profoundly different narrative that exists in film musicals. Rick Altman, *The American Film Musical* (Bloomington: Indiana University Press, 1987), 20.

9   Lester states that the images '. . . were cut to the music' in the documentary *Hollywood, UK*.

10  K. J. Donnelly, *Pop Music in British Cinema: A Chronicle* (London: BFI, 2001), viii.

11  The lip-synch mode is used for *Another Girl* in *Help!*, and the tendency is therefore for the visuals to be articulated around the song's lead singer, Paul McCartney. Its appearance in the film is motivated by a desire for visual variation in the song presentations.

12  Geoffrey Nowell-Smith, *Sight and Sound*, vol. 33, no. 4, Autumn 1964, 191.

13  The film certainly has to be seen as a showcase for the Beatles and their talents, and therefore, it seems reasonable to assume that its representation of the concert performance was one of the film's major attractions.

14 *She Loves You* reached number one in the charts and remained in the charts for twenty-one weeks, while the Beatles' previous singles reached number seventeen (*Love Me Do*) and number two (*Please Please Me*).

15 The hysteria generated during the production of the film was cited by cinematographer Gilbert Taylor as the reason why he did not want to be involved in the Beatles follow-up film. Alexander Walker, *Hollywood, England: The British Film Industry in the Sixties* (London: Harrap, 1986), 269.

16 *A Hard Day's Night* reached number one position in the LP charts and remained in the charts for thirty-eight weeks (compared to *Please Please Me*'s seventy weeks and *With The Beatles* fifty-one weeks).

17 *Kinematograph Weekly*, vol. 566, no. 2965, 30 July 1964, 4.

18 'Box Office Business' in *Kinematograph Weekly*, vol. 566, no. 2963, 16 July 1964, 8.

19 'The Beatles Film: Dispute Settled' in *Kinematograph Weekly*, vol. 563, no. 2948, 12 April 1964, 3.

20 The budget for *Help!* was over £400,000, over twice that of *A Hard Day's Night*. Walker, *Hollywood, England*, 267.

21 The film was made with the same team: United Artists under producer George Ornstein.

22 Thus, the album has to be seen as primary and the film as an adjunct of the successive collection of Beatles' songs released to the public. The incidental score by George Martin would have been of little interest to Beatles' fans, and indeed, the only soundtrack album to a Beatles' film which includes incidental music was *Yellow Submarine* from 1968, where the group fulfilled a contract to provide a minimum of material for the animated feature in which they showed little interest.

23 John C. Winn, *That Magic Feeling: The Beatles' Recorded Legacy, Volume Two, 1966–1970* (London: Random House, 2009), 85–87.

24 Peter Harcourt, *Sight and Sound*, vol. 3, no. 4, Autumn 1965, 199.

25 Nick Cohn, *Awopbop Alubop Alopbam Boom: Pop in the Beginning* (London: Pimlico, 2004), 226.

26 Neaverson, *The Beatles Movies*, 48.

27 Neil Sinyard, *The Films of Richard Lester* (London: Croom Helm, 1985), 33.

28 Wilfrid Mellers, *The Twilight of the Gods: The Beatles in Retrospect* (London: Faber, 1973).

29 H. V. Fulpen, *The Beatles: An Illustrated Diary* (London: Plexus, 1998), 48.

# Chapter 3

1 Michael Hicks, *Sixties Rock: Garage, Psychedelic and Other Satisfactions* (Chicago: University of Illinois Press, 2000), 58.

2   Tony Jasper, *Fab!: The Sounds of the Sixties* (Poole, Dorset: Blandford Press, 1984), 201–204.

3   George Melly, *Revolt into Style: The Pop Arts in Britain* (London: Penguin, 1970), 115, 106.

4   Andy Davis, Mark Paytress and John Reed, 'The Beatles and Psychedelia' in *Record Collector*, no. 166, June 1993, 20.

5   Mark Kurlansky, *1968: The Year that Rocked the World* (London: Vintage, 2005).

6   Hicks, *Sixties Rock*, 63.

7   Michael Watts, 'The Call and Response: The Impact of American Pop Music in Europe' in C. W. E. Bigsby, ed., *Superculture: American Popular Culture and Europe* (London: Paul Elek, 1975), 136.

8   Stuary Laing notes the significant impact of psychedelia in terms of graphic design more generally. 'Economy, Society and Culture in the 1960s: Contexts and Conditions for Psychedelic Art' in Christoph Grunenberg and Jonathan Harris, eds., *Summer of Love: Psychedelic Art, Social Crisis and Counterculture in the 1960s* (Liverpool: Liverpool University Press, 2006), 32.

9   Alan Williams, 'The Musical Film and Recorded Popular Music' in Rick Altman, ed., *Genre: The Musical* (London: Routledge and Keegan Paul, 1981), 149.

10  R. Serge Denisoff and William Romanowski, *Risky Business: Rock on Film* (New York: Transaction, 1991), 159.

11  The film is 'A Dick Clark Production', co-produced by the company founded by Dick Clark, the presenter of music show *American Bandstand* which began in 1957 and ran for thirty years on ABC Television.

12  Peter Biskind, *Easy Riders, Raging Bulls: How the Sex-and-Drugs-and-Rock'n'Roll Generation Changed Hollywood* (London: Bloomsbury, 1999), 15.

13  Produced by other creator Bert Schneider, *Head* was co-produced by Rafelson with Jack Nicholson.

14  One might note that the American was a COUNTER-culture while the British was a counter-CULTURE.

15  Dave Laing claims that the British underground emerged as a completely different thing from its American counterpart. 'Roll Over Lonnie (Tell George Formby the News)' in Charlie Gillett and Simon Frith, eds., *The Beat Goes On: The Rock File Reader* (London: Pluto, 1996), 14.

16  Ian McDonald, *Revolution in the Head: The Beatles Records and the Sixties* (London: Pimlico, 1995), 187, 208.

17  Ibid., 260–261.

18  The Beatles' early music promos also helped to set the visual parameters of psychedelia, with the influential promos for the *Strawberry Fields* and *Penny Lane* double A-sided single. These were directed by Swedish film-maker Peter Goldmann and vividly displayed the characteristics associated with psychedelia, utilizing reverse motion images and aimless and confusing activities.

19  Anon., review in *Kinematograph Weekly*, vol. 619, no. 3196, 11 January 1969, 8.

20  Sleevenotes for George Harrison, *Wonderwall Music* (Commercial Marketing CD, 2014, B00MI712KA).

21  In January of 1968, Harrison had completed the Wonderwall score including ten days in Bombay. Alan Smith, 'Future Pop Star Features' in the *New Musical Express*, Summer Special, 1968, npn.

22  Indian sitar music adopted an important position in the counterculture of the West, with Ravi Shankar appearing to great acclaim at the Woodstock festival.

23  Harrison's music was being recorded just after *Magical Mystery Tour*, and there are some similarities. *Flying* by the Beatles is reminiscent of some of *Wonderwall*, specifically the track *Party Secombe*.

24  On the scientist's side, the wall has two quotations on it: from Alfred Tennyson's *The Daydream* (about sleeping beauty) and from Christina Rosetti's *An End*.

25  Sergei M. Eisenstein, Vsevolod Pudovkin and Grigori Alexandrov, 'Statement on Sound' in Richard Taylor, ed. and trans., *S. M. Eisenstein: Selected Works, Volume 1, Writings 1922–1934* (London: BFI, 1988), 113.

26  According to Nannette Aldred, 'Although *Performance* didn't go into production until 1968, [director Donald] Cammell was clearly thinking about it the previous year and it has a feel of 1967 about it. While the figure of Turner in the film was played by the frontman of the Stones, Mick Jagger, it was based on Brian Jones, then going through a sort of psychic disintegration, with elements of "cool" Keith Richard.' '"The Summer of Love" in *Performance* and *Sgt.Pepper*' in Christoph Grunenberg and Jonathan Harris, eds., *Summer of Love: Psychedelic Art, Social Crisis and Counterculture in the 1960s* (Liverpool: Liverpool University Press, 2006), 112.

27  'Hollywood composer Jack Nitzsche has been engaged to arrange, conduct and orchestrate Mick Jagger's score for "Performance", the Warner Bros. motion picture release filmed in London by Goodtime Enterprises. The score will be recorded in Hollywood beginning next week.' Rod Cooper, 'Production' in *Kinematograph Weekly*, vol. 629, no. 3240, 1968, 12.

28  It clearly was not totally unbelievable to suggest that a pop singer was going to provide a musical score. Indeed, Jagger went on to provide the music for Kenneth Anger's *Invocation of My Demon Brother* (1969), producing some very austere and repetitive synthesizer music.

29  See more detailed discussion in K. J. Donnelly, '*Performance* and the Composite Film Score' in K. J. Donnelly, ed., *Film Music: Critical Approaches* (Edinburgh: Edinburgh University Press, 2001) and 'The *Performance* Soundtrack' in Mark Goodall, ed., *The Gathering of the Tribes: Music and Heavy Consciousness Creation* (London: Headpress, 2013).

30  Jonathan Romney, 'Tracking across the Widescreen' [interview with Ry Cooder], in *The Wire* issue 138, August 1995, 42.

31  Brian Hogg, 'Psych-Out!' in *Record Collector*, no. 135, November 1990, 20.

# Chapter 4

1   *Dark Side of the Moon* remained in the charts for 294 weeks, first charting in March of 1973.

2   Long playing records (LPs) had become widely known as 'albums' exactly like art folios since the advent of *Sergeant Pepper's Lonely Hearts Club Band*. It was the first LP to include a lyric sheet and have a gatefold sleeve and arguably was the first concept album.

3   See some further discussion in K. J. Donnelly, 'Angel of the Air: Popol Vuh's Music for Werner Herzog's Films' in Miguel Mera and David Burnand, eds., *European Film Music* (London: Ashgate, 2006).

4   John Cavanagh, *Pink Floyd's Piper at the Gates of Dawn* (London: Continuum, 2003), 8–9.

5   Ibid., 34.

6   It was recorded at the end of 1967 and transmitted in early Jan 1968. Nick Hodges and Ian Priston, *Embryo: A Pink Floyd Chronology, 1966–1971* (London: Cherry Red Books/Red Oak Press, 1999), 97.

7   Nicholas Schaffner, *The Pink Floyd Odyssey: Saucerful of Secrets* (London: Helter Skelter, 2005), 50–51.

8   This cohering of a particular experience, big screen films, lights, good sound, volume and visual anonymity, leads directly to the phenomenon of 'stadium rock' as pioneered by Pink Floyd, who completed a US tour of 1971 as the only band on the bill and needed 'peripheral' elements to be more central.

9   David Parker, *Random Precision: Recording the Music of Syd Barrett, 1965–74* (London: Cherry Red Books, 2001), 77.

10  Schaffner, *The Pink Floyd Odyssey*, 199.

11  Ibid., 134.

12  Two years later, *Dark Side of the Moon* was recorded using twenty-four tracks.

13  Michael Watts, 'Pink Floyd's Muddled *Meddle*' in *Melody Maker*, 13 November 1971, 48.

14  Schaffner, *The Pink Floyd Odyssey*, 121.

15  Ibid., 150.

16  'Hollywood composer Jack Nitzsche has been engaged to arrange, conduct and orchestrate Mick Jagger's score for "Performance", the Warner Bros. motion picture release filmed in London by Goodtime Enterprises. The score will be recorded in Hollywood beginning next week.' Rod Cooper, 'Production' in *Kinematograph Weekly*, vol. 629 no. 3240, 1968, 12.

17  Hodges and Priston, *Embryo*, 57, 107.

18  This is an earlier version of the piece than that on *Piper at the Gates of Dawn* and demonstrates the group's improvisational character at that time.

19  Hodges and Priston, *Embryo*, 110–111.

20 Nick Mason writes that the music was completed in a morning and not worth releasing. *Inside Out: A Personal History of Pink Floyd* (London: W and N, 2005), 200.

21 Schaffner, *The Pink Floyd Odyssey*, 122.

22 Clearly, there was an intention that they should supply far more music than ended up in the film. Pink Floyd spokesman Steve O'Rourke stated: 'Although groups have been used for music on films as in *Easy Rider* and of course the Beatles for their films, this is the first time a British group has done a soundtrack for a major production. The music is costing MGM in excess of 200,000 dollars.' The article states that eight songs were required for the film from the group. 'Floyd Write Major Score' in *Melody Maker*, 13 December 1969, 3.

23 Schaffner, *The Pink Floyd Odyssey*, 129, 134.

24 While this procedure was not common, it appeared for sections of Led Zeppelin's film *The Song Remains the Same* (1975).

25 Schaffner, *The Pink Floyd Odyssey*, 147.

26 For example, there is a quiet single organ chord at the film's conclusion, when the travellers see the valley they seek.

27 Schaffner, *The Pink Floyd Odyssey*, 127.

28 Ibid., 127.

29 It still is used. Indeed, *The Valley*'s *Childhood's End* was used by Channel 5 in the UK on May 2004 during a montage advertising a screening of the Steven Seagal film *On Deadly Ground*.

30 Hodges and Priston, *Embryo*, 116.

31 This version was 5.40 long, but the version released later on *Relics* was 6.45 long.

32 John Cotner, 'Careful with That Axe, Eugene' in Kevin Holm-Hudson, ed., *Progressive Rock Revisited* (London: Routledge, 2001), 84.

33 The dynamic explosion was accompanied by a sonic spatialization effect. Alan Parsons notes, '... in *Careful with That Axe, Eugene* the quad carries no sound at all until the famous horrific scream at which every amplifier and speaker is driven to its absolute maximum, accompanied by an explosion of flash powder behind the stage.' 'Four Sides of the Moon' in *Studio Sound*, June 1975, 52.

34 Edward Macan, *Rocking the Classics: English Progressive Rock and the Counterculture* (Oxford: Oxford University Press, 1997), 21.

35 *Heartbeat*, episode 'Say It with Flowers' (Yorkshire Television, Tx. Sunday 17 October 2004).

36 *Melody Maker*, 6 April 1967, 5.

37 Michael Walls, 'The Floyd on Rock Today' in *Melody Maker*, 26 September 1970, 15.

38 Pink Floyd's 1969 tour poster advertised this: 'introducing the Azimuth Co-ordinator'.

39 The Azimuth Co-ordinator '... was not a magic box for aligning type machine heads as the name might suggest but a very glorified term for what we now know as a quad pan pot. Its use at live concerts at that time very likely inspired considerable audience interest in multichannel sound systems ...' Alan Parsons, 'Four Sides of the Moon' in *Studio Sound*, June 1975, 50.

40 Hodges and Priston, *Embryo*, 281.

41 There was a stereo mix of *Piper at the Gates of Dawn* (1967) aimed primarily at the US market. The LP had been recorded on four tracks and there are significant differences between the stereo and mono mixes. In 1971, when Pink Floyd's early material was released as the compilation album *Relics*, it was remixed into 'fake stereo', where a hint of added delay gave a more full sound.

42 At times, *Dark Side of the Moon* appears inspired very directly by film and radio drama 'sound effects'.

43 Gianluca Sergi, 'A Cry in the Dark' in Steve Neale and Murray Smith, eds., *Contemporary Hollywood Cinema* (London: Routledge, 1997), 158.

44 Parsons, 'Four Sides of the Moon', 52.

# Chapter 5

1 A good example is an early critical piece: Adrian Wootton, 'Looking Back, Dropping Out, Making Sense: A History of the Rock-Concert Movie' in *Monthly Film Bulletin*, vol. 55, no. 659, December 1988, 355–356.

2 See more discussion in K. J. Donnelly, 'Visualizing Live Albums: Progressive Rock and the British Concert Film in the 1970s' in Robert Edgar, Kirsty Fairclough-Isaacs and Benjamin Halligan, eds., *The Music Documentary: From Acid Rock to Electropop* (New York: Routledge, 2013), 171–182.

3 Discussed further in Jonathan Romney, 'Access All Areas: The Real Space of Rock Documentary' in Jonathan Romney and Adrian Wootton, eds., *Celluloid Jukebox. Popular Music and the Movies since the 50s* (London: BFI, 1995, 82–93.

4 Julie Lobalzo Wright notes the polar characters of the films Woodstock and Gimme Shelter, defining later perception of the counterculture. 'The Good, The Bad and The Ugly '60s: The Opposing Gazes of *Woodstock* and *Gimme Shelter*' in Robert Edgar, Kirsty Fairclough-Isaacs and Benjamin Halligan, eds., *The Music Documentary: From Acid Rock to Electropop* (New York: Routledge, 2013), 84.

5 For instance, the Live Aid concert event in 1985 was televised live (and more recently made available on DVD), as was the 2004 Millennium Stadium Tsunami Concert.

6 Wootton, 'Looking Back, Dropping Out, Making Sense', 355.

7 John Caughie, 'Progressive Television and Documentary Drama' in *Screen*, vol. 21, no. 3, 1980, 31.

8   Keith Emerson noted that ELP had made a video of *Pictures at an Exhibition* to be ready for when video became more pervasive. 'A Quad View of Quadraphonic Sound' in *Melody Maker*, 23 January 1972, 34.

9   Carl Palmer, quoted in George Forrester, Martyn Hanson and Frank Askew, *Emerson, Lake and Palmer: The Show that Never Ends* (London: Helter Skelter, 2001), 70.

10  Ibid., 70–71.

11  Peter Clifton constructed and directed most of the film. Some had been shot by Joe Massot, and Led Zeppelin manager Peter Grant went to extreme and intimidatory efforts to secure this footage. Stephen Davis, *Hammer of the Gods: Led Zeppelin Unauthorized* (London: Pan, 1985), 269–270.

12  An extraordinarily detailed analysis of album and film is provided by Eddie Edwards. 'The Garden Tapes', www.thegardentapes.co.uk/ [accessed 8 May 2011].

13  Wootton, 'Looking Back, Dropping Out, Making Sense', 356.

14  Barry Keith Grant, 'The Classic Hollywood Musical and the "Problem" of Rock'n'Roll' in *Journal of Popular Film and Television*, vol. 18, part 4, 1986, 201.

15  Another significant point was the promise of easy profit. *Woodstock* (1970) cost $500k and made $50 mill. David Sanjek, '"You Can't Always Get What You Want": Riding on the Medicine Ball Caravan' in Robert Edgar, Kirsty Fairclough-Isaacs and Benjamin Halligan, eds., *The Music Documentary: From Acid Rock to Electropop* (New York: Routledge, 2013), 100.

16  Simon Reynolds, 'Tombstone Blues: The Music Documentary Boom' in *Sight and Sound*, May 2007, 32.

17  Indeed, film was quicker than TV to show rock'n'roll in the 1950s and always erred on the side of caution, although there were a few celebrated punk outbursts on British television in the late 1970s, but by this point, making even cheap films was expensive and securing distribution was difficult. Again, cheap 'amateur' films, such as *Punk in London* (1978) and *The Punk Rock Movie* (1978) documented the musical outpouring more than television managed.

18  Anno Mungen, 'The Music is the Message: The Day Jimi Hendrix Burned his Guitar – Film, Musical Instrument, and Performance as Music Media' in Ian Inglis, ed., *Popular Music and Film* (London: Wallflower, 2003), 72–74.

19  Emblematized by songs such as the Sex Pistols' *Anarchy in the UK* and the Clash's *I'm So Bored of the USA*, punk caused great controversy, stoked by the British media.

20  Two concerts from the Sex Pistols' abortive tour of the USA in 1978 had been filmed and ended up released for home video: *Live at Longhorns* and *Live at Winterland*.

21  Such "mockumentaries" have received a certain amount of scrutiny, including Carl Plantinga, 'Gender, Power, and a Cucumber: Satirizing Masculinity in *This is Spinal Tap*' in Barry Grant and Jeanette Slonoiwski, eds., *Documenting the Documentary: Close Readings of Documentary Film and Video* (Detroit, MI: Wayne State University Press, 1998), 318–332, Jane

Roscoe and Craig Hight, *Faking It: Mock-Documentary and the Subversion of Factuality* (Manchester: Manchester University Press, 2001), and Alexandra Juhasz and Jesse Lerner, eds., *F is for Phoney: Fake Documentary and Truth's Undoing* (Minneapolis: University of Minnesota Press, 2006).

22 Indeed, Young had already provided a bizarre score of solo improvised electric guitar to Jarmusch's *Dead Man* (1995).

23 Robert Edgar, Kirsty Fairclough-Isaacs and Benjamin Halligan, 'Preface' in Robert Edgar, Kirsty Fairclough-Isaacs and Benjamin Halligan, eds., *The Music Documentary: From Acid Rock to Electropop* (New York: Routledge, 2013), xi.

24 'Hendrix Film Tour' in *Melody Maker*, 8 January 1972, 1.

# Chapter 6

1 Lawrence Novotny, *Blaxpoloitation Films of the 1970s: Blackness and Genre* (London: Routledge, 2008), 20.

2 Andrew Walker, Andrew J. Rausch and Chris Watson, *Reflections on Blaxploitation: Actors and Directors Speak* (Lanham, MD: Scarecrow, 2009), ix.

3 Another definition comes from Canadian film fanzine *Trash Compactor* suggested that '... true Blaxploitation ... occurred when wagon jumping white boy producers hired primarily black casts to provide chiefly black audiences with "what they wanted". Namely this was to witness "The Man" held up for ridicule by the jive-strutting soul brothers. Of course most of the green from these "black" only films found its way deep into white lined pockets that were basically just mining the then current off Hollywood "in thing" of Black Awareness.' Anon., 'Back in Black (Again)' in *Trash Compactor*, vol. 2, no. 6, Summer 1992, 15.

4 Darius James, *That's Blaxploitation* (New York: St. Martin's Griffin Press, 1995), 90.

5 For a more technical analysis of the notion of groove, see G. Siros, M. Miron, M. Davies, F. Gouyon and G. Madison, 'Syncopation Creates a Sense of Groove in Synthesized Musical Examples' in *Cognitive Neuroscience*, vol. 5, no. 1036, 2014.

6 Josiah Howard, *Blaxploitation Cinema: the Essential Reference Guide* (Godalming, Surrey: FAB Press, 2008), 10.

7 Ibid., 10.

8 Ibid., 15.

9 Ibid., 7.

10 Novotny, *Blaxploitation Films of the 1970s* 18.

11 Mikel Koven, *Blaxploitation Films* (London: Kamera, 2010), 11.

12 Howard, *Blaxploitation Cinema*, 12.

13 Some of the actors involved came from positions of celebrity elsewhere. For instance, athletes featured in many films, with Fred Williamson (football

player), Jim Brown and Rosey Grier, singers such as Isaac Hayes, Curtis Mayfield and Gladys Knight, comedians like Rudy Ray Moore, Richard Pryor and Redd Foxx and glamour models such as Gloria Hendry, Jean Bell and Marki Bey.

14  This musical style has a rapid influence on US TV shows, particularly cop shows with urban settings, perhaps most notably *Starsky and Hutch* (1957–79, Spelling-Goldberg/ABC).

15  At the same time, Roger Moore's debut film as James Bond, *Live and Let Die* (1973), took direct inspiration from Blaxploitation films particularly in its New York scenes. However, the score, written by ex-Beatles' producer George Martin, owes little to these films as does Paul McCartney and Wings' title song. Perhaps this was an assertion of the Britishness of the series through music in the face of a film which is wholly set in the United States and focuses particularly on the African-American community.

16  Van Peebles' basic notation is reproduced in Melvin Van Peebles, *The Making of Sweet Sweetback's Baadasssss Song* (Edinburgh: Payback Press, 1996), 158.

17  Walker, Rausch and Watson, *Reflections on Blaxploitation*, 171.

18  Van Peebles, *The Making of Sweet Sweetback's Baadasssss Song*, 91.

19  While *Sweet Sweetback's Baadasssss Song* uses some radical techniques, perhaps this is the most startling due to it still being a rarity in cinema. An argument might be made for this homologizing later hip hop record 'scratching' where the same piece of music was moved back and forth, to repeat the same excerpt.

20  The large ensemble that recorded Parks' music included well-known jazz musicians Joe Pass on guitar and Freddie Hubbard on trumpet.

21  James, *That's Blaxploitation*, 80.

22  Howard, *Blaxploitation Cinema*, 11.

23  Larry Cohen interviewed in ibid., 27

24  Howard, *Blaxploitation Cinema*, 12.

25  Ed Guerrero, *Framing Blackness: The African-American Image in Film* (Philadelphia, PA: Temple University Press, 1993), 68–69.

26  Howard, *Blaxploitation Cinema*, 12.

# Chapter 7

1  'Bowie Movies into Films' in *Melody Maker*, 7 June 1975, 5.

2  Phillips started out on the New York folk scene before becoming successful with the Mamas and the Papas. He wrote *San Francisco (Be Sure to Wear Flowers in Your Hair)* for Scott Mackenzie and later supplied the music for Mike Sarne's *Myra Breckinridge* (1970). By the mid-1970s, he was far less productive and in 1980 was sentenced to prison on drugs charges.

3   Bob Hughes, 'Loving the Alien' in *Uncut*, no. 103, December 2005, 74.

4   No soundtrack album was released for the film, although unofficial ones appeared later.

5   It seems accepted that *Subterraneans* had its genesis as music for *The Man Who Fell to Earth*. Wilcken notes that the piece 'could easily be' Newton remembering family. Hugo Wilcken, *David Bowie's Low* (London: Continuum, 2014), 132; Bob Hughes notes that Bowie used some of the music in *Subterraneans*, although it is a misnomer that Bowie's 'score' became his later *Low* album (1977). Hughes, 'Loving the Alien,' 86.

6   This was often perceived negatively. Concerning *Young Americans* by 'M.W.' noted: '... a new high in lows ... The problem with Bowie is that he changes contexts with such rapidity that he's hardly entitled to feel sore when he's accused of merely observing passing fashion'. *Melody Maker*, 15 March 1976, 44. Rock writer Lester Bangs noted in *Creem*: 'Young Americans alienated Bowie fans – becoming a fake US soul act ... As for his music, he was ... an accomplished eclectician (a.k.a.thief) ... he had showbiz pro written a over him.' Lester Bangs, *Psychotic Reactions and Carboretor Dung*, Greil Marcus, ed. (London: Serpent's Tail, 1996), 161, 162.

7   'Bowie jumped the glam-rock ship just in time, before it drifted into a blank parody of itself.' David Buckley, *Strange Fascination – David Bowie: The Definitive Story* (London: Virgin, 1999), 217.

8   Bowie took an ambiguous inspiration from Nazism. The British Musicians Union made strong responses to some of his political statements in 1976. See details here: www.muhistory.com/?p=304 [accessed 20 May 2014].

9   'Philly' was the common corruption of Philadelphia, referencing Bowie's short-lived inspiration from Philadelphia soul musicians.

10  Criterion DVD commentary.

11  Ibid.; Hughes, 'Loving the Alien', 76.

12  Twenty minutes were cut out by the US distributor. The film's UK premiere took place in March of 1976.

13  Anthony O'Grady, 'Watch Out Mate! Hitler's on His Way Back' in *New Musical Express*, August 1975. Republished in *The Quietus*, 25 January 2010. www.thequietus.com/articles/03598-david-bowie-and-new-nazi-rock-movement [accessed 27 April 2012].

14  Jon Savage, *England's Dreaming: The Sex Pistols and Punk Rock* (London: Faber, 2005), 3.

15  Lisa Robinson, 'The First Synthetic Rock Star. There Is No Other' in *New Musical Express*, March 1976. Republished at: www.bowiegoldenyears.com/articles/750300-nme.html [accessed 27 April 2012].

16  Bowie's son is now more prosaically named Duncan Jones but has gone on to become an acclaimed film director.

17  David Toop, 'Rock Musicians and Film Soundtracks' in Jonathan Romney and Adrian Wootton, eds., *Celluloid Jukebox: Popular Music and the Movies Since the 50s* (London: BFI, 1995), 79.

18  Bob Dawbarn, 'The Swing is to Albums' in *Melody Maker*, 19 October 1968, 15.

19  Mark Sinker, 'Music as Film' in Jonathan Romney and Adrian Wootton, eds., *Celluloid Jukebox: Popular Music and the Movies since the 50s* (London: BFI, 1995), 111.

20  Robinson, 'The First Synthetic Rock Star. There Is No Other'.

21  Steve Shroyer and John Lifflander, 'Spaced Out in the Desert' in *Creem*, December 1975. Republished at: www.bowiegoldenyears.com/articles/751200-creem.html [accessed 27 April 2012].

22  Ibid.

23  See further discussion in K. J. Donnelly, *British Film Music and Film Musicals* (London: Palgrave 2007).

24  www.tonyvisconti.com/faq/bowie.htm [accessed 20 April 2012].

25  The musicians were Pete Kelly – keyboards; guitars – Mick Taylor, Ricky Hitchcock; B.J. Cole – pedal steel; Dave Marquee – bass; Frank Ricotti – percussion; Henry Spinetti – drums. Taylor had left the Rolling Stones in December of 1974.

26  Other tracks include *Boys from the South*, *Rhumba Boogie*, *Bluegrass Breakdown*, *Black Broadway* and *Devil on the Loose*.

27  The spectrum of writing runs from well-researched and detailed material to basic fan material often premised on pictures. Since the advent of the internet, there has been more volume of material, but perhaps more space for more esoteric fan material.

28  JtheGoblinKing. TMWFTE message board http://imdb.com/title/tt0074851/board/nest/14868995 posted 13 January 2005 [accessed 6 September 2005].

29  Fake recordings are not unheard of. Ian MacDonald notes about the Beatles' unreleased *Carnival of Light*: 'For various reasons, it will never be released, although it may, of course, eventually find its way onto a bootleg. Almost no one outside the Apple circle has heard it and interest in it among "Beatleologists" is consequently high. In fact, an enterprising fraudster could easily counterfeit a black-market version, since the real thing sounds nothing like The Beatles.' Ian Macdonald, *Revolution in the Head: The Beatles' Records and the Sixties* (London: Pimlico, 2005), 224.

30  Roeg points this out on the DVD commentary for the Anchor Bay release of the film.

31  'Fantastic Response to "Piano Man"', *BBC News*, www.bbc.co.uk [accessed 20 February 2006].

32  Neil Spencer, 'Spaced Invader' [interview with Nic Roeg] in *Uncut*, 1998. [www.teenagewildlife.com/Appearances/Press/1998/0700/uncut.html [accessed 29 April 2012].

33  www.lukeford.net/profiles/profiles/si_litvinoff.htm] [accessed 27 April 2012].

34  Spencer, 'Spaced Invader'.

# Chapter 8

1   Claudia Gorbman, *Unheard Melodies: Narrative Film Music* (London: BFI, 1987), 70, Kathryn Kalinak, *Settling the Score: Music and the Classical Hollywood Film* (Madison: University of Wisconsin Press, 1992), xv–xvi.

2   Kalinak, *Settling the Score*, 189.

3   David Bordwell, Janet Staiger and Kristin Thompson, *The Classical Hollywood Cinema Style and Mode of Production to 1960* (London: Routledge, 1985), 368.

4   Kalinak, *Settling the Score*, 187.

5   Rod Cooper, 'Beating the Drum for the Music Makers' (Interview with Ron Goodwin) in *Kinematograph Weekly*, vol. 634, no. 3279, 15 August 1970, 3.

6   William Darby and Jack Dubois, *American Film Music: Major Composers, Techniques, Trends 1915–90* (Washington, DC: MacFarland, 1982), 486.

7   R. Serge Denisoff and George Plasketes, 'Synergy in 1980s Film and Music: Formula for Success or Industry Mythology?' in *Film History*, vol. 4, 1990, 257.

8   Thomas Schatz, 'The New Hollywood' in Jim Collins, Hilary Radner and Ava Preacher Collins, eds., *Film Theory Goes to the Movies* (London: Routledge, 1993), 32.

9   R. Serge Denisoff and William D. Romanowski, *Risky Business: Rock in Film* (London: Transaction, 1991), 694.

10  John Burlingame, 'Danny Elfman on the Move' in *Soundtrack!* September 1990, 21; Daniel Schweiger, 'Danny Elfman Returns' in *Soundtrack!*, September 1992, 19.

11  Barry McIlheny, review of Elfman and Prince soundtracks in *Empire*, 1990, 108.

12  Kim Newman, review of *Batman* in *Monthly Film Bulletin*, vol. 56, no. 668, September 1989, 269.

13  Denisoff and Romanowski, *Risky Business*, 693.

14  Janet K. Halfyard notes a superficial similarity between Elfman's score and classical film scoring. *Danny Elfman's Batman: A Film Score Guide* (Lanham, NJ: Scarecrow, 2004), 62.

15  Kalinak, *Settling the Score*, 187.

16  Schweiger, 'Danny Elfman Returns', 19.

17  Ibid., 18.

18  Quoted in Roy M. Prendergast, *A Neglected Art: Film Music* (New York: New York University Press, 1977), 42.

19  Arnold Whitall, entry in Stanley Sadie, ed., *The New Grove Dictionary of Music and Musicians, vol. 2* (London: Macmillan, 1984), 104.

20  Schweiger, 'Danny Elfman Returns', 17.

21  Fredric Jameson, 'Progress versus Utopia, or, Can We Imagine the Future?' in Brian Wallis, ed., *Art After Modernism: Rethinking Representation* (New York: New Museum of Contemporary Art, 1984), 244.

22 Kalinak, *Settling the Score*, 189.

23 Didier Deutsch, 'Interview with Danny Elfman' in *Soundtrack!*, December 1993, 9.

24 Although Elliot Goldenthal praises Danny Elfman's music, he asserts that his music never looks back to it. Michael Singer, *Batman, and Robin: The Making of the Movie* (London: Hamlyn, 1997), 125.

25 This approach was taken by Goldenthal in *Alien3* (1992), where the sound of thrash metal riffing is used to underscore an attack on Ripley.

26 Gorbman, *Unheard Melodies*, 162; K. J. Donnelly, 'Altered Status: A Review of Music in Postmodern Cinema and Culture' in Steven Earnshaw, ed., *Postmodern Surroundings* (Amsterdam: Rodopi, 1994), 50.

27 Schweiger, 'Danny Elfman Returns', 19.

28 *The Dark Knight* included four obscure remixes on its double-CD edition (by artists such as the Crystal Method and Paul van Dyk) although two songs by Boom Boom Satellites which appeared in the club scene were not on the soundtrack album. *The Dark Knight Rises* (2012) included a download code for a Junkie XL remix of a track not included in the film. No tied-in songs in the traditional sense were part of the films.

# Chapter 9

1 See further discussion about Sting's acting in Phil Powrie, 'The Sting in the Tale' in Ian Inglis, ed., *Popular Music and Film* (London: Wallflower, 2003), 39–40.

2 Frank Zappa scored some low budget films in the early 1960s, before finding success in rock music. *The World's Greatest Sinner* (1962) was a project that starred and was directed by Timothy Carey, while *Run Home Slow* (1963) was a cheaply made western starring Mercedes McCambridge.

3 Barry followed a similar strategy but with different musical palettes for the very different British spy film *The Ipcress File* (1965) and the Kenyan-set *Born Free* (1965).

4 Mark Sinker, 'Music as Film' in Jonathan Romney and Adrian Wootton, eds., *Celluloid Jukebox: Popular Music and the Movies since the 50s* (London: BFI, 1995), 111.

5 David Toop, 'Rock Musicians and Film Soundtracks' in Jonathan Romney and Adrian Wootton, eds., *Celluloid Jukebox: Popular Music and the Movies since the 50s* (London: BFI, 1995), 73.

6 Neil Norman, 'Green Ice for a Grey Stone' (Interview with Bill Wyman) in *New Musical Express*, 30 May 1981, 11.

7 Toop, 'Rock Musicians and Film Soundtracks', 79.

8 Other 'early adopters' composing scores for films include Tangerine Dream, Popol Vuh and Fred Frith and Lindsay Cooper of avant garde rock group Henry Cow.

9   Christopher Palmer, *The Composer in Hollywood* (New York: Marion Boyars, 1990), 19–23.

10  The group had scored minor hits in the 1990s with records such as *Def Con One*, *Touched by the Hand of Cicciolina* and the film-inspired *Get the Girl – Kill the Baddies*.

11  James Newton Howard has worked with Elton John, Earth, Wind and Fire, Chaka Khan, Olivia Newton John and Leo Sayer, among others; Mark Mancina has played with Yes and Seal, while Nick Glennie-Smith has played with Pink Floyd, Phil Collins, Tina Turner and Paul McCartney.

12  It is interesting to note that among top creative rock guitar players, Robert Fripp has not written film music. He was involved with ambient music along with Brian Eno but appears to have resisted the pull toward film music (although some of his music was used in Amos Poe's *Subway Riders* [1981]).

13  Another was Roger Waters, the bassist in Pink Floyd, provided music (collaborating with Ron Geesin) for *The Body* (1970), music for a documentary about Rene Magritte, for the animated film *When the Wind Blows* (1987) and writing the music and script for *Pink Floyd: The Wall* (1983).

14  Mark Snow once drummed for the New York Rock'n'Roll Ensemble, which also featured Michael Kamen. He is famed for composing and performing the music for *X-Files* and primarily is known for television music.

15  Kathryn Kalinak, *Settling the Score: Music and the Classical Hollywood Film* (Madison: University of Wisconsin Press, 1992), xv–xvi.

16  Jeff Smith, *The Sounds of Commerce: Marketing Popular Film Music* (New York: Columbia University Press, 1998), 6.

17  Ibid., 6.

18  Philip Tagg, *Kojak: Fifty Seconds of Film Music: Toward the Analysis of Affect in Popular Music* (Goteborg: Musikvetenskapliga Inst., Goteborg University, 1979), 59.

19  Simon Frith, 'Mood Music' in *Screen*, vol. 25, no. 3, 1984, 83.

20  Smith, *The Sounds of Commerce*, 6.

21  Ibid., 231.

22  Graeme Revell quoted in Jeff Berkwits, 'Graeme Revell – Journeys to Dune' [interview] in *Soundtrack*, vol. 19, no. 76, Winter 2000, 6.

23  Ian MacDonald, *Revolution in the Head: The Beatles' Records and the Sixties* (London: Pimlico, 2005), 373.

# Chapter 10

1   See further discussion of the situation in Britain in the introduction to K. J. Donnelly, *Pop Music in British Cinema: A Chronicle* (London: BFI, 2001).

2    As noted by Ronald Rodman, 'Popular Song as Leitmotiv in *Pulp Fiction* and *Trainspotting*' in Phil Powrie and Robynn Stilwell, eds., *Changing Tunes: The Use of Pre-existing Music in Film* (Aldershot: Ashgate, 2006), 120–137.

3    Arved Ashby convincingly argues that Tarantino changed his musical signature approach after his first three films. Ken Garner, 'You've Heard this One Before: Quentin Tarantino's Scoring Practices from Kill Bill to Inglourious Basterds' in Arved Ashby, ed., *Popular Music and the New Auteur: Visionary Filmmakers after MTV* (New York: Oxford University Press, 2013), 160.

4    A point noted in relation to a pop video maker turned film director. Russell Mulcahy '... has worked extensively in rock videos, which is evident enough in the way *Highlander* has been made as a succession of set-pieces'. Tim Pulleine, review, *Monthly Film Bulletin*, vol. 53, no. 631, August 1986, 237.

5    Some commentators have noted the increased status of music in contemporary films. Claudia Gorbman, *Unheard Melodies: Narrative Film Music* (London: BFI, 1987), 162.

6    Kathryn Kalinak, *Settling the Score: Music and the Classical Hollywood Film* (Madison: University of Wisconsin Press, 1992), 186, 187.

7    Jon Lewis, *The Road to Romance and Ruin: Teen Films and Youth Culture* (London: Routledge, 1992), 136.

8    Andrew Yule, *Enigma: David Puttnam, the Story so far* (Edinburgh: Mainstream, 1988), 86.

9    Oddly, *That'll Be The Day* has only two short bursts of non-diegetic score; only uses a song as non-diegetic music once, with only a small number of group performances using the performance mode.

10   Its esoteric references are most obviously the casting of Ringo Starr and Keith Moon (of the Who), while nostalgia aficionados could appreciate Billy Fury acting and singing – making a comeback of sorts, singing *A Thousand Stars* – while playing a character called Stormy Tempest, a play not only on Fury's name but also a direct allusion to another rock'n'roll singer of the period, Rory Storme. Musical direction for the film, overseeing choices of music, was by Neil Aspinall, once a Beatles road crew member, and Keith Moon.

11   R. Serge Denisoff and William Romanowski, *Risky Business: Rock on Film* (New York: Transaction, 1991), 299–300.

12   Gary LeMel, president of the music division at Warner Brothers, claims that the early and mid-1980s were a time when there was intense pressure to deliver hit records with films but the pressure lessened late in the decade. Jean Rosenbluth, 'Soundtrack Specialists: Maximizing Crfoss-Market Connections' in *Billboard*, 16 July 1988, S-9.

13   Its highest placing was No. 16, and it was on the charts for eight weeks, entering on 14 August 1980.

14   Melissa Carey and Michael Hannan, 'Case Study 2: *The Big Chill*' in Ian Inglis, ed., *Popular Music and Film* (London: Wallflower, 2003), 166–167.

15   Indeed, an associated album release was called *Music of a Generation*.

16  David Shumway contends that music appears in films like this not as commentary but furnishing a sense of 'generational solidarity' through 'commodified nostalgia'. In the case of *The Big Chill* it is difficult to disagree. 'Rock'n'Roll Sound Tracks and the Production of Nostalgia' in *Cinema Journal*, vol. 38, no. 2, Winter 1999, 38–39.

17  The promos for *Groovy Kind of Love* and *Going Loco in Acapulco* used clips from the film and thus functioned like cinema trailers, yet oddly *Two Hearts* included no reference to the film.

18  Steven Romer, 'Production Strategies in the UK' in Duncan Petrie, ed., *New Questions of British Cinema* (London: BFI, 1992), 66–67.

19  Denisoff and Romanowski, *Risky Business*, 679.

20  R. Serge Denisoff and George Plasketes, 'Synergy in 1980s Film and Music: Formula for Success or Industry Mythology?' in *Film History*, vol. 4, no. 3, 1990, 21.

21  Quoted in Mark Cooper, 'Heard Any Good Films Lately?' in *Q*, August 1989, 17–18.

22  Claudia Gorbman, 'Auteur Music' in Lawrence Kramer, Richard Leppert and Daniel Goldmark, eds., *Beyond the Soundtrack: Music in Cinema* (Berkeley: University of California Press, 2007), 149.

23  This sequence is discussed in detail in Phil Powrie, 'Blonde Abjection: Spectatorship and the Abject Anal Space In-between' in Steve Lannin and Matthew Caley, eds., *Pop Fiction: The Song in Cinema* (Bristol: Intellect, 2005), 100–119.

24  Michel Chion, *Audio-Vision: Sound on Screen*, Claudia Gorbman, ed. and trans. (New York: Columbia University Press, 1994), 8.

25  Estella Tincknell notes that *Pulp Fiction* was a 'self-consciously "cool"' text'. 'The Soundtrack Movie, Nostalgia, and Consumption' in Ian Conrich and Estella Tincknell, eds., *Film's Musical Moments* (Edinburgh: Edinburgh University Press, 2006), 139.

26  Missing songs include The Robins' *Since I First Met You*, Link Wray's *Rumble* and *Ace of Spades*, Woody Thorne's *Teenagers in Love*, The Brothers Johnson's *Strawberry Letter #23*, Gary Shorelle's *Waitin' in School* and The Marketts' *Out of Limits*.

27  See further and compelling discussion in Lisa Coulthard, 'The Attractions of Repetition: Tarantino's Sonic Style' in James Wierzbicki, ed., *Music, Sound and Filmmakers: Sonic Style in Cinema* (New York: Routledge, 2012).

28  Ken Garner, '"Would You Like to Hear Some Music?" Music in-and-out-of-Control in the Films of Quentin Tarantino' in K. J. Donnelly, ed., *Film Music: Critical Approaches* (Edinburgh: Edinburgh University Press, 2001), 188–189.

29  Apart from the Robert Gordon recording mentioned above, it does not include Mussorgsky's *Night on a Bare Mountain*, the Melvins' *Spread Eagle Beagle*, Peter Gabriel's *The Rhythm of the Heat*, Leonard Cohen's *In Doubt*, Rage Against the Machine's *Bombtrack* and *Take the Power Back*, Marilyn Manson's *Cyclops*, The Specials' *Ghost Town* and the Cowboy Junkies' *If You Were the Woman and I Was the Man*.

30  The film includes references to The Beatles, most notably the configuration of the four friends copying the cover of *Sgt. Pepper's Lonely Hearts Club Band* when standing at the train halt and *Abbey Road* when they cross the road in London.

31  The same event is shown later in the film, although shot and edited differently and with different music.

32  For further analysis of this sequence and its music, see Murray Smith, *Trainspotting* (London: BFI, 2002), 67–70.

33  Including Underworld's *Dark & Long (Dark Train Mix)*, Sleeper's *Statuesque*, Heaven 17's *Temptation*, Ice MC's *Think About the Way* and the *Habanera* from Bizet's *Carmen*. It also includes an extended version of Leftfield's *A Final Hit*, an alternative mix of Underworld's *Born Slippy/NUXX*, by Darren Price and a remix by Baby Doc of Iggy Pop's *Nightclubbing*.

34  Geoffrey McNab, 'The Boys are Back in Town' (interview with the makers of *Trainspotting*) in *Sight and Sound*, vol. 6, no. 2, February 1996, 10.

35  *Boston Kickout* (1995) included Primal Scream and Oasis, *House of America* (1996 UK/Holland) included Blur and Primal Scream, *Velvet Goldmine* (1998 UK/US) and *The Full Monty* (1997) included Pulp, while *The Acid House* (1998) included Primal Scream and Oasis. *Lock, Stock and Two Smoking Barrels* (1998) featured a number of Britpop songs.

36  See further discussion in Elena Boschi, '"Please, Give Me Second Grace": A Study of Five Songs in Wes Anderson's *The Royal Tenenbaums*', in David Cooper, Christopher Fox and Ian Sapiro, eds., *Cinemusic?: Constructing the Film Score* (Newcastle: Cambridge Scholars Publishing, 2008).

37  Bowie's song is one of the many mentioned in Irvine Welsh's original novel, which espoused an older repertoire of music than the film's translation.

38  Denisoff and Plasketes, 'Synergy in 1980s Film and Music', 257.

39  Tom Gunning, 'The Cinema of Attractions' in Thomas Elsaesser and Adam Barker, eds., *Early Cinema: Space, Frame, Narrative* (London: BFI, 1990), 61.

40  Smith, *Trainspotting*, 20.

# Chapter 11

1  Ferrara also directed two episodes of TV show *Miami Vice* and the films *China Girl* (1987, a remake *West Side Story*), acclaimed TV movie *The Gladiator* (1987) and *Cat Chaser* (1989).

2  Janet Maslin, 'Bad Lieutenant: Jaded Cop; Raped Nun; Bad Indeed' movie review in *The New York Times*, 20 November 1992. www.nytimes.com/movie/review?res=9E0CE0D6133EF933A15752C1A964958260 [accessed 20 December 2014].

3  'Film Maker Paul Rachman Remembers Zoe Lund' in *Film Maker*, Winter 2015. www.Filmmakermagazine.com/33153-filmmaker-paul-rachman-remembers-zoe-tamerlis-lund/#.VQMMyPhFDGU [accessed 20 January 2014].

4   Portrayal was often negative but sensational. The front cover of the *New Musical Express* (13 September 1986) showed Schoolly D with his hood up and pointing a handgun.

5   Stanley Cohen wrote a highly influential book about the near-hysterical media reaction to urban fighting between mod and rocker subcultures in the early 1960s, which coined the term 'moral panic'. *Folk Devils and Moral Panics* (London: MacGibbon and Kee, 1972).

6   Clyde Taylor, 'New U.S. Black Cinema' in *Jump Cut*, no. 28, April 1983, 47.

7   'Hip-Hop in Politics: What a Difference a Generation Makes' in *ABC News*. www.abcnews.go.com/Politics?OTUS/hip-hop-politics-difference-generation-makes/story?id=18495205 [accessed 20 December 2014].

8   Dawn M. Norfleet, 'Hip-Hop and Rap' in Mellonee V. Burnim and Portia K. Maultsby, eds., *African American Music: An Introduction* (London: Routledge, 2005), 365.

9   John Springhall, *Youth, Popular Culture and Moral Panics: From Penny Gaffs to Gangsta Rap, 1830–1996* (Basingstoke: Palgrave, 1999).

10  From Philadelphia, he was born Jesse B Weaver Jr, in 1966.

11  Eithne Quinn, '"Who's the Mack?": The Performativity and Politics of the Pimp Figure in Gangsta Rap' in *Journal of American Studies*, vol. 34, no. 1, 2000, 120.

12  Henry Louis Gates, Jr., *The Signifyin' Monkey: A Theory of African-American Literary Criticism* (Oxford: Oxford University Press, 1988).

13  Claudia Mitchell-Kernan, 'Signifying, Loud-Talking, and Marking' in Thomas Kochman, ed., *Rappin' and Stylin' Out: Communication in Urban Black America* (Chicago: University of Illinois Press, 1972), 326.

14  Quinn discusses how Ice Cube's *Who's the Mack?* has three characters like in the signifying monkey story. Quinn, *Who's the Mack?*, 129.

15  Ibid., 117.

16  Don Jeffrey, 'Plant, Page Oust Song from Film' in *Billboard*, 5 March 1994, 12.

17  He discusses the notion of 'Forced Marriage', changing either music or image and seeing the difference. Michel Chion, *Audio-Vision: Sound on Screen*, ed. and trans. Claudia Gorbman (New York: Columbia University Press, 1994), 188.

18  Reminiscent of the insidious 'looped' and bowdlerized edited TV versions of some films.

19  The 'Rated NC-17' category was then only 2 years old and receiving this meant that the Blockbuster video chain would not stock it. An R-rated cut of the video was made especially for them.

20  'Live Must Destroy "Bad" Vids sez Judge' in *Variety*, 14 December 1994.

21  Another instance is the *Doctor Who* story 'The Chase', Tx. 22 May 1965, which used the Beatles' *All You Need Is Love*. Unable to secure the rights for home release, the song was redubbed into the decades-later releases on both VHS video and DVD.

22 Rick Altman, 'General Introduction: Cinema as Event' in Rick Altman, ed., *Sound Theory Sound Practice* (London: Routledge, 1992), 14.

23 In fact, I had recourse to this unofficial 'archive' of the 'grey' Internet for this book's chapters on Pink Floyd and David Bowie, where the former's unreleased scores could be found with a little searching around, and in the latter's case clearly fake audio files of Bowie's 'score' for *The Man Who Fell to Earth*.

24 Another example of censorship changing history is that the current UK DVD release of *Sweet Sweetback's Baadasssss* Song (1971) – censored opening where a young boy is forced into sex with a woman. The boy is in fact Mario Van Peebles, being directed by his father Melvin, but nevertheless this is a clear depiction of abuse of a minor (seemingly real and staged for the camera).

# Bibliography

Adorno, Theodor. 'On Popular Music' in Andrew Goodwin and Simon Frith, eds., *On Record: Rock, Pop and the Written Word*. London: Routledge, 1990.

Aldred, Nannette. '"The Summer of Love" in *Performance* and *Sgt. Pepper*' in Christoph Grunenberg and Jonathan Harris, eds., *Summer of Love: Psychedelic Art, Social Crisis and Counterculture in the 1960s*. Liverpool: Liverpool University Press, 2006.

Altman, Rick. *The American Film Musical*. London: BFI, 1987.

Altman, Rick. 'General Introduction: Cinema as Event' in Rick Altman, ed., *Sound Theory Sound Practice*. London: Routledge, 1992.

Anon. 'Back in Black (Again)' in *Trash Compactor*, vol. 2, no. 6, Summer 1992.

Ashby, Arved, ed. *Popular Music and the New Auteur: Visionary Filmmakers after MTV*. New York: Oxford University Press, 2013.

Auslander, Philip. *Liveness: Performance as Mediatized Culture*. London: Routledge, 1999.

Bangs, Lester. *Psychotic Reactions and Carboretor Dung*, Greil Marcus, ed., London: Serpent's Tail, 1996.

*Billboard*

Biskind, Peter. *Easy Riders, Raging Bulls: How the Sex-and-Drugs-and-Rock'n'Roll Generation Changed Hollywood*. London: Bloomsbury, 1999.

Bordwell, David. *Narration in the Fiction Film*. London: Routledge, 1987.

Bordwell, David. *On the History of Film Style*. Cambridge, MA: Harvard University Press, 1998.

Bordwell, David, Janet Staiger and Kristin Thompson. *The Classical Hollywood Cinema Style and Mode of Production to 1960*. London: Routledge, 1985.

Boschi, Elena. '"Please, Give Me Second Grace": A Study of Five Songs in Wes Anderson's *The Royal Tenenbaums*' in David Cooper, Christopher Fox and Ian Sapiro, eds., *Cinemusic?: Constructing the Film Score*. Newcastle: Cambridge Scholars Publishing, 2008.

Buckley, David. *Strange Fascination – David Bowie: The Definitive Story*. London: Virgin, 1999.

Caine, Andrew. 'Can Rock Movies Be Musicals?' in Lincoln Geraghty and Mark Jancovich, eds., *The Shifting Definitions of Genre: Essays on Labelling Films, Television Shows and Media*. Jefferson, NC: McFarland, 2008.

Carey, Melissa and Michael Hannan. 'Case Study 2: *The Big Chill*' in Ian Inglis, ed., *Popular Music and Film*. London: Wallflower, 2003.

Caughie, John. 'Progressive Television and Documentary Drama' in *Screen*, vol. 21, no. 3, 1980, 9–35.

Cavanagh, John. *Pink Floyd's Piper at the Gates of Dawn*. London: Continuum, 2003.

Chion, Michel. *Audio-Vision: Sound on Screen*, Claudia Gorbman, ed. and trans. New York: Columbia University Press, 1994.

Cohen, Annabel J. 'Congruence-Association Model and Experiments in Film Music: Toward Interdisciplinary Collaboration' in *Music and the Moving Image*, vol. 8, no. 2, Summer 2015.

Cohen, Stanley. *Folk Devils and Moral Panics*. London: MacGibbon and Kee, 1972.

Cohn, Nick. *Awopbop Alubop Alopbam Boom: Pop in the Beginning*. London: Pimlico, 2004.

Collins, Tom. 'Popular Music and Technology' in Mark Christopher Carnes, ed., *The Columbia History of Post-World War II America*. New York: Columbia University Press, 2007.

Conrich, Ian, and Estella Tincknell, eds. *Film's Musical Moments*. Edinburgh: Edinburgh University Press, 2006.

Cook, Nicholas. 'Music and Meaning in the Commercials' in *Popular Music*, vol. 13, no. 1, 1994, 27–40.

Cotner, John. 'Careful with That Axe, Eugene' in Kevin Holm-Hudson, ed., *Progressive Rock Revisited*. London: Routledge, 2001.

Coulthard, Lisa. 'The Attractions of Repetition: Tarantino's Sonic Style' in James Wierzbicki, ed., *Music, Sound and Filmmakers: Sonic Style in Cinema*. New York: Routledge, 2012.

*Creem*

Darby, William and Jack Dubois. *American Film Music: Major Composers, Techniques, Trends 1915–90*. Washington, DC: MacFarland, 1982.

Davis, Andy, Mark Paytress and John Reed. 'The Beatles and Psychedelia' in *Record Collector*, no. 166, June 1993, 20.

Davis, Stephen. *Hammer of the Gods: Led Zeppelin Unauthorized*. London: Pan, 1985.

Denisoff, R. Serge and George Plasketes. 'Synergy in 1980s Film and Music: Formula for Success or Industry Mythology?' in *Film History*, vol. 4, no. 3, 1990, 257–276.

Denisoff, R. Serge and William Romanowski. *Risky Business: Rock on Film*. New York: Transaction, 1991.

Donnelly, K. J. 'Angel of the Air: Popol Vuh's Music for Werner Herzog's Films' in Miguel Mera and David Burnand, eds., *European Film Music*. London: Ashgate, 2006.

Donnelly, K. J. 'British Cinema and the Visualized Live Album' in Robert Edgar, Kirsty Fairclough-Isaacs and Benjamin Halligan, eds., *The Music Documentary: Acid Rock to Electropop*. London: Routledge, 2013.

Donnelly, K. J. *British Film Music and Film Musicals*. Basingstoke: Palgrave Macmillan, 2007.

Donnelly, K. J. 'The Classical Film Score Forever?: Music in the *Batman* Films' in Steve Neale and Murray Smith, eds., *Contemporary Hollywood Cinema*. London and New York: Routledge, 1998.

Donnelly, K. J. '*Performance* and the Composite Film Score' in K. J. Donnelly, ed., *Film Music: Critical Approaches*. Edinburgh: Edinburgh University Press, 2001.

Donnelly, K. J. *Pop Music in British Cinema: A Chronicle*. London: BFI, 2001.

Eckstein, Jeremy, ed. *Cultural Trends 19*, vol. 3, no. 3. London: Policy Studies Institute, 1993.

Edgar, Robert, Kirsty Fairclough-Isaacs and Benjamin Halligan. 'Introduction: Music Seen: The Formats and Functions of Music Documentary' in Robert Edgar, Kirsty Fairclough-Isaacs and Benjamin Halligan, eds., *The Music Documentary: From Acid Rock to Electropop*. New York: Routledge, 2013.

Edgar, Robert, Kirsty Fairclough-Isaacs and Benjamin Halligan. 'Preface' in Robert Edgar, Kirsty Fairclough-Isaacs and Benjamin Halligan, eds., *The Music Documentary: From Acid Rock to Electropop*. New York: Routledge, 2013.

Eisenstein, Sergei M. *The Film Sense*, Jay Leyda, ed. and trans. London: Faber and Faber, 1963.

Eisenstein, Sergei M., Vsevolod Pudovkin and Grigori Alexandrov. 'Statement on Sound' in Richard Taylor, ed. and trans., *S. M. Eisenstein: Selected Works, Volume 1, Writings 1922–1934*. London: BFI, 1988.

Ellis, John. *Visible Fictions: Cinema, Television, Video*. London: Routledge, 1982.

*Empire*

Ewens, David. *All the Years of American Popular Music*. London: Prentice-Hall, 1977.

Feuer, Jane. *The Hollywood Musical*. London: Macmillan, 1982.

*Film Score Monthly*

Forrester, George, Martyn Hanson and Frank Askew. *Emerson, Lake and Palmer: The Show that Never Ends*. London: Helter Skelter, 2001.

Frith, Simon. 'Mood Music: An Inquiry into Narrative Film Music' in *Screen*, vol. 25, no. 3, 1984, 78–87.

Fulpen, H. V. *The Beatles: An Illustrated Diary*. London: Plexus, 1983.

Garner, Ken. 'Would You Like to Hear Some Music? Music in-and-out-of-control in the Films of Quentin Tarantino' in K. J. Donnelly, ed., *Film Music: Critical Approaches*. Edinburgh: Edinburgh University Press, 2001.

Garner, Ken. 'You've Heard this One Before: Quentin Tarantino's Scoring Practices from Kill Bill to Inglourious Basterds' in Arved Ashby, ed., *Popular Music and the New Auteur: Visionary Filmmakers after MTV*. New York: Oxford University Press, 2013.)

Garwood, Ian. 'Must You Remember This?: Orchestrating the "Standard" Pop Song in *Sleepless in Seattle*' in *Screen*, vol. 41, no. 3, 2000, 282–298.

Gates Jr., Henry Louis. *The Signifyin' Monkey: A Theory of African-American Literary Criticism*. Oxford: Oxford University Press, 1988.

Glynn, Stephen. *A Hard Day's Night*. London: I.B. Tauris, 2005.

Gorbman, Claudia, 'Auteur Music' in Lawrence Kramer, Richard Leppert and Daniel Goldmark, eds., *Beyond the Soundtrack: Music in Cinema*. Berkeley: University of California Press, 2007.

Gorbman, Claudia. *Unheard Melodies: Narrative Film Music*. London: BFI, 1987.

Grant, Barry Keith. 'The Classic Hollywood Musical and the "Problem" of Rock'n'Roll' in *Journal of Popular Film and Television*, vol. 18, part 4, 1986, 195–205.

Guback, Thomas H. 'American Interests in the British Film Industry' in *Quarterly Review of Economics and Business*, no. 7, 1967, 7–21.

Guerrero, Ed. *Framing Blackness: The African-American Image in Film*. Philadelphia, PA: Temple University Press, 1993.

Gunning, Tom. 'The Cinema of Attractions' in Thomas Elsaesser and Adam Barker,
     eds., *Early Cinema: Space, Frame, Narrative*. London: BFI, 1990.
Halfyard, Janet K. *Danny Elfman's* Batman: *A Film Score Guide*. Lanham, NJ:
     Scarecrow, 2004.
Heldt, Guido. *Music and Levels of Narration in Film*. Bristol: Intellect, 2014.
Hicks, Michael. *Sixties Rock: Garage, Psychedelic and Other Satisfactions*.
     Chicago: University of Illinois, Press, 2000.
Hill, John. '*A Hard Day's Night*' in Nicholas Thomas, ed., *The International
     Dictionary of Films*. London: St. James Press, 1990.
Hill, John. 'Television and Pop: The Case of the 1950s' in John Corner, ed.,
     *Popular Television in Britain: Studies in Cultural History*. London: BFI, 1991.
Hodges, Nick, and Ian Priston. *Embryo: A Pink Floyd Chronology, 1966–1971*.
     London: Cherry Red Books/Red Oak Press, 1999.
Hogg, Brian. 'Psych-Out!' in *Record Collector*, no. 135, November 1990, 20.
*Hot Press*
Howard, Josiah. *Blaxploitation Cinema: The Essential Reference Guide*.
     Godalming: FAB Press, 2008.
Inglis, Ian. 'Introduction: Popular Music and Film' in Ian Inglis, ed., *Popular Music
     and Film*. London: Wallflower, 2003.
Inglis, Ian. *Popular Music and Film*. London: Wallflower, 2003.
Ireland, David. 'Deconstructing Incongruence: A Psycho-Semiotic Approach
     Towards Difference in the Film-Music Relationship' in *Music and the Moving
     Image*, vol. 8, no. 2, Summer 2015.
James, Darius. *That's Blaxploitation*. New York: St. Martin's Griffin Press, 1995.
Jameson, Fredric. 'Progress versus Utopia, or, Can We Imagine the Future?' in
     Brian Wallis, ed., *Art After Modernism: Rethinking Representation*. New York:
     New Museum of Contemporary Art, 1984.
Jasper, Tony. *Fab!: The Sounds of the Sixties*. Poole, Dorset: Blandford Press,
     1984.
Juhasz, Alexandra and Jesse Lerner, eds. *F is for Phoney: Fake Documentary and
     Truth's Undoing*. Minneapolis: University of Minnesota Press, 2006.
Kalinak, Kathryn. *Settling the Score: Music and the Classical Hollywood Film*.
     Madison: University of Wisconsin Press, 1992.
Kassabian, Anahid. 'The End of Diegesis as We Know It (And I Feel Fine)'
     in Claudia Gorbman, John Richardson and Carol Vernallis, eds., *Oxford
     Handbook of New Audiovisual Aesthetics*. New York: Oxford University Press,
     2013.
Kealy, Edward R. 'From Craft to Art: The Case of Sound Mixers and Popular
     Music' in Simon Frith, ed., *On Record: Rock, Pop and the Written Word*. New
     York: Pantheon, 1990.
Kernfeld, Barry, ed. *The New Grove Dictionary of Jazz*. London: Macmillan,
     1988.
*Kinematograph Weekly*
Koven, Mikel. *Blaxploitation Films*. London: Kamera, 2010.
Kurlansky, Mark. *1968: The Year that Rocked the World*. London: Vintage,
     2005.
Laderman, David. *Punk Slash! Musicals: Tracking Slip-Sync on Film*. Austin:
     University of Texas Press, 2011.

Laderman, David. '(S)lip-Sync: Punk Rock Narrative Film and Postmodern Musical Performance' in Jay Beck and Tony Grajeda, eds., *Lowering the Boom: Critical Studies in Film Sound*. Chicago: University of Illinois Press, 2008.

Laing, Dave. 'Roll Over Lonnie (Tell George Formby the News)' in Charlie Gillett and Simon Frith, eds., *The Beat Goes On: The Rock File Reader*. London: Pluto, 1996.

Laing, Stuart. 'Economy, Society and Culture in the 1960s: Contexts and Conditions for Psychedelic Art' in Christoph Grunenberg and Jonathan Harris, eds., *Summer of Love: Psychedelic Art, Social Crisis and Counterculture in the 1960s*. Liverpool: Liverpool University Press, 2006.

Lannin, Steve and Matthew Caley, eds. *Pop Fiction: The Song in Cinema*. Bristol: Intellect, 2005.

Lewis, Jon. *The Road to Romance and Ruin: Teen Films and Youth Culture*. London: Routledge, 1992.

Lobalzo Wright, Julie. 'The Good, The Bad and The Ugly '60s: The Opposing Gazes of Woodstock and Gimme Shelter' in Robert Edgar, Kirsty Fairclough-Isaacs and Benjamin Halligan, eds., *The Music Documentary: From Acid Rock to Electropop*. New York: Routledge, 2013.

Macan, Edward. *Rocking the Classics: English Progressive Rock and the Counterculture*. Oxford: Oxford University Press, 1997.

Mason, Nick. *Inside Out: A Personal History of Pink Floyd*. London: W and N, 2005.

McDonald, Ian. *Revolution in the Head: The Beatles Records and the Sixties*. London: Pimlico, 1995.

Mellers, Wilfrid. *The Twilight of the Gods: The Beatles in Retrospect*. London: Faber, 1973.

Melly, George. *Revolt into Style: The Pop Arts in Britain*. London: Penguin, 1970.

*Melody Maker*

Mitchell-Kernan, Claudia. 'Signifying, Loud-Talking, and Marking' in Thomas Kochman, ed., *Rappin' and Stylin' Out: Communication in Urban Black America*. Chicago: University of Illinois Press, 1972.

*Mojo*

*Monthly Film Bulletin*

Mungen, Anno. 'The Music Is the Message: The Day Jimi Hendrix Burned His Guitar – Film, Musical Instrument, and Performance as Music Media' in Ian Inglis, ed., *Popular Music and Film*. London: Wallflower, 2003.

Murphy, Robert. *Sixties British Cinema*. London: BFI, 1992.

Neaverson, Robert. *The Beatles Movies*. London: Cassell, 1997.

*New Musical Express*

Norfleet, Dawn M. 'Hip-Hop and Rap' in Mellonee V. Burnim and Portia K. Maultsby, eds., *African American Music: An Introduction*. London; Routledge, 2005.

Novotny, Lawrence. *Blaxploitation Films of the 1970s: Blackness and Genre*. London: Routledge, 2008.

Palmer, Christopher. *The Composer in Hollywood*. New York: Marion Boyars, 1990.

Parker, David. *Random Precision: Recording the Music of Syd Barrett, 1965–74*. London: Cherry Red Books, 2001.

Plantinga, Carl. 'Gender, Power, and a Cucumber: Satirizing Masculinity in *This is Spinal Tap*' in Barry Grant and Jeanette Slonoiwski, eds., *Documenting the Documentary: Close Readings of Documentary Film and Video*. Detroit, MI: Wayne State University Press, 1998.

Powrie, Phil. 'Blonde Abjection: Spectatorship and the Abject Anal Space In-between' in Steve Lannin and Matthew Caley, eds., *Pop Fiction: The Song in Cinema*. Bristol: Intellect, 2005.

Powrie, Phil. 'The Sting in the Tale' in Ian Inglis, ed., *Popular Music and Film*. London: Wallflower, 2003.

Prendergast, Roy M. *A Neglected Art: Film Music*. New York: New York University Press, 1977.

Quinn, Eithne. "Who's the Mack?': The Performativity and Politics of the Pimp Figure in Gangsta Rap' in *Journal of American Studies*, vol. 34, no. 1, 2000, 115–136.

*Record Collector Magazine*

Rodman, Ronald. 'Popular Song as Leitmotiv in *Pulp Fiction* and *Trainspotting*' in Phil Powrie and Robynn Stilwell, eds., *Changing Tunes: The Use of Pre-existing Music in Film*. Aldershot: Ashgate, 2006.

*Rolling Stone*

Romer, Steven. 'Production Strategies in the UK' in Duncan Petrie, ed., *New Questions of British Cinema*. London: BFI, 1992.

Romney, Jonathan. 'Access All Areas: The Real Space of Rock Documentary' in Jonathan Romney and Adrian Wootton, eds., *Celluloid Jukebox. Popular Music and the Movies Since the 50s*. London: BFI, 1995.

Romney, Jonathan. 'Tracking Across the Widescreen' in *The Wire*, no. 138, August 1995, 42.

Romney, Jonathan and Adrian Wootton, eds. *Celluloid Jukebox. Popular Music and the Movies since the Fifties*. London: BFI, 1995.

Roscoe, Jane and Craig Hight. *Faking It: Mock-Documentary and the Subversion of Factuality*. Manchester: Manchester University Press, 2001.

Sadie, Stanley, ed. *The New Grove Dictionary of Music and Musicians, vol. 2*. London: Macmillan, 1984.

Sanjek, David. '"You Can't Always Get What You Want": Riding on the Medicine Ball Caravan' in Robert Edgar, Kirsty Fairclough-Isaacs and Benjamin Halligan, eds., *The Music Documentary: From Acid Rock to Electropop*. New York: Routledge, 2013.

Savage, Jon. *England's Dreaming: The Sex Pistols and Punk Rock*. London: Faber, 2005.

Schaffner, Nicholas. *The Pink Floyd Odyssey: Saucerful of Secrets*. London: Helter Skelter, 2005.

Schatz, Thomas. 'The New Hollywood' in Jim Collins, Hilary Radner and Ava Preacher Collins, eds., *Film Theory Goes to the Movies*. London: Routledge, 1993.

Sergi, Gianluca. 'A Cry in the Dark' in Steve Neale and Murray Smith, eds., *Contemporary Hollywood Cinema*. London: Routledge, 1997.

Shumway, David. 'Rock'n'Roll Sound Tracks and the Production of Nostalgia' in *Cinema Journal*, vol. 38, no. 2, Winter 1999, 36–51.

*Sight and Sound*

Singer, Michael. *Batman, and Robin: The Making of the Movie*. London: Hamlyn, 1997.

Sinker, Mark. 'Music as Film' in Jonathan Romney and Adrian Wootton, eds., *Celluloid Jukebox: Popular Music and the Movies Since the 50s*. London: BFI, 1995.

Sinyard, Neil. *The Films of Richard Lester*. London: Croom Helm, 1985.

Smith, Jeff. 'Bridging the Gap: Reconsidering the Border between Diegetic and Non-Diegetic' in *Music and the Moving Image*, vol. 2, no. 1, 2009, http://mmi.press.uiuic.edu/index.html.

Smith, Jeff. *The Sounds of Commerce: Marketing Popular Film Music*. New York: Columbia University Press, 1998.

Smith, Murray. *Trainspotting*. London: BFI, 2002.

*Sounds*

*Soundtrack!*

Springhall, John. *Youth, Popular Culture and Moral Panics: From Penny Gaffs to Gangsta Rap, 1830–1996*. Basingstoke: Palgrave, 1999.

Stilwell, Robynn J. 'The Fantastical Gap between Diegetic and Non-Diegetic' in Daniel Goldmark, Lawrence Kramer and Richard Leppert, eds., *Beyond the Soundtrack: Representing Music in Cinema*. Berkeley: University of California Press, 2007.

*Studio Sound*

Sutton, Martin. 'Patterns of Meaning in the Musical' in Rick Altman, ed., *Genre: The Musical*. London: Routledge and Kegan Paul, 1981.

Tagg, Philip. *Kojak: Fifty Seconds of Film Music: Toward the Analysis of Affect in Popular Music*. Gothenberg: Musikvetenskapliga Inst., Gothenberg University, 1979.

Taylor, Clyde. 'New U.S. Black Cinema' in *Jump Cut*, no. 28, April 1983, 46–48.

Tincknell, Estella. 'The Soundtrack Movie, Nostalgia, and Consumption' in Ian Conrich and Estella Tincknell, eds., *Film's Musical Moments*. Edinburgh: Edinburgh University Press, 2006.

Toop, David. 'Rock Musicians and Film Soundtracks' in Jonathan Romney and Adrian Wootton, eds., *Celluloid Jukebox: Popular Music and the Movies Since the 50s*. London: BFI, 1995.

*Uncut Magazine*

Van Peebles, Melvin. *The Making of Sweet Sweetback's Baadasssss Song*. Edinburgh: Payback Press, 1996.

*Variety*

Walker, Alexander. *Hollywood, England*. London: Harrap, 1986.

Walker, Andrew, Andrew J. Rausch and Chris Watson. *Reflections on Blaxploitation: Actors and Directors Speak*. Lanham, MD: Scarecrow, 2009.

Watts, Michael. 'The Call and Response: The Impact of American Pop Music in Europe' in C. W. E. Bigsby, ed., *Superculture: American Popular Culture and Europe*. London: Paul Elek, 1975.

Wilcken, Hugo. *David Bowie's Low*. London: Continuum, 2014.

Williams, Alan. 'The Musical Film and Recorded Popular Music' in Rick Altman, ed., *Genre: The Musical*. London: Routledge and Keegan Paul, 1981.

Winn, John C. *That Magic Feeling: The Beatles' Recorded Legacy, Volume Two, 1966–1970*. London: Random House, 2009.

Winters, Ben. 'The Non-Diegetic Fallacy: Film, Music and Narrative Space' in *Music and Letters*, vol. 91, no. 2, 2010, 224–244.

Wootton, Adrian. 'The Do's and Don'ts of Rock Documentaries' in Jonathan Romney and Adrian Wootton, eds., *Celluloid Jukebox. Popular Music and the Movies Since the 50s*. London: BFI, 1995.

Wootton, Adrian. 'Looking Back, Dropping Out, Making Sense: A History of the Rock-Concert Movie' in *Monthly Film Bulletin*, vol. 55, December 1988, 356–358.

Yule, Andrew. *Enigma: David Puttnam, The Story So Far*. Edinburgh: Mainstream, 1988.

# Index